Wildflower Gardening

THE TIME-LIFE ENCYCLOPEDIA OF GARDENING

Wildflower Gardening

by

JAMES UNDERWOOD CROCKETT,

OLIVER E. ALLEN

and

the Editors of TIME-LIFE BOOKS

Watercolor Illustrations by

Richard Crist

An Owl Book

Henry Holt and Company

NEW YORK

THE TIME-LIFE ENCYCLOPEDIA OF GARDENING

EDITOR: Robert M. Jones
EDITORIAL STAFF FOR WILDFLOWER GARDENING:
Assistant Editor: Jeanne LeMonnier
Text Editor: Betsy Frankel
Picture Editor: Jean Tennant
Designer: Albert Sherman
Staff Writers: Susan Feller, Kathleen Shortall
Researchers: Loretta Britten, Reese Hassig,
Marilyn Murphy, Judith W. Shanks, Reiko Uyeshima
Copy Coordinators: Kathleen Beakley, Elizabeth Graham
Picture Coordinator: Jessy Faubert
Special Contributors: Carol Clingan, Barbara Ensrud,
Angela Goodman, Jane Opper Grace, Cinda Siler

Published by Henry Holt and Company,
521 Fifth Avenue, New York, New York 10175.
Published simultaneously in Canada.

Library of Congress Cataloging in Publication Data
Crockett, James Underwood.
Wildflower gardening.
(The Time-Life encyclopedia of gardening)
Reprint. Originally published: Alexandria, Va. :
Time-Life Books, c1977.
Bibliography: p.
Includes index.
1. Wild flower gardening. I. Allen, Oliver E.
II. Crist, Richard. III. Time-Life Books. IV. Title.
V. Series.
[SB439.C76 1986]   635.9'676   85-27290
ISBN 0-03-008522-5 (pbk.)

First published by Time-Life Books in 1977.
First Owl Book Edition—1986
Printed in the United States of America
10 9 8 7 6 5 4 3 2 1

ISBN 0-03-008522-5

CO-AUTHOR: The late James Underwood Crockett, a graduate of the University of Massachusetts, received an Honorary Doctor of Science degree from that University and was cited by the American Association of Nurserymen and the American Horticultural Society. He worked with plants in California, New York, Texas and New England. He was the author of books on greenhouse, indoor and window-sill gardening, and wrote a monthly column for *Horticulture* magazine and a monthly bulletin, "Flowery Talks," for the retail florists. His weekly television program, *Crockett's Victory Garden,* was seen by more than three million viewers on 125 public broadcasting stations throughout the United States.

CO-AUTHOR: Oliver E. Allen was for many years on the staff of LIFE magazine and TIME-LIFE BOOKS. He served as Editor of the LIFE World Library and the TIME-LIFE Library of America, and as Editorial Planning Director.

ILLUSTRATOR: Richard Crist provided the watercolor paintings for this book. He studied at Carnegie Institute of Technology and The Art Institute of Chicago. An amateur botanist, Mr. Crist is author of several children's books.

GENERAL CONSULTANTS: Arthur Ode is Director of Horticulture at the New York Botanical Garden; Hal Bruce is Assistant Professor of English at the University of Delaware, Consulting Taxonomist at Winterthur Gardens, Delaware, and author of *The Gardens of Winterthur in All Seasons* and *How to Grow Wildflowers and Wild Shrubs and Trees in Your Own Garden;* Dr. T. R. Dudley is Research Botanist at the U.S. National Arboretum; George A. Kalmbacher is Plant Taxonomist at the Brooklyn Botanic Garden.

THE COVER: Raindrops moisten the petals of a purple globe tulip, photographed in springtime in the lower reaches of the California High Sierras. This dainty wildflower, *Calochortus amoenus,* is usually a rosy color when young but turns purple as it ages. It is one of 50 species of a bulbous plant commonly known as the Mariposa tulip or Mariposa lily.

CONTENTS

A garden like nature's own 1

The effect can be startling. In the woods on a spring morning a sweep of white trilliums suddenly comes into view, undulating gently in the fresh breeze: a garden in the wilderness. Along a country road in August a succession of sparkling blossoms unfolds in orange, purple, yellow, white—butterfly weed, New England aster, goldenrod and Queen Anne's lace, humble plants all. Or a woodland brook is festooned with the dark red of the cardinal flower and the delicate blue of the monkey flower, while not far off a luxuriant colony of rose-purple swamp milkweed covers a meadow. All of these blooms appear with no help from man, growing spontaneously in the wild. They are so lovely and satisfying it seems odd these plants are not grown more often in gardens.

Until quite recently, wildflowers have been the outcasts of horticulture. Gardens were filled with exotics and hybrids—most of them imported from distant lands and crossbred for splendid blooms and dependable growing habits. The reasons American gardeners ignored the native bounty of their land go far back. When European naturalists first came to North America they found a large number of beautiful native plants that truly astonished them. What Europe admired the colonists denigrated. The English formal garden was glorified and the natives of American field and forest were left out in the wild—or intentionally eradicated.

This practice has continued. In a garden, Americans have said, color should be concentrated; the majority of native flowers have not fitted into this system. But a certain snobbery has also excluded these native flowers from cultivation. Growing everywhere, they have not been thought deserving of the attention and care lavished on the tulip and the rose.

Conversely, some gardeners have avoided native flowers because they were thought to be too hard to grow to be worth the effort. Although a few survive almost any conditions, many de-

A cluster of wild geraniums, their unusually vibrant pink color set off by deeply cut leaves, bursts into spring bloom. This hardy wildflower grows in eastern woods and meadows and is easy to domesticate.

7

mand special treatment that did not seem practical. Finally, there were few wildflower experts or nurseries that stocked native plants or their seeds.

Now this neglect of a rewarding native resource is ending. Concern for the environment is one factor. As wilderness areas shrink, many wild plants have become rare, and many gardeners have come to view wildflowers as valuable and therefore desirable. They have found it exciting to restore a bit of unspoiled nature to the suburban landscape. As one gardener said, "I like to work with nature, not against it." Membership in wildflower societies is on the increase. As interest in conservation has mounted, well-established societies—The North Carolina Wildflower Preservation Society, the New England Wildflower Society, the Western Pennsylvania Conservancy—have grown by 10 per cent or more a year; the California Native Plant Society, started by five people in 1965, had 16 chapters and several thousand members a decade or so later. To meet the demand, some 65 specialized nurseries sprang up to serve the wildflower enthusiast. And many gardeners learned that wildflowers are easier to raise than they had thought.

But raising wildflowers does demand a special approach, an acceptance of the landscape's natural subtlety. Wildflower colors can be spectacular, but more often they are muted and intermittent. One enthusiast gazed at his carefully managed field of flowering spurge, goldenrod, fleabane and yarrow and remarked, "Lots of gardeners would say these are just weeds, but I find them absolutely beautiful." Another observed, "Wildflowers are lean and pure. There's no fat on them. Garden flowers and vegetables have been developed by man, but without man's constant care they would expire. Wildflowers have existed for thousands of years without human intervention, and they will endure. They are absolutely functional." This contrast with more conventional garden plants attracts many gardeners. "I have marigolds in the front yard," one said, "but the regular garden flowers seem rather brazen at times. I like the wildflowers out back. I get along with them better."

SPECIES BY THE THOUSANDS

An appearance of simplicity may be part of the appeal of wildflower gardening. But this simplicity is more apparent than real, for the wildflower world is huge, diverse and complex. Strictly speaking, a wildflower is any herbaceous plant, whether notable for its blooms or not, that grows naturally in the wild—not just in the woods and on the prairies and mountains, but in marshes, swamps, bogs and even in the desert. Botanists have counted some 4,000 species in the northeastern United States, 5,000 in the Southeast, 4,000 in the Rockies, at least 3,000 in

Arizona alone (largely cacti and other desert plants), 5,000 in the Northwest and more than 4,000 in California. Although there is some duplication in the lists, the total of all flowering-plant species growing wild in the United States is in excess of 15,000. This list of native plants includes not only those that bloom brightly in forest and field but a great many others associated with them in one way or another. A large number are grasses whose blossoms are barely noticeable. Some are herbs and ferns. Others are trees and shrubs. But most wildflower gardeners leave to academic botanists the bulk of native plants and concentrate on small plants with decorative flowers or berries. It is this limited group of plants that is the subject of this book.

Even when so rigorously restricted in variety, the wildflowers favored by gardeners still number in excess of 6,000 species. Many are in the horticultural underworld of weeds, but are so delightful they have been nurtured like their more proper cousins. Many others, such as the day lily, are wild only because they are strays from cultivation. Many are aliens from Europe, such as Queen Anne's lace, accidently introduced to a land where it prospered. But even the true native wildflowers are astonishingly diverse. There are at least 30 varieties of trillium, more than 75 goldenrods, more than 100 asters.

Wildflowers range in size from minuscule varieties—whose flowers you can appreciate only by getting down on your knees and peering through a magnifying glass—all the way up to giant sunflowers 8 or 9 feet tall. Their needs vary radically: desert plants will die if they are given more than a small amount of moisture, while the waterlily's roots demand the mud and water at the bottom of a pond.

Wildflowers are notable not only for their diversity but for preposterous common names—imagine inventing such bizarre labels as liverleaf, cow vetch and spiderwort—and for the charming legends that have sprung up about them. Yarrow, a field plant that blossoms in the spring in various parts of the world, is said to have been used by Achilles to treat Myrmidon's wounds at the siege of Troy; forget-me-nots memorialize a German folk tale—a drowning knight tossed a sprig of the plant to his distraught lover ashore, beseeching her not to forget him.

Many common names confusingly denote more than one species. Several plants are referred to as mayflowers, for example, because so many bloom in that month; in fact only one, trailing arbutus, said to have been the first flower sighted by the Pilgrims after their first winter in America, truly deserves that name in the

FLOWERS WITH A HISTORY

Mating wildflowers and environment

The secret of growing wildflowers is to choose plants whose natural environment can be duplicated in your backyard. North America can be divided into nine basic wild environments *(map, page 149)*, sketched here beside cross sections of their soil to a depth of about 5 feet. To reestablish the conditions of moisture, wind, sunlight and soil that once typified your region so you can grow wildflowers adapted to those conditions generally takes little effort; with more work, you can also reproduce the wilderness of environments outside your own area.

NORTHEASTERN CONIFEROUS WOODLAND

Northern pines, spruces, hemlocks and beeches control this environment, shady all year. The soil is moist and acid, below pH 5.5, partly due to ground-litter—mostly foliage dropped by trees—and partly due to the acidic granite bedrock. Frequent rains dissolve away, or leach, nutrients from the upper soil.

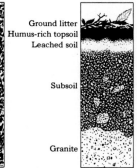

Ground litter
Humus-rich topsoil
Leached soil

Subsoil

Granite

DECIDUOUS WOODLAND

In this environment, oak, beech, maple and hickory trees reign. Dappled sunlight in spring encourages a variety of forest flowers to blossom; in summer dense foliage produces partial to deep shade. Falling leaves, especially from oaks, make a moderately acid ground-litter and humus, giving a porous structure and a pH of 5.5 to 6.5 to the deep soil.

Ground litter
Humus-rich topsoil
Leached soil

Subsoil

SOUTHEASTERN CONIFEROUS WOODLAND

Because branching begins high up on the trunks of Southern conifers, like the yellow and loblolly pine, and their foliage is airy, more sun reaches the ground through them than is true of their Northeastern counterparts. Sandy subsoil allows good drainage; acid ground-litter decomposes to give this region's soil a pH below 5.5.

Ground litter
Humus-rich topsoil
Leached soil

Subsoil

WETLAND

Glaciers pockmarked much of the northern U.S. with scattered wetlands: ponds, marshes and bogs. Similar areas border rivers and the ocean in the Southeast. Soils are waterlogged and very acid—below 5.5 pH. Pines, willows, alders and larches rim a northern pond (right). In southern wetlands, cypress, sweet bay and tupelo trees predominate.

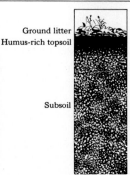

Ground litter
Humus-rich topsoil

Subsoil

PRAIRIE

This environment splits, on a line from Bismarck to Dodge City, into eastern and western zones, both too dry for many trees; the sun eliminates acidic ground-litter. In the East, with 20 or more inches of annual rain and a deep, slightly acid soil, grasses reach 8 feet. In the West, with neutral soil and less rain, grasses are shorter. Prairie pH ranges from 6.0 to 7.0.

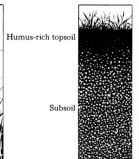

Humus-rich topsoil

Subsoil

SEMIARID GRASSLAND

A stubby sea of coarse buffalo and grama grass, only 1 or 2 feet high, covers this terrain, interrupted along the rivers by tough vegetation like junipers and cottonwoods. The topsoil is thin, lacking humus, and chemically neutral, about pH 7.0, and rainfall is light, below 12 inches a year. Only hardy wildflowers, adapted to sun and little rain, survive here.

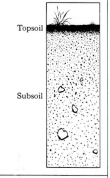

Topsoil

Subsoil

ROCKY MOUNTAIN WOODLAND

This high, windy habitat has only a thin layer of slightly acid topsoil, pH 5.5 to 6.5, atop a granite base. Ground-litter is sparse. The most common trees are aspen, fir and spruce. Truly vigorous wildflower specimens will grow at this height; above the tree line, in frosty meadows, the choice narrows to alpine flowers that need cool temperatures with constant sun.

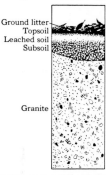

Ground litter
Topsoil
Leached soil
Subsoil

Granite

DESERT

Strong winds have blown the topsoil off this almost barren landscape, leaving a surface of sand littered with pebbles. Cacti are typical of the vegetation. Their leathery skin shields them from relentless sun and wind, reducing moisture loss to a minimum. The alkaline soil, pH 8.0 or higher, is so salty in places that almost no vegetation can endure it.

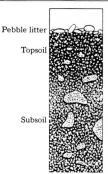

Pebble litter

Topsoil

Subsoil

WESTERN CONIFEROUS WOODLAND

Earthquakes and volcanoes have cracked deep fissures into this area's typical bedrock—basalt, siltstone and sandstone. Into them sifts slightly acid topsoil (pH 5.5 to 6.5)—shallow but rich, providing root runs for cedar, sequoia and redwood, Douglas fir and hemlock. These evergreens create dense shade year round.

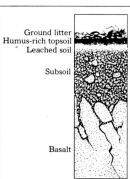

Ground litter
Humus-rich topsoil
Leached soil

Subsoil

Basalt

United States. It is the state flower of Massachusetts. (The Pilgrims' ship, however, was named for yet another mayflower; trailing arbutus does not grow in England.) One authority noted that cypress spurge, *Euphorbia cyparissias,* is also known as welcome-to-our-house, Irish moss, tree moss, quacksalver's spurge, cypress, garden spurge, balsam, graveyard weed, and even welcome-home-husband-though-never-so-drunk. Wildflower authorities avoid such confusion by referring to plants by their specific Latin names, and indeed when you order plants and seeds it is important to use these more exact labels. The botanical identification is used in the encyclopedia section of this volume, but elsewhere in the book the less formidable common names are generally employed.

This huge assortment of native plants can supply delightful examples for every garden. Looking about you as you travel, you will see that no area that supports any greenery lacks wildflowers. If you cannot have one kind of wild garden, you can have another.

The native plants' adaptability was demonstrated to a South Dakota nursery owner by an astonishing setting he came upon. A stretch of prairie had been stripped of soil, leaving nothing but gravel and silt. In this barren landscape a series of wild plants established themselves and presented the succession of bloom that every gardener seeks. The show got under way each June with the reddish-lavender blossoms of the purple locoweed, *Oxytropis lamberti.* This gave way in July to the tall, slender silver-and-white pea-bush flowers of *Dalea enneandra,* accompanied by the lavender and purple bonnets of *Astragalus goniatus.* In August came the foot-high purple spikes of gay-feather, *Liatris punctata,* together with copious stands of goldenrod; the season ended in September with two varieties of aster that seemed to light up the plains.

Such accidental gardens spring up everywhere. But everywhere they are different. The wildflowers that will grow in a particular place depend on its climate, of course, but that dependence is much more subtle than the influence of climate on domesticated plants. Temperature, for example, is far less critical a factor than it is for most ordinary garden species. Some wildflowers are annuals so that winter freezes are irrelevant; the major effect of a cold or hot climate is a change in the date of blossoming. Even the wild perennials grow over a wide geographic span, and are likely to be more sensitive to summer heat than winter cold.

PRIMEVAL HABITATS More important than climate are moisture and soil composition. These factors determine the natural plant environment now as they did in the past. And they were set by the plants that did grow in the past. To a considerable extent, what you can grow in your own wild garden today depends on what grew there 500 years ago, before the white man arrived and began rearranging the landscape. At that time one massive feature blanketed much of the eastern part of North America: a vast deciduous forest dominated by oaks, maples and beeches. In the northern part of this region and in the mountains, deciduous trees gave way to coniferous forests of pines, spruces and hemlocks; along the shore there were sandy stretches with more pines. Of course there were swamps and marshes here and there, and tropical growth in Florida, but for the most part east of the Mississippi the great forest held sway, magnificent and silent. Even beyond the Mississippi, in the Ozarks and elsewhere, forest stretched into mountainous areas. But as the rainfall decreased westward, the maples and beeches gave way to hickory and lighter oaks and then to locust, cottonwood and willow, and finally to the open prairie, some of its grasses taller than a man. Then, as the rainfall in the west slackened off still further, even the tall grass stopped and there was semidesert or desert, broken by the Rockies with their coniferous woods and alpine stretches but reasserting itself beyond the Rockies and in the dry southwest. Arid regions filled most of the western part of the land except along the northerly reaches of the Pacific Coast, where redwoods and other great conifers stood.

The countryside has changed radically since those days. In the East the forests were cleared away, although in some areas like New England they are returning. In the Midwest the prairie was plowed and planted with crops, and in the Southwest the desert was irrigated until everyone in the cities who wanted a lawn could have one. But wildflowers pay no heed to man's changes. The flowers of the deciduous forest will grow almost any place where a similar forest once stood. Thus trilliums, May apple and baneberry will grow in a woodland area of Arkansas as successfully as they will in a similar area in Massachusetts. The primeval environment is more important to wildflowers than the latitude.

How the past affects present ecology can be seen by examining the forest. Although the usual stretch of woods may seem simple to the uninformed eye, forest plants are the beneficiaries of an extremely complicated arrangement of elements. In control of these elements are the tall trees: if they are mostly pines or hemlocks or other conifers the shade beneath them will be deep and the soil very acidic, and the plants growing there will reflect those conditions. If the trees are deciduous the ground will be sunlit in early spring, the later shade will be lighter and the ground less acidic, and a different set of flowers will live there. In either case a large

CONDITIONS ALTERED BY MAN

number of the plants will bloom in the spring, when they have the sunlight that will later be shielded from them. In addition to the tall trees in such a woods there is often an "understory" of lesser trees like dogwoods, and possibly a layer of shrubs, laurel or blueberry. Then come the wildflowers, some as tall as a foot or 18 inches but many much smaller and some merely creeping along the ground. Finally comes the soil itself, actually a many-leveled construction of fallen leaves, rotting twigs and logs, humus and, beneath it all, the subsoil and rock. It is this mixture that conserves moisture and makes possible the constant renewing of plant life.

CLUES FROM THE TREES

Just as the kinds of trees govern the nature of a forest, so do the native trees on any property suggest the kind of wild forest garden that will grow best there. If a preponderance of pines or hemlocks creates deep shade, you may choose to grow trailing arbutus, red or white trillium, shiny-leaved galax, or bunchberry (for large white flowers in spring and rich red berries in August). But if you have the intermittent shade of maples, oaks or similar trees, you might begin with round-lobed hepatica with its delicate blossoms, white bloodroot (whose roots if broken exude orange-red juice), Jack-in-the-pulpit or the magnificent large white trillium.

Few yards are completely shaded, so even if you live in a

HOW TO PRESS WILDFLOWERS

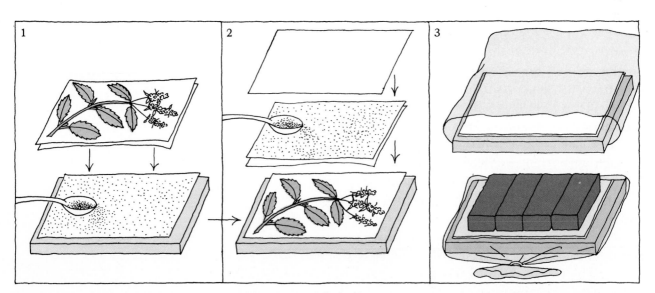

Place paper towels on a board large enough to hold the flattened flowers. Shake 2 tablespoons of silica gel drying agent, available at flower shops, on the surface; cover with cleaning tissue. Arrange flowers on the tissue.

Completely cover the flowers with another layer of cleaning tissue. Sprinkle an additional 2 tablespoons of silica gel over the second layer of cleaning tissue and then cover the gel with another layer of paper towels.

Slide the board into a plastic bag and tie the bag closed. Place bricks on top of the board, distributing them so that all parts of the plant material are evenly weighted. In a week, the flower will be pressed and dried.

region that was once forested, part of your land is likely to be sunny. For this particular section you have many choices among the sun-loving wildflowers.

If you are an Easterner, your open area is likely to be man-made: it will revert to scrub growth and eventually to woods if not cut periodically. But if you mow it once a year, it can be a sunny wildflower garden that requires little upkeep, for the mown grass furnishes the mulch such wild plants demand. A sunny expanse might be either dry or wet. If it is dry it is a field and will support a variety of the plants you see growing beside the road—ox-eye daisies, blue-eyed grass and hawkweed among many others. If the area is wet, it is properly called a meadow; many cow pastures are meadows and have mucky soil. Meadow flowers are different from field plants, and include such beauties as boneset, the orange Canada lily and asters.

If you are lucky enough to possess a pond, brook or stream, you might consider growing native flowers that "like wet feet," as nurserymen put it. Among these are monkey flower, white turtle-head and great blue lobelia and its noble relative, the cardinal flower. Pond owners often raise waterlilies—though waterlilies, if not confined, spread to clog the pond.

A swamp—defined as a wet place filled with trees and shrubs so it is shady most of the time—may seem an unlikely spot for wildflowers, but its rich soil can support a host of them. Taking advantage of that fact, a Connecticut couple who bought a suburban house backing on a dense wet thicket and a small stream decided not to clear out the scrubby growth as so many of their neighbors had done; instead they developed a swamp garden. Today their patch of moist woods is filled not only with woodland plants and a large number of wetland shrubs, but with marsh marigold, pinkish-red swamp milkweed and flowering sweet pepperbush. On a hot afternoon in July the luxuriating shrubbery, through which winding pathways lead, makes the garden a cool oasis, the air filled with the gentle scent of pepperbush.

Marshes are often confused with swamps, but they differ in one major respect: marshes have no trees and only low shrubs. A marsh is always sunlit and the vegetation is rarely more than 3 or 4 feet high. The most familiar marsh plant is the cattail with its hot-dog-like brown seed head, but a fresh-water marsh may be awash with luxuriant growths of white or pink rose mallow or the orchid-like blue-violet flowers of pickerelweed.

There is still another kind of wetland, the bog, a seemingly desolate area that is actually teeming with insect and plant life and

PLANTING WETLANDS

THE NINE ENVIRONMENTS

hence is treasured by wildflower devotees. Bogs are similar to swamps but have no visible outlet; water collects in them and gradually sinks into the ground, its surface covered by decaying vegetation. True bogs are filled with very acid sphagnum moss, its spongy consistency giving them the name of quaking bogs. Walking on a bog can be both exciting and dangerous, and if you jump up and down on one side, you may see shrubs rocking slightly on the other side. Despite such forbidding traits, these sinkholes support a wide array of flora and fauna. Chief among the fauna are insects, whose presence might be distressing but for the fact that many of the flora are insectivorous. You might see the pitcherplant with its funnel-like container of water and acid that digests its prey; or the sundew, amply endowed with sticky hairs in addition to tiny white flowers that appear in midsummer.

Such potential garden sites can be found in most of North America, since all are associated with the forests of one kind or another that once covered much of the continent. Where no trees grew, there were plants less demanding of moisture.

West of the Mississippi, where rainfall averages less than 30 inches a year, the gardener can combine long grasses with field flowers, including most of those that grow in forest meadows plus magenta-flowered poppy mallow and queen-of-the-prairie, a lofty plant 5 or 6 feet tall bearing minute deep-pink flowers in June and July. Farther west, anyone with a large open space could give much of it to the famous California poppy and the white evening primrose, whose flowers last only a single day but are produced in such profusion that the display lasts throughout the spring and into summer. Even in such an unlikely place as the seashore, wild plants exist. Many of those found near the Atlantic are unexpectedly ornamental, such as beach goldenrod, beach plum and a white-flowering ground cover called bearberry. Californians at the shore can grow beach strawberry and rose-colored sand verbena.

Since the choice of wildflowers for a home garden depends so much on its past environment, an environmental classification scheme used by botanists has been adapted for this book with the aid of plant experts at the U.S. Department of Agriculture. This classification divides North America into nine environmental types, all of which you will have encountered in this chapter: Northeastern Coniferous Woodland, Deciduous Woodland, Southeastern Coniferous Woodland, Wetland, Prairie, Semiarid Grassland, Rocky Mountain Woodland, Desert, and Western Coniferous Woodland. These environmental types are based on the primeval plant cover that established the present environment for wildflowers. Thus the pine, spruce, and hemlock trees that once populated the region from eastern Canada to the Pennsylvania mountains flourished in shallow, moist, acid soil and created dense shade; those conditions are typical of the Northeastern Coniferous Woodland environment. Similarly the Deciduous Woodland environment is that once covered by oaks, maples and beeches in the East, and by hickories, light oaks, locusts and cottonwoods in the Midwest. Other woodland environments were established by other types of trees: loblolly pine and bald cypress in the Southeastern Coniferous environment, aspen and pine in the Rocky Mountain environment, Douglas fir and redwoods in the Western Coniferous environment. Grasses helped set the pattern elsewhere—marsh grass and sedges in the bogs, swamps and marshes of the Wetland environment; needle, bluestem and wheat grass in the Prairie environment; buffalo and grama grass in the Semiarid environment—while cacti and sagebrush dominated the Desert environment.

The nine wildflower environments are delineated on the map on page 148; the soil characteristics and distinguishing landscape of each are diagramed and described on pages 10-11. Instructions for cultivating the 123 wildflower species described in the encyclopedia section are keyed to the map and its nine environmental types. Thus, you can readily find which wildflowers will grow in your own garden by looking up a species in the encyclopedia and checking whether it is suitable for the environment you have—or can create.

Unlike conventional gardens, wildflower gardens follow no set pattern, for every piece of property is unique in some way. What you have is different from every other piece of land on earth, so there is every opportunity to pioneer. In fact, one Toronto man experimented with wildflowers without owning any land at all—his home was an apartment with a balcony. He resolved to construct a woods garden right there. He built a big planter box, 2 feet by 10 and 18 inches deep, put a layer of gravel on the bottom and then filled the rest of the space with a mixture of potting soil and peat moss. He topped it all off with a generous layer of twigs and dead leaves. Into this mix he set one plant each of trillium, hepatica and spring beauty, together with a number of ferns. Because the box was near the apartment wall it was protected from the rigors of the Toronto winter, and in the summer it was shaded by nearby trees. The plants bloomed on schedule, and the box became the talk of the owner's friends. They were both surprised and pleased, he said, to be able to come to dinner in early spring, look out through the plate-glass windows, "and see what appeared to be a small but flourishing slice of the forest floor."

A BALCONY WOODLAND

Glories of native flowers, coast to coast

It is easy to understand why gardeners who live in botanically difficult areas—the Western desert, say, or the windswept coast of Maine—have turned to wildflower gardening. In either case, creating a garden with cultivated plants can mean a major reconstruction of the soil. It is better to use indigenous plants that grow naturally in their harsh environment and flourish without human help.

But wildflower gardening is also indulged in by people living in more hospitable regions, where many kinds of plants will grow readily. Sometimes these gardeners too are drawn to native plants by the prospect of minimal care. More often, they are intrigued by the character of the plants themselves. Every part of North America, whatever its climate or geological character, has its complement of regional wildflowers that grow there as naturally as beach grass grows on sand dunes, and that are an integral part of the local landscape. And every part of the continent has gardeners who, responding to a variety of personal interests, cultivate these plants.

The people who created the gardens on the following pages speak of the delicacy of their wildflowers, of the childhood memories they evoke, of the need to preserve a fast-disappearing heritage. The attention these gardeners lavish on their task often turns them into amateur ecologists. They spend hours studying and analyzing the natural growing conditions of their subjects—their preferences as to soil, exposure, moisture and drainage—in the hope of duplicating these conditions. When they fail, they try again. When they succeed, it is occasionally owing to a plant's unexpected behavior. Thus, one gardener discovered that many wildflowers accustomed to the moist soil of coastal plains actually needed less moisture in the heavier soil of the mountains. A desert gardener's domesticated wildflowers, given extra water to get them established, thereafter demanded an extra ration of water to survive.

"Sometimes," observed one enthusiast, "our backs ached and I wondered why we worked so hard." To this question the gardens themselves, shown on the next ten pages, give the answer.

An array of wild lupines, lovingly nurtured, borders the tailored lawn of a Southern California home.

Bahia absynthifolia blooms all summer.

Blooms of the desert sands

A thermometer placed in the desert sands of the South-west at noon may register more than 140°, yet nature has provided some plants with mechanisms that compensate for this heat and its accompanying dryness—deep root systems and leaves that are either small and leathery or protected by hairs. Furthermore, as if to make up for their austere setting, desert wildflowers are often amazingly beautiful. The Arizonan whose garden plants are pictured here capitalized on this fact. When he built his desert home, he left the resident flowers undisturbed, and since then he has added still others. Thus his home and garden, instead of disrupting the natural setting, are an extension of it, enhancing what was already there.

A paloverde tree is surrounded by low-growing desert plants. The yellow flowers in the left background are bahia, the orange are anisacanthus. In the foreground are pink sand verbenas. The spikes are agaves.

Penstemon eatonii is sometimes called firecracker plant.

Fairy-duster bears stamens 5 inches long.

Paper flower's golden blossoms turn papery when dry.

Red globe mallow blooms in airy clusters.

21

Fragile beauty in southern warmth

The conservation-minded owners of this Georgia garden claim that the Southland, with its long growing season, is the best region for raising wildflowers. Their garden—actually a series of gardens—occupies more than 20 acres and contains a number of native trees and wildflowers, some of which are pictured here. It was assembled over many years to show how attractive native plants can be, and to encourage others to grow them and protect them. The search for specimens took the owners on repeated trips throughout the region, but the most spectacular find—the rare white iris *(far right)*—turned up on their own land when the removal of some trees gave a dormant plant the light it needed to reappear.

Creeping phlox rarely tops a foot in height.

Ground-hugging golden star blooms in woodland shade.

A spiderwort flower opens for just one morning, then fades.

The crimson pitcher plant is a bog dweller.

Dwarf crested iris, normally blue, also can be white.

Mountain oaks flank a stone wall in this southern wildflower garden.

Color amid prairie grasses

Because it contains the most valuable farmland in the world, the American prairie has been almost entirely denuded of its native flowers. Only a scattering of blood-root remained in an uncultivated wood lot when the Illinois owner of this prairie wildflower garden decided to return a half-acre field adjoining her suburban lawn to its natural condition. Approaching her task with appropriate seriousness, she spent four years reading about prairie plants, visiting them in their natural habitats, attending classes at the local arboretum and studying the conditions on her own property. Three years passed before there were any results, but today flowers appear each spring on their own where at one time there was only grass.

A bed of spring-flowering blue-eyed grass dominates a corner of this prairie garden. The deep purple flowers are Johnny-jump-ups, a relative of the pansy, while at lower left is the plumed head of an early-blooming pasqueflower that has already gone to seed.

Blue-eyed Mary is an annual that seeds itself.

An aptly named shooting star dips earthward.

Blue-eyed grass, an iris relative, grows amid field grasses.

The flowers of prairie smoke are followed by plumed fruit.

A rue anemone faces the sun.

Merrybells is a cousin of the lily.

Rich woodlands of the Northeast

One of the richest natural environments in the United States is the Eastern Deciduous Woodland; a piece of it in Westport, Connecticut, forms this wildflower garden. A leafy canopy of trees provides a cool, damp habitat for shade-loving plants and—more important—an enriching and ever-renewing forest floor of decomposing foliage. Compared with common garden soil which holds 15 to 30 per cent of its weight in water, the humus-filled soil of a woodland holds 10 times its own weight. This garden was begun at a time when wildflower gardening was in its infancy; the owner learned his plants' preferences by trial and error. Today the garden looks much as the whole Northeast once did, before the white man came.

White dogwoods form a backdrop for a man-made bosky dell of wild pink azaleas, ferns and giant white trilliums. The shade is provided mostly by native oak and pine. A rustic chair adds to the peaceful scene.

A Jack-in-the-pulpit hides beneath its hood.

Crimson and gold columbine bloom brightly in dappled shade.

Great Solomon's seal hugs a tree trunk.

A rocky headland on the sea

Of all the unpromising locales for a garden—even a garden of wildflowers—none could be more daunting than a rocky finger of land jutting into the North Atlantic Ocean off the Maine coast. But the owner of this garden made a virtue of adversity by filling the rocky ledges with different mixtures of soil, creating minigardens in which acid-loving plants exist side by side with plants that thrive on alkaline soil. Only the bluets and false lilies of the valley are original residents of the site; the other plants were transferred from elsewhere in the area. A few are not native at all, but are alpine wildflowers that successfully made the transition from high altitude to sea level, thanks to the Maine coast's notorious cold mists and fogs.

Creeping dogwood thrives in the cool air.

Yellow lady's slipper is a native North American orchid.

Bluets do well in a cool, damp soil.

Difficult twinflowers fill a rocky pocket.

False lily of the valley is a true native.

*Sharing a rocky ledge with
rhododendrons and red spruce, a
clump of nodding pink lady's
slippers blooms in sight of the sea in
soil so shallow that spruce roots
protrude through the surface.*

Planning for a private wilderness 2

When you decide to take up wildflower gardening, you are entering a rich domain. With 6,000-odd species of native American plants awaiting, you have more choices as candidates for your garden than you will ever need to keep the beauty of the wilderness on display year round in your own backyard. But to exploit this treasure of plants you must begin to think differently about the whole concept of gardening.

In conventional gardening, you can decide rather arbitrarily what plants to grow and where to place the plots; then you cultivate the soil, plant seeds or bulbs or seedlings, and sit back to await the blooms. Most wildflowers will not stand for that sort of treatment. The close-packed soil found around a house is likely to suffocate them. And for anything but a cactus plant, this type of soil may be too alkaline as well, especially if it has been limed frequently to support a healthy lawn.

If you cannot readily create compatible conditions for any specific wildflower, it does not belong on your list. So what you must do is determine what kind of environment already exists on your property—or once existed there. Then you proceed to figure out how much you can modify it without investing an unreasonable amount of time or money in the changes and what plants will not only survive but thrive in the environment that results. Sometimes the results will surprise you.

One couple moved from the suburbs to Brooklyn and planted conventional garden flowers, the only plants they expected the backyard of their brownstone to support. The deep shade and difficult soil defeated all their efforts. But Brooklyn once had been part of the great Deciduous Woodland of the Northeast, so finally the couple tried some forest wildflowers. They were astonished to discover that the soil consistency, the shade from nearby buildings and the degree of acidity were just right for this choice. They soon

Illuminated by the setting sun, cardinal flowers flourish alongside a stream. The abundant moisture supplied by the watercourse is helpful to the well-being of this exuberantly blooming plant.

were enjoying large stands of wild violets and woodland ferns; eventually they were able to report a Jack-in-the-pulpit that had grown to be 3 feet tall.

ANALYZE YOUR LAND

It is evident that success with wildflower gardening is often at least partly accidental. But you can increase your own chances if you take a hard look at your property, study its characteristics and then plan your approach methodically.

The first thing to do in planning a wild garden is to check the map on page 149, which shows the types of environments that existed in America when it was all a wilderness. Was your land originally part of the Deciduous Woodland or the Prairie? Or the Western, Northeastern or Southeastern Coniferous Woodland? Perhaps even the Desert or Semiarid Grassland environment? How the land began long ago should largely dictate what wildflowers you first attempt to grow.

Next, observe your land closely: note how it slopes (if it does), where the prevailing winds come from (many wild plants need some protection from it), and the location of any protruding rocks. A south-facing slope will be warmer and sunnier than one facing north; a hillside will have faster drainage than land perfectly level. Finally, consider the water supply. How much rainfall do you get in the course of a year? What is the general level of humidity? Most important, what happens to water on the ground—does it sink in and disappear quickly, simply stand there in pools, or drain off toward lower sections?

The answers to these questions will tell you in general terms what kind of wild garden you can have—or gardens, for most certainly you can have more than one. In the past the untouched woodlands were dotted with open glades that supported sun-loving wildflowers, and the vast virgin prairies were crisscrossed with tree-shaded river bottoms.

NEIGHBORHOOD WILDLINGS

To get more precise clues to the plants you should choose, study existing vegetation, not only on your land but also on neighboring properties and particularly in undeveloped parkland nearby: what kinds of trees and shrubs are there? If you find pine trees, your wildflowers should be those that thrive in shade and acid soil. If you see beeches or hickories, choose plants at home in lighter shade and less acid soil. If there are maples or fruit trees, the soil will be even closer to neutral, making possible other choices. If all of your trees were planted by man and not by nature, look around your community to find out what plants grow wild. In any environment it is a good idea to begin, at least, by concentrating on local plants. You might start with those that still grow wild within 100 miles of where you live, although many aggressive wildflowers are remarkably tolerant and will make themselves at home in patches thousands of miles from their native sites.

If, for example, you have half an acre with a couple of conifers and three or four deciduous trees, none of them very large, plus an ample expanse of lawn, you already have the elements of three different kinds of wild gardens: an acid-soil, deep-shade garden of one of the Coniferous environments grouped around the evergreens, a Deciduous Woodland garden nestled under the other trees, and a sunny Prairie garden taking over an unshaded corner of your lawn. If in addition to these types of gardens you also have surface water in any form—a brook, a pond, even a swampy area— you can also have a Wetland garden.

But that probably would be striving for too much, at least at first. Wildflower gardening can be conducted on various levels of intensity. At the simplest level you need only buy some of the most adaptable and undemanding wildflowers compatible with your basic environment and set them beside your other plants. At a more advanced level you can move wild plants into an existing environment in which they are likely to flourish by, for example, adding appropriate kinds of wildflowers to an open field that is seldom mowed, a muddy area beside a brook, or perhaps an uncultivated patch of woodland. At the most complex level you can expend the effort to create an environment that is especially suited to the wildflowers you want to grow.

If you have a soggy, badly drained stretch of ground, for example, it is not terribly difficult to convert it into a bog (page 53). However, it is best to start small.

Many a wildflower gardener began by developing a pocket in a triangular area that was enclosed by three trees, say about 10 feet apart, where the trees cast enough shade and dropped enough leaves to shelter and encourage forest plants. If such a beginning fails, you can try something else. If it succeeds, you are on the right track and can expand your operations.

You will need patience. Many wildflowers are slow to develop. Many of them have adapted to a precise set of circumstances that exists only in one particular patch of ground—a unique combination of soil texture and chemistry, sunlight and shade, moisture and drainage, even soil bacteria and fungi. But they might accept a new scene in time; meanwhile they might appear to be very listless. Some will wait several years before they actually bloom. This is most likely to happen when you raise the plants from seeds, for many wildflowers produce seeds that germinate only at widely

STARTING SIMPLY

spaced intervals—a protective adaptation that enables the various wildflower species to survive despite such natural catastrophes as fire and drought.

The unpredictability of wildflowers was demonstrated to one Connecticut gardener when she planted golden seal, an attractive plant that puts out bright red berries in late summer. She set the seedling in a partially shaded place that seemed ideal for it. But although she mulched it faithfully, the plant languished. After several years she decided it was in the wrong place, so she dug it up and moved it to a spot elsewhere in her garden. It still languished. But in the place where it had been growing, a completely new crop of golden seal plants appeared the next spring—having apparently come from seed—and there they have continued to grow handsomely ever since.

You will need to stay flexible. You should have a well-defined plan for planting sections of your property with various wildflowers, but you might be surprised to discover that plant B has moved right in on plant A and has elbowed it aside. One gardener reported that he had planted some wintergreen along a path with hopes that it would stabilize and not only define the edge of the path but border it each year with its aromatic red berries. "Then I put some false lily of the valley next to it, and the lily of the valley is taking over," he said. He doesn't mind: the intruder's cheerful white blossoms in spring are a welcome sight in themselves. He plans to try the wintergreen elsewhere.

(continued on page 38)

Trillium: bounty of spring

Among the best-known inhabitants of the North American woods are the trilliums. They grow in forests nearly everywhere. In the Appalachian, Blue Ridge and Great Smoky mountains a spring hiker is almost certain to come upon the brilliant great white trillium or the deep crimson wake-robin growing singly or in masses that splash light and color on the emerging foliage around them. But these flamboyant forms are just a few of the 30 to 40 trillium species that have an ecological niche in woodlands and a welcome place in wildflower gardens from Canada to Georgia in the East, westward into the prairies and along the Pacific Coast.

Some trilliums, like the red-throated painted trillium (page 37), have exquisite flowers; others, such as prairie trillium and T. stamineum, are appealing for their handsome mottled leaves; still others, such as the compact Ozark trillium, are prized as delicate miniatures. But whether they produce spectacular blossoms, subtle foliage or rich spots of color, the arrival of the trilliums is a peculiarly American sign of spring.

Rarest and most brilliant of the species, the double trillium has up to 30 petals; a clump may spread to 3 feet.

First a splash of white (above), the
great white trillium later fades (below).

About two weeks after opening, the
great white trillium turns pink.

After about a month, the same flower
blushes rose and begins to wither.

Strong-scented purple trillium is also called stinking Benjamin.

T. flexipes is tall, with long-lasting flowers and leathery leaves.

The subtle flower of T. viridiscens has furling, upright green petals.

Canopied by leaves, nodding trillium is best admired from an ant's-eye view.

Snowy T. simile carpets rocky areas of the Smokies in early spring.

With its arching petals, prairie trillium looks closed even in full bloom.

36

White wake-robin is one of many mutant forms of T. erectum.

Widespread leaves reveal the nodding flower of T. catesbaei.

The twisted petals and pale sepals of T. stamineum rest on mottled leaves.

Painted trillium needs cold, wet, acid soil and is hard to cultivate.

Sweet Beth is related to stinking Benjamin—but is soft scented.

Ozark trillium's flower, about 1 inch long, is prized for rock gardens.

Once you have analyzed your property and decided what sort of garden or gardens you will have, draw a map of the area, recording in detail the characteristics that you have considered in making your choices. Indicate existing trees, rocks, changes in level and other features of the terrain. Mark the directions of the compass so you can note the location of the sun in relation to the property at various times of the day, and list areas that are sunny, partly shaded or fully shaded. (Be aware that your house casts shade more dense than that of any tree, and that some areas will be sunny in the spring but shaded in the summer.) Record the direction of the prevailing wind. Test the soil *(Chapter 3)* and designate areas that are very acid, moderately acid, neutral or alkaline. Determine which places are especially warm or cool; the range of temperature variations even within a small plot of ground can be surprising. Finally, decide which views you want to enjoy, or which ones you want to screen out. For example, you might want to build your wild garden around a particularly handsome clump of shrubs or a graceful dogwood.

OBSERVING NATURE

Before using your new map to plot your plantings, wait if you can through a full growing season to observe what grows naturally in uncultivated areas. You will be able to identify existing species as they appear and remove unwanted underbrush or other plants—including poison ivy and poison oak. Retain all healthy, mature trees, of course, but remove those that seem spindly or diseased, as well as seedlings that eventually would crowd the garden. Save some underbrush, too, or your wild garden will not look wild. As any existing wildflowers appear, place temporary markers next to them—the plants may vanish after blooming, becoming dormant for the rest of the year. In the autumn the markers will tell you where there are empty spaces in the garden to fill with new plants according to your overall plan.

In developing a wildflower garden, think of it as existing on several different levels, depending on the number of horizontal layers of greenery the finished area will eventually display. From top to bottom you may have first the taller trees, either dense conifers or the more open deciduous trees; shorter trees such as dogwoods and hollies; shrubs such as azaleas or laurels; taller wildflowers and ferns (that is, those 2 to 4 feet high); shorter wildflowers and ferns (6 inches to 2 feet); and finally such ground covers as partridgeberry or wild ginger may be included. In and around these various elements there might be rocks of various sizes and shapes. A good wildflower garden combines several of these elements for natural variety and a sense of scale.

Because you cannot do much about the trees and large rocks you already have, make them the foundation of the plan, arranging the other elements to complement them. Rocks are particularly desirable because they not only recall outcroppings and ledges in a natural landscape but also help conserve moisture for plants. For these reasons, you may want to bring in more rocks. If you add them to a level site, you usually get the most harmonious effect if you place them with the flattest side down and the longer sides running in the same general direction. On a slope, bury the rocks at least halfway, with the back ends set lower than the front ends in order to channel water into the soil rather than letting it run over the surface downhill.

When you collect rocks to add to a garden, look for weathered ones. Since you are setting out to re-create a natural scene, govern your choice and placement of landscaping elements by what you have seen in nearby wild areas.

Your garden may need shelter against strong winds, especially if it is in the Prairie or Semiarid Grassland environments. The hot winds of summer are particularly lethal, but a shelter belt should serve as a windbreak the year round and therefore should include some evergreens.

If you are planning to add any trees or shrubs to your wild-flower garden, you must be careful to set them far enough apart to let them develop properly as they mature, so that they will not become crowded. Try to imagine how they will look when they are fully grown, and then place them in an arrangement that will appear to be naturally random.

Another important consideration is foot traffic. Wildflowers, whether in sunny Grassland or Prairie, Woodland or Wetland, will not thrive in compacted soil. So make it a rigid rule not to step on your garden soil once you have prepared it (Chapter 3). You must, of course, be able to reach any part of it for planting, mulching and other tasks, so you will need access paths—winding strips, varying in width, of wood chips or gravel will help to keep mud and weeds at bay without looking artificial. Set in stepping stones at convenient intervals wherever they are needed. As ground covers grow or ground-litter increases, raise the stones or exchange them for larger ones. They should always be plainly visible, so that visitors to your garden will be able to see exactly where it is safe for them to step and where it is not.

With stepping stones and paths plotted, the skeleton of your garden is complete. Now it must be fleshed out with plants. The objective, of course, is an attractive display year round, and if you

THE MEAT-EATING PLANTS
Gardeners frustrated by insects that prey upon their favorite plants might turn the tables and grow wild plants that eat insects. The sundew, for example, a native of wetlands throughout North America, catches its prey on leaf hairs, which curl down around it and digest the pest. The Venus's-flytrap, which grows in bogs of the Southeast, snaps its clam-shell leaves around insects attracted to them. Pitcher plants, native to wetlands of eastern forests, get insects with a Mickey Finn—a sweet fluid that entices them down the throat of the leaf, from which there is no return.

go about it in the right way, this goal is generally attainable even though your choice of plants is to a considerable degree limited by the existing environment.

East of the Mississippi River, where great forests of the Deciduous Woodland once held sway, many novice wildflower gardeners experience what might be called the June blues. They set out to create a perfect patch of woods in a corner of the yard, turn over the soil, dutifully mix it with peat moss and leaf mold, dig in a variety of suitable plants and carefully mulch the whole affair. In the spring these gardeners are overjoyed to see the tender plants begin to bloom in spectacular hues of red, white, yellow, lavender and blue for a spine-tingling six weeks. Then suddenly the display is all over. Nothing is left in the garden but some green leaves and the mulch. The spring ephemerals—those plants that come into bloom before the trees leaf out and thus cut off the sunlight, have already finished for the entire year. The next show will not come until the following spring.

LATE BLOOMERS

No gardener, even one growing only flowers of the Deciduous Woodland, needs to suffer the June blues. If you will note the blooming times of spring flowers and other wild plants in your environment, you will see that the season does not need to be short. In the Northeast, hepatica and trailing arbutus might flower while there is still snow on the ground, but with a careful selection of species for a garden, you can have blooms of one kind or another well into the summer and even beyond. Among the late bloomers in the Deciduous Woodland are bunchberry, which flowers from

TWO WAYS TO MAKE A PATH

1. *If the soil is not soggy, fill the path with a 2- to 3-inch layer of wood chips or pebbles, humping up the center to allow for settling. Scatter flat rocks through the garden area to step on when you weed or pick flowers.*

2. *Where the ground is soggy, dig a trench along the route of the path 4 inches deep. Place a layer of 1- to 2-inch pebbles, and cover with 2 inches of sand. For walking, set in the sand sections of tree trunk 3 inches thick; the wood weathers fast and blends into the setting. Scatter rocks for stepping stones.*

late spring into summer; the Canada violet, which also continues blooming into summer; partridgeberry and Canada lily, which
bloom in early to midsummer; and pink bleeding heart, which
maintains its rose-pink blooms through the summer and until the
first frost. If you are able to find them, you can experiment with
such plants as Culver's root, which blooms all summer, and American bugbane and white boneset, both of which blossom in late
summer. In other environments, the species may be different, but
the principle is the same one; simply select plants for your environment according to their blooming season as they are listed in the
encyclopedia section of this book.

You can also take advantage of the late blooming times of
certain wild shrubs. Even though azaleas are famed for their spring
beauty, a number of native species of the Southeast and Northwest
bloom much later. The plumleaf azalea, for example, stages its
show of orange-red flowers in midsummer, and the Florida swamp
azalea blooms in late summer. The fragrant blossoms of the sweet
pepper bush grace many a Wetland wildflower garden in midsummer, as do various other flowering shrubs.

But flowers are not the only source of spectacle in the wilderness. An opportunity for late color is provided by the berries of
wildflowers, shrubs and trees. Baneberry presents its tiny white
flowers in spring but in late summer bursts forth with clusters of
red berries. Bunchberry, a ground-cover plant, puts out red berries
in the fall, and the red berries of wintergreen last from autumn well
into the winter. In California, the bright red, fist-sized clusters of
Christmas berries can be seen growing beside highways for up to
six months of the year.

To complement such a succession of displays of flowers and
berries, you can in addition plan for a variety of levels, shapes and
textures of foliage. Wildflower plants themselves offer a delightful
array of leaf patterns that put on a show after the blossoms fade.
But the best source of attractive foliage is the ferns. With such
striking species as the maidenhair, royal and cinnamon ferns, you
can achieve wonderfully cool and pleasing effects—and you can
select ferns that will not appear in the spring until after the early
flowers have had their chance. Most will flourish in any shady area
that does not dry out; along the north foundation of a house they
are one of the most dependable possibilities. Ground covers are
similarly useful: the round, shiny leaves of galax contrast delight-
fully with the small, spatula-shaped leaves of wintergreen. Above
the ground covers can rise the bizarre shapes of green dragon or
Jack-in-the-pulpit, or the large glistening leaves of May apple or

BERRIES FOR FALL COLOR

SEEDING BARREN HILLSIDES

1. *To aerate the soil of a barren hillside and help it hold moisture for future flowers, enrich it with organic matter. First mark off the area you intend to cultivate. Then cover the slope with a layer of decayed vegetation such as compost, leaf mold or peat moss to a depth of 2 to 3 inches. Dig in the new material with a spading fork.*

2. *With a heavy steel-tined garden rake, smooth the surface of the planting bed. If necessary, add more soil and humus to ensure smooth, even coverage of any protruding rocks in the area.*

3. *Scatter the wildflower seeds over the hillside bed, but do not cover them with soil. Instead, press them in with a wooden tamp, to approximate the way seeds are incorporated into the soil by nature. You can make a tamp from ordinary hardware-store materials (inset). For the handle, buy a section of pipe about ¾ inch in diameter, threaded at one end and long enough to be comfortable to work with. Attach it to a threaded metal flange, and fasten the flange with screws to a block of wood measuring 8 inches square and 2 inches thick.*

4. *To keep the newly planted seeds and the new topsoil layer from being blown away by wind or washed down by rain, blanket the hillside with a protective covering. Use a coarse, open-mesh fabric (tobacco cloth or erosion netting, usually available at garden centers). Anchor the covering to the hillside with U-shaped wire pins, cut and bent from 8-inch lengths of coat hangers (detail). The young plants will push up through openings in this covering; as they become established, the covering will be hidden and, if made of natural fiber, it will gradually disintegrate.*

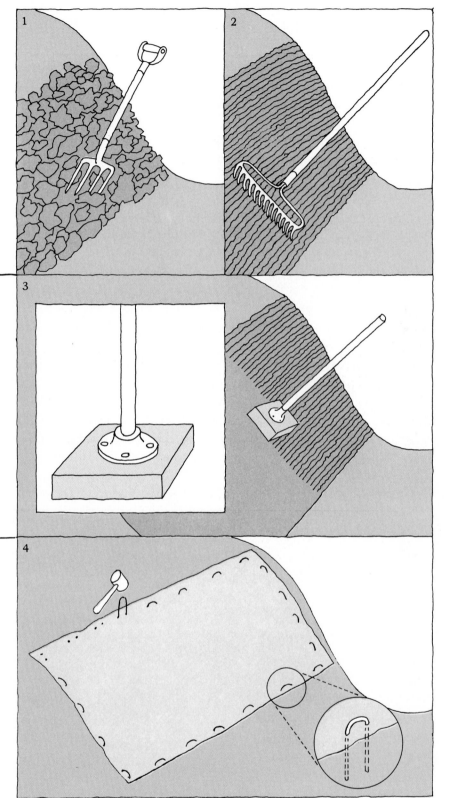

the silvery, deeply notched leaves of bloodroot. All these myriad shapes, textures and subtle shades of green, when they are viewed against various types of trees, shrubs and rocks, can make a wild garden a place of quiet beauty even during those times when no flowers are to be seen.

You can do still more. With imagination and a modest amount of work you can create a wildflower garden offering a constantly changing variety of both scale and color. On a large plot, one that will permit the establishment of several environments of different types, a tremendous range is possible.

One Illinois gardener reported that on his four-acre property he and his wife were growing more than 1,000 species of wildflowers. A level area was given over to Prairie flowers such as fragrant meadowsweet and cattail gay-feathers; they were surrounded by crab apples, hawthornes and other trees to protect them against winter damage. A shaded pond was the center of a Wetland garden of Jack-in-the-pulpit, cardinal flowers, blue lobelia, marsh marigolds and lady's slippers. Oaks and hickories provided the trees for a Deciduous Woodland environment that was host to hepatica, trilliums of several varieties, rue anemone, bloodroot, spring beauty and various violets. Ferns abounded everywhere in the four acres. There were also a moss garden and several separate rock gardens. The area was never without some kind of bloom from April straight through until the fall. Although few gardeners are lucky enough to have four acres to command, many wildflower enthusiasts do just as well in achieving continuous bloom on a considerably smaller scale.

In much of North America, it is fairly easy to ensure variety and a long season of color by developing at least two different environments in a single backyard: a Woodland garden and a sunny Prairie garden. For this combination you will need sun, shade and an adequate supply of moisture—either natural or manmade. The succession of bloom in any sunny expanse—for example, in the space beside a driveway—can easily be planned so it will continue to flower throughout the growing season. In spring come flowers such as blue-eyed grass and the red and yellow wild columbine. Summer is ushered in by bee balm, Canada lily, common yarrow, blue flag, the orange butterfly weed and the blue, white or purple blossoms of wild lupine. During the summer the pink-red blossoms of Joe Pye weed and the lavish purple loosestrife will appear, followed by the many goldenrods, red and white turtlehead, and finally the asters, notably the blue-violet New England aster, which continues to bloom until midautumn.

GARDENS FOR SUN AND SHADE

Creating a special world 3

As Richard Pough, a leader of conservation groups and one of the world's most skillful wildflower gardeners, walked through the yard around his suburban home, he picked up a short branch that had blown down. He broke it into small pieces, and casually tossed them onto the leaves surrounding the Jack-in-the-pulpit, green dragon and double bloodroot. "Best thing in the world for the plants," Pough said. "I wouldn't think of putting any branch or twig out by the street to be hauled away. Twigs keep the soil light and airy, and when they decay they supply valuable nourishment." He picked up another twig and repeated the process. "We've lived here for 35 years, and in all that time we've never thrown out a single thing from the trees or the yard. It all stays here: leaves, branches, dead plants, everything. In some places the oak leaves are several feet thick. Any time I want some leaf mold for a new plant, I just dig down and get what I need."

Pough's property demonstrated a special point of view typical of devoted wildflower gardeners. It was bursting with greenery of startling variety. Along with imported herbs and ivies, it displayed a profusion of wild plants—trillium, shortia, Canada lily, and native shrubs, set amid half a dozen kinds of ferns. There was no lawn at all; in fact, there was barely room for a small terrace. In 35 years this gardener had never bought any weed killer or fertilizer—but there were virtually no weeds. By conscientiously allowing all plants to live out their normal spans, then die, decay and return their elements to the soil, he had duplicated the process by which a wild environment is created naturally. His only problem was to keep one vigorous wild species from crowding another out. "Watch out for May apple," Pough said. "It wants to take over."

Not everyone would like to have this kind of garden, with its abundance of shrubbery and lack of open space. And not everyone is willing to wait 35 years while the forces of nature reclaim an

Almost no soil is too poor, dry or hot for bitter-root, a refreshing spring flower of the western mountains. It is common in Montana, where Meriwether Lewis discovered it during his 1806 expedition.

TESTING FOR SOIL CONSISTENCY

*To see if your soil is suitable
for wildflowers, dig a hole 6 inches
deep. Note the depth of the darker
topsoil—you need at least 4 inches—
and check its texture by wetting a
handful and squeezing it in your fist.
A soil heavy with clay will form a
smooth, dense ball (left); a sandy soil
will crumble (center). The most
desirable soil, rich in leaf mold and
decayed vegetable matter, will separate
into several large lumps (right). If
you are lucky enough to have such soil,
no modification is needed. But if the
test shows that the soil is heavy with
clay or light with sand, spread 3
inches of leaf mold or compost over the
planting bed and spade it in.*

environment, cycling and recycling the things that want to grow of themselves until there is ecological balance. Fortunately, it is not necessary to be so patient. You can nudge nature along to re-create fairly quickly the effect of the primeval environment.

Once you have decided what kind of garden—or gardens—to create and what kind of plants to grow *(Chapter 2),* several factors must be considered in adjusting the environment to suit them. One is sunlight and wind, which will largely be controlled by existing trees and shrubs, but can be modified by additional plantings. The relative wetness of the ground may vary from section to section of even a small yard. Moisture depends partly on rainfall and surface contours, of course, but is also influenced by the soil. And it is the soil that is perhaps the most important factor in the success of your wildflower garden, for its structure and chemical composition determine which plants will grow.

SOIL: THE KEY TO SUCCESS

All gardeners have to think about their soil, but a wildflower gardener must view it in a special way. The soil needed by most conventional garden flowers is a rich, deep surface layer called loam, composed of clay, sand, silt and organic matter, in varying proportions; it is turned over periodically to loosen its consistency and eliminate weeds. Limestone may have to be added if it is too acid, or sulfur if it is too alkaline, and it may need to be watered periodically and fertilized. Such soil is generally suitable for vegetables and garden flowers. But most wildflowers demand a more stable growing medium, and the requirements vary depending on the type of environment you wish to create—or rather re-create, in returning the land to its ancient form. Wildflower soil differs from cultivated soil principally in that it is very porous—it holds more water than cultivated land, and this water passes through it more freely—so it can easily transfer nutrients for plant growth.

Wildflowers of fields and meadows, such as those that grow in the Prairie and Semiarid Grassland environments and in sunny parts of forest regions, thrive in soil that is not very different from conventional garden loam; they require in addition only a protective mulch of dead grasses to nurture their growth, and they are adapted to the neutral chemical composition that suits both lawns and most domesticated plants. But the most popular wildflowers, those of the forest as well as those of some wetlands, demand something different. They thrive in acid soil. And they need a texture that is very porous.

Such a soil structure is a complex engine for the renewal of fertility. At the top of this structure is a layer of ground-litter, a mixture of fallen leaves, twigs, branches and other decaying vegetation. This vegetable litter decomposes into what is called leaf mold. Mixed in with it is a certain amount of decaying animal matter—the droppings and occasional carcasses of forest creatures, from worms and insects to birds and squirrels. All this decomposed material, animal and vegetable, makes up the rich substance called humus. Humus contributes to the porous texture of the soil. It also provides growth-promoting organic substances, principally compounds of nitrogen. In addition, it contains many essential minerals, substances that were in the soil, were taken out of it by plants, and are then returned to it by the decay of the plant material (or of the animals that had eaten the plants).

LAYERED FOREST FLOOR

The organic humus composed of decaying plant and animal matter mixes with tiny particles of various earth minerals to make the nutritious, porous topsoil in which forest plants grow. Below this layer is a subsoil that becomes increasingly less organic and more mineral with depth; underneath all these layers is solid rock or hard clay that is almost entirely mineral. The underlying rock helps determine the soil's chemical content—in the eastern United States it tends to be granite, which is acid, while in all of the West but the Rocky Mountains there is a preponderance of limestone, which is alkaline. The limestone influence, however, is tempered by the decaying matter above, which is acid, and by rain, which can wash away the alkalinity.

All through this structure, organic matter is constantly breaking down to enrich the topsoil while dissolved minerals are working their way up from lower layers into the subsoil and even into the

LEAVES FOR LEAF MOLD

Leaf mold, like soil, should have approximately the level of acidity to which the plant is accustomed. The acidity of leaf mold depends on the type of materials that are used in making it (opposite). The leaves or needles of hemlock, spruce, fir, pine, oak, beech, blueberry, rhododendron, azalea and laurel are, for instance, very acid, with a pH of 4.0 to 5.0. Red maple and most birches are moderately acid, with a pH of 5.0 to 6.0. Slightly acid (pH 6.0) to neutral (pH 7.0) leaves come from cedar, basswood, hickory, ash, poplar, butternut, most maples, elm, tulip, willow and dogwood trees.

USING A pH KIT

topsoil by capillary attraction. It is on these various components—organic and mineral—that all wildflowers live. They do so in soil that is almost constantly moist, because the humus-rich soil of the forest has an extraordinary capacity for storing water. Soft and spongy, this soil can hold several times as much water as can ordinary garden soil.

It is this intricate structure that you will try to reproduce if you set out to create a swamp, marsh or bog of the Wetland environment or a Woodland environment of any type—Deciduous, Northeastern Coniferous, Southeastern Coniferous, Rocky Mountain Woodland or Western Coniferous. It may take some doing; the soil around many American houses is horticulturally deprived. You must test your soil both for consistency and for acidity.

Dig a hole where you plan to locate your wild garden and see how the consistency of the soil changes as you go down *(page 46)*. This will tell you how much topsoil you have. Pick up a handful of topsoil and crumble it with your fingers. What is its texture? Is it sandy—with many small stones in it—or smooth like clay? Or is it humusy, full of rich organic matter? Wet another handful and roll it into a ball. Does it hold together tightly or fall into pieces? Ideally it should do neither: soil for woodland flowers should hold generally firm but break into a few sections. If the soil is too sandy or too clayey, it will need to have some humus added to it in the form of leaf mold *(left)*.

Now for the chemical test. You may have already deduced the acidity of your soil from the kinds of trees in your area *(Chapter 1)*. You should, however, be more precise at this point, for such observations may be misleading. Many a gardener has assumed that his soil was acid because plants adapted to this characteristic, such as oaks and rhododendrons, grew there, only to find that many applications of limestone on the lawn had made the ground neutral. Using a testing kit from a garden center, test several samples, from different locations and different depths.

This testing will immerse you in the world of pH values—the numbers that indicate the relative acidity or alkalinity of the soil. The pH values cover a scale of 1.0 to 14.0, with 1.0 designating the ultimate in acidity and 14.0 the peak in alkalinity. The numbers you will be concerned with are 4.0 to 8.0, with 7.0 designating neutral soil. Any pH value above 7.0 is alkaline, and any below 7.0 is acid. To do the test, mix a soil sample with a chemical in the kit. The solution will turn color, depending on the acidity or alkalinity of the soil, and by matching that color on an accompanying chart you will get the pH reading. Be sure to keep the soil sample pure.

Do not even touch it—perspiration is alkaline and thus might throw off your reading.

A pH value below 5.0 is very acid, and soils with this rating are generally found only in peat bogs of the Wetland environment or directly under coniferous trees of Northeastern and Southeastern Coniferous environments (decaying needles are highly acid). Ratings between 5.5 and 6.5 mean the soil is slightly acid: you find such soil in the Western Coniferous environment and in the Deciduous environment, and even in gardens that have been heavily fed with a fertilizer such as cottonseed meal, which leaves an acid residue. Rhododendrons and azaleas flourish in such soil, as do many wildflowers. Any rating close to 7.0—near neutral—is fine for most field flowers of the Prairie and Semiarid Grasslands environments. A rating of 8.0 or above means that the soil is decidedly alkaline; such a level is typical of the Desert environment, suitable for cacti and other succulents.

With the soil tests finished, you will know the chemistry and texture of your soil and how much you need to change it. You can alter a soil's consistency, say from sandy to humusy. But an attempt to change its chemical nature will be successful only to a limited extent. Factors beyond your control, such as the underlying

MAKING LEAF MOLD FOR WILDFLOWERS

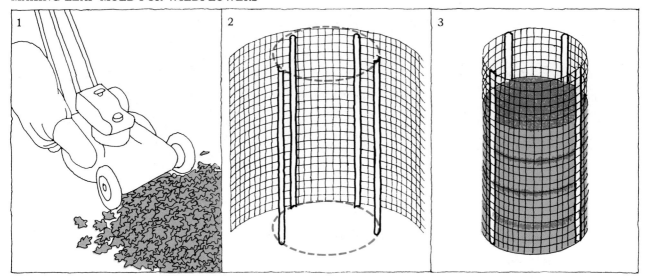

Fallen leaves left to decompose will form leaf mold in about two years, but the time can be halved by chopping the leaves with a power mower equipped with a collecting bag before forming the leaf-mold pile.

Support a leaf bin with four grooved metal fence posts 5 feet tall, set a foot deep in a square of any convenient size; encircle them with 1-inch hardware cloth 4 feet wide, fastened by twisting together the ends.

Fill the bin with alternate layers of acid soil and chopped-up leaves, 6 inches of leaves to 1 of soil. Shape the soil like a saucer to retain water. As each soil layer is added, water well; keep the pile moist at all times.

rock of your area, the trees above or the chemical composition of your rainfall (rain has a pH rating, too, as does the tap water from your garden hose), tend to return the soil to its natural rating. Rather than attempting to push the pH rating very far in either an acid or alkaline direction, you would be much better off choosing plants that will do well in your soil as it is or as it can be made with slight changes.

Both of the important characteristics of soil—texture and acidity—are adjusted in the same operation. You simply mix in leaf mold or peat moss. Whether the existing soil is too sandy, too clayey or too dense from compaction by foot traffic, adding decayed leaves will correct the deficiency. Simultaneously, the leaf mold can modify the pH if you concoct it of the appropriate kinds of leaves and modify it with chemical additives. One note of caution: do not use such popular soil conditioners as manures, even those that are well aged. Although venerated by gardeners everywhere, they are not suited for most wild plants, and can set off an unbridled growth that is unnatural.

QUICK LEAF MOLD   Since leaf mold is nature's own soil conditioner of decayed leaves and twigs, it is simple enough to prepare in nature's own way, although there are a couple of tricks that make the process go faster than it does in the wild forest. Autumn is the time to make it, when the leaves drop. Build a container of wire mesh about 3 feet square and 3 or 4 feet high, its corners held stable by stakes *(page 49)*—or use a heavier metal mesh and simply tie it in a circle—and fill it with chopped leaves. What is of special importance to wildflower growers is the chemical nature of the leaves, since the resulting leaf mold will be exactly as acid as what goes into it. If you want to produce a very acid compost you should use the needles of conifers or the leaves of oaks, beeches, blueberries, azaleas and rhododendrons. Moderately acid are the leaves of red maples and most birches. Only slightly acid or neutral are the leaves of most common deciduous trees not already mentioned. To create leaf mold that is alkaline, or to temper natural acidity when necessary, simply add lime, testing the pH until you get it right. If you keep the pile of chopped leaves moist but not sopping, rich, crumbly brown leaf mold will be yours in about a year; the process takes about two years if you use unchopped leaves.

A SPECIAL COMPOST   A still faster but more artificial method for producing the decayed vegetable material you need to condition your soil is to make a compost formulated especially for a wild forest garden. Like ordinary compost, it will be ready for use in three to six months. But it should be made only of chopped leaves and twigs—

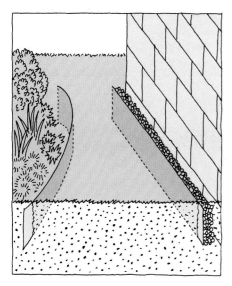

A BARRIER AGAINST ALKALINITY
To keep undesirable plants or soil chemicals from intruding on your wildflower garden, you can construct a hidden barrier of rigid plastic or rust-resistant metal bands 9 inches wide. To bar any invading roots, bury the barrier around the garden perimeter so that its upper edge is just even with the surface of the soil. To keep out unwanted chemicals, such as lime from an adjacent masonry wall (which would tend to make the soil in the flower garden more alkaline), bury the barrier in the soil 2 inches away from the wall and then fill the intervening space with sand so that any chemical runoff from the wall will drain away from the wildflowers.

no garbage, corncobs or lawn clippings—that have been treated with chemical additives in order to adjust acidity. It is, in effect, a leaf compost.

Every expert has his favorite compost method. Piles can be made in pits, in concrete-block bins, in wooden-slat structures or in the wire-mesh contraption described for leaf mold. All are good, although the pit requires more turning because it gets less ventilation. Whatever method is used, composters agree on two things: the ingredients should be added in layers, and the whole pile should be kept moist at all times. The acidity of the mixture, like that of leaf mold, is determined by the ingredients. Choose leaves as you would for leaf mold. In addition, you can increase acidity, if necessary, by adding powdered sulfur, superphosphate, ammonium sulfate or aluminum sulfate. To make the mixture more alkaline, dust each layer in the pile with ground limestone. Each 6-inch layer of vegetable matter should be covered with 2 inches of ordinary soil to seal in the heat that was generated by decay bacteria. Turning the pile every six weeks speeds the compost process, but more important is the addition of a pint of 5-8-7 garden fertilizer to each layer, since the nitrogen and phosphorus in the fertilizer will speed the bacterial action.

REPLACING THE SOIL

The addition of such a leaf compost or of leaf mold itself is generally sufficient to bring soil close to the woodland state. But perhaps the spot you have chosen for a wild garden is too far gone to be easily repaired, with poor soil or the wrong vegetation or both, and a drastic change is needed.

Among the best methods for total replacement of soil is still the one described in 1951 by Clarence Birdseye—the pioneering developer of quick-frozen foods—who, with his wife Eleanor, wrote the classic book, *Growing Woodland Plants*.

"The original soil should be excavated to a depth of 18 inches, unless ledge or hardpan intervenes, in which case the surface of the finished garden will be somewhat higher than the surrounding soil," explained Birdseye. "As the earth is dug out, roots, even of valued shade trees, should be cut off and removed—so long as not more than about 20 per cent of the total roots of any one tree are severed. If you are in any doubt on this matter, ask the advice of a nurseryman.

"After excavation has been completed, place a 2-inch layer of crushed granite, cinders, or sharp sand in the bed to assure adequate drainage and to deter earthworms from carrying alkaline subsoil upward into your acid garden loam. If you are building your garden over a sloping or well-drained granite ledge, this drainage layer is not necessary; but if the garden surmounts a limestone or marble ledge, the drainage layer is important if acid-loving plants are to be grown."

INGREDIENTS OF THE BED

Birdseye then prescribed the ingredients for the wildflower bed. "Over the layer of drainage material, spread 6 inches of the excavated soil, or of any good garden loam; on top of that, sprinkle a ⅛-inch layer of equal parts of commercial superphosphate, ammonium sulphate and powdered sulfur. Next, apply a 2-inch layer of garden loam and 2 inches of woods-compost," which Birdseye prepared as described above for leaf compost. Over this he spread ½ inch of cottonseed meal "and another ⅛-inch layer of the three chemicals. Again mix thoroughly and water adequately.

"Now lay on 6 inches of compost, which, if rightly prepared, will have an acid value of about pH 5.0 to 6.0. If the pH number is lower than 5.0, add about 2 pounds of garden lime per 100 square feet to raise it slightly; or if the pH is above 6.0, sprinkle on 1 to 2 pounds of powdered sulfur and ammonium sulphate, mixed. Thoroughly mix the compost and chemicals; again water well."

To ensure the integrity of this wildflower-bed mixture, line the pit with a band of metal lawn edging set flush with ground level. This will prevent the encroachment of grass and weeds or the entry of alkaline substances.

The effort required to establish a garden for woodland flowers is considerable simply because the trees of the Woodland environments were erased so long ago from much of the continent. Less manipulation of soil is needed if your aim is one of the other types of wildflower gardens. For an open patch of flower-dotted grass-land—such as that typical of the Prairie or Semiarid environments, or even of the sunny meadows and fields that are normally scattered through woodlands—you can engage in what might be called carefully controlled neglect. Field flowers will grow in poor soil, but they too will be much healthier if given a good humusy base. If your sunny area is not cluttered by shrubbery, dig the soil to a depth of 1 foot and incorporate leaf compost, peat moss or leaf mold to hold moisture through heat waves and dry spells.

Field flowers are fairly easy to grow for another reason. They are less finicky about the acidity or alkalinity of the soil than forest plants, and will generally grow over a broader pH range than that specified for their environment. Consequently you may be able to grow field flowers that are native to environments different from your own, although this flexibility cannot be pushed too far—you are, for instance, unlikely to have much luck raising California lupines in a Massachusetts bog.

Plant the field with grasses, then sit back and wait. In due course it will be covered with grass as well as weeds and other vegetation; some of these plants will be wildflowers that you will want to keep—daisies and asters in a Deciduous Woodland field, perhaps, or yarrow and milkweed in a Semiarid Grassland environment. The weeds can be pulled. At any time you can introduce new varieties of field flowers that you have collected or propagated. Thereafter, if you live in the dry Prairie or Semiarid Grassland environment you need do nothing more; there is no danger that

ADAPTABLE FIELD FLOWERS

HOW TO BUILD A BOG GARDEN

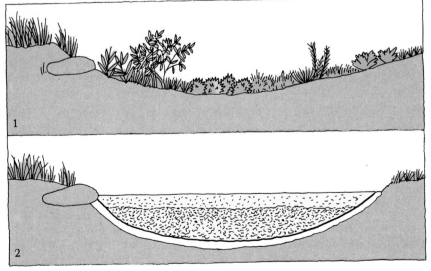

1. To create a bog garden, select a low spot; dig up undesirable plants.

2. Remove soil to make a bowl-shaped depression 18 inches deep, with sloping sides. Line it with 1 inch of sand; cover the sand with 20-mil-thick black vinyl sheeting. To prevent floods during heavy rains, cut a runoff trench, 6 inches deep, into the bog's top edge. Put a mixture of half peat moss, half humus 1 foot thick into the bottom of the bog. Fill the remaining space with sphagnum moss; water until the moss is saturated but not submerged. In six weeks to two months test the bog; it should have a pH below 6.0. Add ground sulfur if it is not acid enough.

shrubs and trees will take over. In moister regions, you must mow the field once a year to discourage trees—early fall is a good time because most wildflowers have set seed by then, though some gardeners favor spring because they prefer to let the plants distribute their own seed. Mowing also improves the mulch of dead grasses atop the soil.

If you have water of any kind on your land, even rainwater that does not drain away quickly, you have the chance to own some kind of wet wildflower garden—a brookside, pond, marsh, swamp or bog. For most of these types of gardens there is no soil problem: the wet area will surely be rich and mucky—and ideal for some kind of plant life. The only question will be whether to restrict or decrease the wet area. Marshes and swamps can be partially drained, brooks can be dammed to make a pond, a bog can be built from scratch (page 53). In all such cases you will probably want to place rocks or strong-rooted plants along the banks to forestall any possible erosion.

PLANTING IN SAND

Seashore and desert gardens are practical only for those who live in those environments. For them, little preparation is necessary. The existing soil will be sand or a combination of sand and loam; any plant that grows there naturally is used to it. But you can improve the environment enough to lessen the shock suffered by plants when they are moved into the garden. If you dig peat moss, compost or leaf mold into the seashore soil, you will help the plants' roots to catch hold, and the moisture supply will be more constant

(continued on page 58)

A watery world magically restored

Few gardening sites seem less promising than a bog, and few gardening activities are more rewarding than transforming one. The expansive bog garden at right, described by its photographer-owner Steve Wilson as "a delicate profusion of floral activity," occupies 17 acres near Seattle once used for lumbering and gold mining. When the debris was cleared away, the owner recognized that the site was ideal for bog plants: a granite bottom trapped water; rain plus runoff from adjacent slopes guaranteed moisture; sphagnum moss gave an acid base.

Today hundreds of bog plants grow there. In winter, heavy rains make the garden all but inaccessible, swelling its bed of moss to a depth of 6 feet. But in summer, the owner, walking on quaking moss 2 feet thick or supported by a raft, sets up his tripod and uses his garden for subject matter (pages 56-57). Gnats, flies and mosquitoes are controlled in fact by insectivorous plants, like sundew, and by the frogs, trout and water birds that enjoy the bog as much as its owner does.

Pink salal, white Labrador tea and yellow pond lilies adjoin a raft built of cedars like those around the bog.

Heal-all's dense flower heads and slender leaves form a mass of rich summer color on the surface of the bog.

Sticky, sensitive leaf hairs of sundew glisten as they wait to trap unwary insects that the plant will eat.

The ill-scented western skunk cabbage flower, 6 inches tall, will be dwarfed by 4-foot leaves (emerging left).

Water parsnip's lacy flowers bloom among 2-foot-tall marsh grasses and a single skunk cabbage.

In July the foam flower's tiny bell-shaped blossoms swing from the ends of slender 6- to 18-inch stems.

Nodding clusters of western bleeding heart's May flowers arch over their spreading, fernlike foliage.

An Alaskan buttercup, accustomed to higher latitudes, is grown experimentally in the milder Washington climate.

With the bog at its spongy driest, a yellow pond lily seems suspended in air; in wet months, its leaves float on water.

during the transition period. In the Desert environment, dig in 2 or 3 inches of leaf mold or peat moss to hold moisture that will help flowers get started.

After the soil for a wildflower garden is properly established, its character must be preserved. This is the main job of mulches, which are vital to any kind of wildflower environment. They help enrich the soil as they disintegrate, and they also protect plants from too much sunlight, heat, cold and other extremes of nature. In the forest, ground-litter performs this important function; in an open field or meadow the grass does it—even breaking the force of downpours that might otherwise injure delicate plants. What kind of mulch you should use will depend on what is available and what is best for your garden.

Inorganic mulches provide no soil enrichment but can be used in any environment, Desert to Wetland. Stones and rocks work well—as anyone can testify who has noted the wild plants that flourish along railroad tracks.

For specific environments, a wide variety of organic mulches is available to choose from. The ingredients of a compost suitable to the environment are, of course, satisfactory mulches. For the Deciduous Woodland garden, oak or beech leaves are fine, although they may need to be held down with branches. The small leaves of white birches, willows and mountain ashes are also desirable because they turn to humus quickly. Avoid maple leaves, however, which tend to mat and drain water away like shingles. For a wildflower garden in a Northeastern or Southeastern Coniferous environment, the needles of such evergreens as white or Norway pine make good mulches. For a Western Coniferous or Rocky Mountain Woodland environment, you can use needles or leaves from native trees.

Peat moss is an acceptable mulch in any Woodland environment, but it is more efficiently used as a soil conditioner. Wood chips, including bark, serve well but break down slowly (for this reason, they make an excellent garden path).

There are a number of mulches that can be used in gardens other than forest ones. For woodland meadows and fields, as well as the Prairie and Semiarid Grassland environments, lawn clippings, hay, buckwheat hulls and cranberry clippings are excellent. Seaweed or salt-marsh hay are recommended for seashore gardens.

Because mulches must remain loose and spongy to be effective, you should give your wild garden further protection by installing stepping stones, so you will not have to tread on the actual garden surface and compact it.

With the soil prepared and mulched, the plants of your garden will require little maintenance. Your chief task will be renewing the mulch. Fall and spring are the key seasons. In the fall, make sure there is at least an inch or two of mulch over the entire area. In the spring, thin out any mulch that is so thick it will inhibit growth, but renew any mulch that has grown thin.

A secondary but still important concern will be water, especially in a forest garden. In theory, a wildflower garden should need no artificial watering. If the plants are well established and adequately mulched, should they not survive on their own as they do in nature? Well, maybe. To begin with, your garden is not the plant's original environment—only a skillful re-creation—and inevitably some of the protections found in the wild will be missing. Then, droughts do occur in nature, and take a severe toll. In true wilderness this loss must be tolerated as the price of evolution; in your garden a similar loss leaves you with no garden at all, and there is no reason to tolerate such disaster. So check during dry periods to make sure the soil is generally moist. The top of the mulch can be dry, but if there has been no rain for a couple of weeks, wildflowers will signal their need by wilting. At that point deep-rooted plants need three or four hours of watering with a soaker hose; shallow-rooted plants will make do with a half-hour shower from a sprinkler. In all watering, pay special attention to places where tree roots grow near the surface; give them extra water. In a seashore garden, light but frequent sprinklings will minimize the leaching of nutrients from the sandy soil.

There are two final maintenance chores. One is a continuing check on acidity. Even if you have not actually altered your garden's pH, that rating can shift in time. Use the soil-testing kit whenever you suspect there has been a change. A drift toward alkalinity can be forestalled by mulching with peat moss. If more drastic action is indicated, add ground sulfur. Overacidity is unlikely, but it can be corrected by applying lime.

One final concern is pests (diseases are rare). Borers, slugs, aphids and cutworms can be just as lethal in the wild garden as in the conventional one. Serious attacks should be countered with insecticides, used selectively and cautiously.

One woe of conventional gardeners and lawnkeepers—the growth of mushrooms and toadstools—is actually a sign of health among wild plants that prefer an acid soil. Their flourishing existence proves the habitat suits fungi, and fungi mean there is vigorous bacterial activity underground. To the wildflower devotee they are cause not for dismay but for celebration.

WATERING ON DEMAND

How to get the plants you need 4

Although wildflower gardeners find ever-increasing numbers of commercial suppliers ready to serve them, you are still unlikely to find the seeds you seek in packets in the supermarket rack, next to the tomato and phlox envelopes. Just the matter of stocking your garden becomes a challenge. For many plants you will have to collect seeds, transplant specimens or propagate from whatever stock you might have at hand.

If you can buy nursery-grown plants ready to be set into your own garden, do so by all means; this method of obtaining stock is the easiest and generally the most successful, for plants that are raised commercially are likely to be tougher and more receptive to transplanting than those found in their natural state. But few nurseries carry more than the most popular varieties. The second method is to transplant the flowers from the wild, perhaps from a friend's land or from property that has been condemned; this method is the most economical one, often the most intriguing, and sometimes the only one available—very few seashore species, for example, are sold commercially. Transplanting from the wild, however, may involve a would-be gardener in controversy, as there is wide disagreement about the propriety of such collecting.

The third method is to propagate your own plants, raising them from seeds, multiplying them by taking cuttings or employing other techniques such as layering and dividing. This process is the most complicated and time-consuming but it is relatively inexpensive and in many ways the most interesting.

Your choice of plants will help you to decide which of these methods to use. Although you may have some special preferences, you will probably find yourself selecting, at the beginning, from among a few well-known varieties, particularly those of the Deciduous Woodland environment. Helen S. Hull, who writes on wildflower gardening, once asked people in every state of the United

Dutchman's breeches, one of the easiest wildflowers to grow, is also one of the most ephemeral. Here, in an eastern woodland garden in early spring, it delicately and briefly festoons a rocky slope.

MOVING A DORMANT PLANT FROM THE WILD

1. *When you find the plant you want, label it with a stake. The smaller the plant and the closer to the edge of a clump, the easier it will be to separate and move the root system. Test the soil acidity around the plant; prepare a soil of similar pH (page 50).*

2. *Return for the plant after flowers have faded and leaves have died. For most plants that bloom in early spring, the best transplanting time is fall; those that bloom in the late spring, summer or early fall should be moved in early spring.*

3. *Dig up the dormant plant and its roots in a solid ball of earth, taking as much of the root structure as you can possibly gather. If it seems necessary, cut away the roots of any adjacent plants with pruning shears.*

4. *Put the entire plant in a plastic bag and fasten it tightly to keep the root structure from drying out. Fill another plastic bag with as much soil gathered from around the plant as you can comfortably carry. If at all possible replant your new acquisition on the same day that you collect it.*

5. *At home, dig a hole about 3 inches wider and deeper than the root ball. Line the hole with some of the soil that you brought from the plant's original site. Set the plant in the ground and fill in around the roots with a mixture of equal parts of garden soil and the remaining soil from the plastic bag.*

6. *Tamp the soil around the root ball and water the area until the soil becomes saturated. Cover the soil with 2 inches of mulch. If the plant is one that requires high acidity, use a mulch consisting of oak leaves or pine needles.*

States to name the plants they had grown most happily. She learned that, despite considerable variations in growing conditions among their gardens, there was a large overlap in the lists. Twelve plants, in fact, kept recurring: bloodroot, Jack-in-the-pulpit, American columbine, Virginia bluebells, sweet William, snow trillium, fawn lily, hepatica, Dutchman's breeches, cardinal flower, wild ginger and crested iris—all native to the Deciduous Woodland.

Many of these and other popular wildflowers are available from commercial growers. It is wise to choose a nursery that specializes in wildflowers and, if possible, visit it to examine in person the plants you want. However, many of the best wildflower nurseries are remote from populated areas, and so you may have to order by mail. Even so, order from a nursery that is not far away: its owners will be more aware of your climate and the plants will spend less time in transit. Good nurseries list their plants by both the Latin and the common name; on your order, use the Latin name to prevent mistakes. Make a copy of your order when you buy by mail, with notations as to the eventual locations of your purchases, so that when the plants arrive you will know that *Podophyllum peltatum* is common May apple and is supposed to go over in the east corner next to the azalea. Because some losses are inevitable, it is best to order more than one of each species. Have a space in the garden already prepared *(Chapter 3)* and put them into the ground immediately when they arrive, watering them thoroughly and observing any special instructions the dealer may have included. The roots are usually packed in sphagnum moss; add the moss to the soil if it needs lightening, or to the surface mulch.

While purchase is simple and relatively foolproof, it lacks the romance of the second method of stocking a wildflower garden: collecting from the wild. If you hope to follow this course, be aware that you may find yourself somewhat embroiled in dispute, because many naturalists stoutly oppose any collecting at all. Many beautiful wildflowers are threatened with extinction today, and much damage is done by people who thoughtlessly dig up plants they should not, so any observations about how to collect may provoke an argument. One thing is certain: under no circumstances must you take any plant that is on a state or federal endangered list; it is wrong, and it is illegal. Plants that are thus protected—for example, the carnivorous plants—often have been so ruthlessly harvested that they could disappear completely. To learn what plants are endangered in your area, write to the National Parks and Conservation Association in Washington, D.C., or check with your state conservation department or a local horticultural society.

RULES OF PLANT COLLECTING

Some gardeners feel they have an ecological duty to preserve rare species by lovingly transporting endangered ones to the safety of their own yards. But if the plant then dies, or if the house is later sold to someone who does not care for wildflowers, there is a loss rather than a gain. So do not take any threatened species unless you know it is about to be ripped up by a bulldozer.

THE NEED FOR PERMISSION

The second rule is that you must always ask permission from the owner of a property before collecting. There are no exceptions to this rule; do not assume that the owner does not care. The rule applies even to ordinary roadsides. Indeed it is often argued that no collecting should be done along public roads at all, for if you remove these plants you deprive other motorists of a pleasurable sight. In any case, be careful to check with local highway authorities before you dig—some, such as the Texas Highway Commission, spend great effort in cultivating roadside flowers.

The permission rule even applies to what is often considered an exception: land that is being cleared for construction. Certainly you should expect to get permission to take plants before the bulldozer arrives, but again you must ask—some owners fear legal problems or interference with the construction work.

When you have permission, schedule the hunt. If a bulldozer is due the next day you will have to act immediately, but otherwise you may be better off waiting. Although it is possible to move almost all wildflowers at any time if enough precautions are taken, and although field flowers like daisies and asters can be transplanted even when they are blooming, the majority of wild plants—particularly the woodland varieties—are most likely to survive if they are transplanted when they are dormant. The rule of thumb is that spring-blooming plants should be moved in the fall and all others in the early spring, but you can move any plant a month or so after it has blossomed with a reasonable expectation of success.

The question arises: how can you locate a plant to move it if it becomes dormant and disappears after blooming, as so many wild plants do? The solution is to tour the area when the flowers are out and put small markers in the ground next to the plants you want. You can return a month or so later to do your moving. If marking is impractical, at least wait until the flowers have passed their peak before trying to dig them up.

THE HAZARD OF DRYING

The day before you plan to move a plant, look around your garden and decide where it will go. Any plant that you move will be better off if it is replanted by nightfall, and if you settle on the place you will save valuable time and minimize the drying suffered by the plant during its move. Then check the weather. If there has been a drought or the following day is forecast as hot or windy, you might want to postpone the trip, or at least make it in the early morning or late afternoon. Most plants are damaged by excessive wind or heat. During summer months the best collecting days are those that are cloudy and cool.

You can easily move many flowers with nothing more than a trowel or small shovel, perhaps a water container, and some plastic bags of various sizes. But Woodland and some Wetland plants require extra preparations. Your equipment then should include the following: pruning shears, for cutting any alien roots that may interfere with your own plant's root structure; a sharp-bladed pocket knife; some flat baskets, for carrying your acquisitions; perhaps a soil-testing kit *(Chapter 3)*; and a notebook for jotting down the conditions in the immediate vicinity—other plants, rocks, amount of shade—so you can try to duplicate those conditions at home.

When you arrive at the site, first clear away fallen leaves and other ground-litter around the plant. If there has been a drought and the ground is dry, give it a generous sprinkling from your water jug. Then dig up the plant *(drawings, page 62)*.

You may want to collect more than one plant from a given spot, for certain plants—like common May apple and snow trillium—grow in colonies and will be healthier in your garden if they have company of their own kind. Younger plants are easier to move than old ones, as their root structures are not so elaborate. If you are collecting ground covers like partridgeberry that grow in mats, you can simply lift part of the patch, taking plenty of dirt

EQUIPMENT FOR THE HUNT

HOSPITABLE SETTING FOR A BEACH PLANT

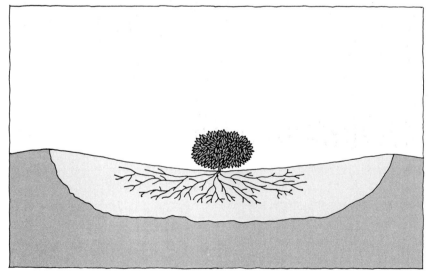

When planting beach plants, take special precautions with their scraggly roots, which are very long. Wrap them in wet newspaper so they do not dry while the planting site is prepared. For the site, dig a hole in the sand twice as wide and deep as the root system. Place the plant in the center, slightly below the surrounding surface so that runoff water will drain toward the plant. Fill the depression with a half-and-half blend of loose peat moss and sand. Water until the mixture is thoroughly damp, then tamp to remove air pockets. Water regularly until the plant is established in its new site.

with it but being careful to leave the rest of the patch intact so that the plants can replenish themselves.

Since everything you dig up should be replanted before the end of the day, take only what you can easily handle. And be sure to clean up the site where you have been digging, replacing and smoothing the soil and covering it with ground-litter.

Back home, pour into the already prepared hole *(Chapter 3)* some soil brought from the woods and insert the plant, making sure it is set just as deep but no deeper than it grew in the wild. Fill in around it with more woods soil or some of the soil you prepared for the bed and tamp it thoroughly to eliminate air pockets. Then cover the surface of the soil with ground-litter or mulch.

Replanting techniques may depend on root structure. Some plants have long-rooted stems just beneath the surface, while others have trailing stems that put down roots here and there. Replanting either of these types can be difficult, but you can sometimes cut the rooted stems into convenient lengths and plant them separately, making certain that each section has its own roots and that any root-crown buds are facing upward. Be careful not to leave any roots exposed to the open air for long; keep them wrapped in damp newspapers so they do not dry out.

After you have replanted the wildflower in your garden, two precautions need to be taken. One is to water the plant occasionally for two or three weeks until it is well established. The other is to protect it from sunlight for at least a week. If its new site is not naturally shady, make a temporary shelter for it out of evergreen boughs or other branches.

Shore plants are a special problem. Most of them have very long roots, and the main chore in digging is to get as much of the root structure as possible. Luckily many of the plants do not have to be moved with their own root ball, so you can retrive the longer roots by digging carefully along their entire length.

Replanting beach plants also may be tricky, for the sandy sides of the holes you dig have a tendency to cave in. Some plants, such as beach grass, can simply be inserted into the sand at their new location and they will take hold. But others, such as beach plum, must be mulched around the roots, a difficult job in shifting sand. Some gardeners put beach wildflowers into mulch in paper containers or large peat pots and bury the containers in the sand. (The containers must be made of paper or pressed peat—plastic will not disintegrate to let roots reach for moisture.) Others simply make a dish-shaped hole, mix peat into the sand at the bottom, set in the plant and fill the hole.

HOW TO GATHER WILDFLOWER SEEDS

If you want to use wild seeds for your garden, you must get to them before they are dispersed by the plant or eaten by birds. Cover the seed head with a bag made of cheesecloth or an old stocking about two weeks after the flowers have finished blooming. Secure the bag with a rubber band or twist tie. In late summer or early fall, when the seeds are ripe, cut the stem below the seed head, untie the bag and remove its contents.

Once your garden is started, you can expand it by propagating the plants you have. The encyclopedia chapter that starts on page 83 specifies how each plant can be multiplied; many can be propagated in alternative ways. Virginia bluebells, for example, can be easily grown in the East from either seeds or root divisions.

Propagating from seeds is perhaps the most widely used method of expanding a garden—and for the adventurous, it is an exciting way to start one. You can buy some seeds by mail, but beware of packaged mixtures of "wildflowers for shade" or "wildflowers for sun"—some of the seeds may be for plants that are inappropriate for your particular environment.

Since the variety of seeds available commercially is limited, you may have to collect those of some species yourself, either from a friend's garden or from the wild. Collecting seeds, unlike digging up the entire plant, does not raise conservation problems—taking seeds does no harm if you leave some—but you still have an obligation to get permission from the property owner if there is any question of trespassing.

Finding the seeds and taking them is tricky and requires patience. Most plants release their seeds a month or so after flowering, and you will have to observe the plant carefully off and on during this crucial time to make sure you get to it when the seed is ripe—or, still better, before.

If plants are left to their own devices, they disperse their seeds in a number of ways. Some simply drop them; others put them out in the form of berries to be eaten by birds and later dropped; still others release them to float in the air; some plants forcibly eject them. To collect the seeds, you must get to them before they are dispersed (*drawing, opposite*). The surest way to do that is to set your trap while the flowers are still blooming. Cut a piece of muslin or nylon netting about 8 inches square, larger if necessary, and tie it over the flower head with a rubber band or twist tie. Wait a couple of weeks and return to collect your booty. After shaking a few of the seeds on the ground to help out nature, put those remaining in an envelope, one envelope for each plant, and write on the outside the name of the plant, date and location, plus any other pertinent facts—surrounding vegetation, condition of soil— that may be of use in raising the seedlings. Then, if you can, collect some soil from near the parent plant. Your seeds will germinate more readily if they are placed in soil that has been brought from their original home in the wild.

Ideally the seeds should be planted at once, since that is what happens to them in the wild. If you must delay, spread them out on sheets of paper and let them dry for a few days. Then clean them by gently rubbing any coating off; if the coatings persist, soak the seeds in warm water overnight. Finally, place them on a fine-mesh metal screen, scrub them with a stiff-bristled brush, allow them to dry, and then return them to their envelopes. Store in a cool, dry place until they are needed.

HELPING SEEDS GERMINATE

When the time for planting arrives, many inexperienced gardeners make an understandable mistake. If nature plants the seeds by simply dropping them on the ground to take root, these people reason, why bother with any other method? Why not take a fistful and broadcast them grandly, forgetting all about flats, cold frames and special soil mixtures? The answer is a simple one: by taking pains you can mitigate the murderous competition that in nature wastes so many seeds. To preserve the species, plants put out an extraordinary number of seeds. A single plant may yield a dozen, or fifty or a thousand. Multiply this by the floral population of a field full of daisies or a forest glade of hepatica and you have an incomprehensible number. But most of these seeds never germinate. They are eaten by birds and bugs, or they fail to reach the soil, or they are choked out by other plants. A microscopic minority make it. So from that fistful you scatter, you might get nothing.

TWO WAYS TO START PLANTS IN RETAINING WALLS

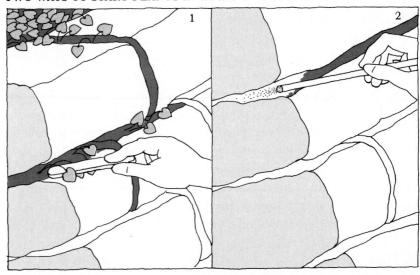

To introduce rock plants such as columbine or harebell into retaining walls or other crevices, wet the entire plant and, using a stick, push the roots into the crevice. Cover the roots with moist soil.

To plant small seeds, such as those of sedum and soapwort gentian, blow the seeds through a drinking straw into the crevice between the rocks. Then tamp dampened soil firmly into the crevice around the seeds.

Of course, some plants can be raised from seeds carefully cast on prepared soil under the right conditions (many California wildflowers qualify for this treatment). But generally speaking, you will waste a high percentage of the seeds this way. You can reverse the odds and have most of them sprout if you control the conditions of germination, emulating nature where it serves the purpose but ruthlessly eliminating competition. The trick is to make your seeds sprout and get a strong start before you plant them in the ground; to achieve this, set them in flats or in pots kept outdoors.

Fall is usually the best time for starting seeds, because many kinds must undergo months of dampness before they will germinate. The seeds of many species—such as Jack-in-the-pulpit or baneberry—planted in the fall this way will sprout the following spring, or even earlier. But some will take longer. One gardener recalls waiting more than a year for some holly seedlings to appear. It was 14 months before even a few showed up; eventually most of the seeds sprouted.

If you are planting seeds that you know are slow to germinate—iris or lewisia, perhaps—you may be able to speed them up with a process known as stratification—that is, by subjecting them to a period of cold and dampness. Freeze them in ice cubes in the refrigerator for a couple of months and then plant them. The seeds react to this stretch of uninterrupted cold as if they had been through an entire winter, and they germinate as if it were spring.

Wildflower seeds are most easily started in flats 3 or 4 inches deep, although some devotees prefer pots and others like to use cans with holes punched in the bottom. In each case there must be good drainage. If pots or cans are used, plan to bury them in soil to within 1 inch of their rims. This will keep them from tipping over and will let them take up moisture from the surrounding soil through their drainage holes.

To fill your containers, the best soil mixture is some that was dug up from the place where the seeds were produced. But if you ordered your seeds from a commercial source or were unable to collect soil, you must prepare your own. One simple and acceptable mix for most seeds is one part sand—it must be coarse, sharp builder's sand, never salty beach sand—to one part compost, leaf mold or peat moss. This mixture should have the same pH (*Chapter 3*) as the soil the plant normally grows in; adjust it as necessary, adding ground sulfur to push it toward acidity or ground limestone to make it more alkaline. You will find the seeds easier to plant if the soil is somewhat dry. Immediately after sowing, dampen the soil, and keep it moist—but not soggy—thereafter. Germination is

AN ARTIFICIAL WINTER

the most critical time in a plant's life; if the soil dries out during this period, the plant will perish.

Plant the seeds sparingly in the flat or pot, so the seedlings will have room to grow without being crowded. The seedlings will be less subject to a disease called damping-off, which makes them rot at the soil line, if you cover the seeded soil lightly with milled sphagnum moss. Although seeds in the wild seem not to be covered, the fact is that the successful ones usually are. Many have appendages that expand and contract to push the seeds underground; others are buried when alternate freezing and thawing open crevices in the soil into which the seeds fall. The gardener can improve on nature's one-in-a-million odds by covering large seeds about three times their dimension with soil. Only tiny dustlike seeds do not need to be covered.

The planted flat or pot needs to be set outdoors in a place where it will be protected from harsh sunlight and rain. Set it in a cold frame or make a miniature greenhouse of clear plastic bags—simply cover the container with plastic held up from the soil with coat-hanger wire or sticks and secured with tacks or tucks under the pot. The seedbed must be shaded. It can be placed under an evergreen, or set in a frame shaded with evergreen boughs. Grown this way, the seedlings require little attention and need watering only every few weeks. They can stay outdoors all winter—even in regions of heavy snowfall. However, the soil must be kept moist. This is vital: the seedlings must not dry out, nor should they be so wet that they succumb to damping-off. If you use plastic covering remove it as soon as the seedlings emerge from the soil. If you find that slugs or snails are seriously damaging the seedlings, spread a bait contining metaldehyde—a specific poison for these garden pests—around the pots.

WHEN TO MOVE SEEDLINGS

When the seedlings develop their first true leaves, identifiable as those of the species—usually by midspring—transfer them to individual pots or to a prepared nursery bed where they will have more room to grow. Peat pots are ideal, for when the plants are large enough to move into the garden, the entire pot can simply be buried in the ground where it will disintegrate. The new soil mixture should be the same as the old one—one part sand to one part compost, leaf mold or peat moss, with its pH adjusted to the requirements of the plant.

To transplant the seedling, prick it out of the flat with an ice-cream stick, together with some of its soil, and place it in the new container, gently firming the new soil around it. Steady the seedling by holding a leaf—do not touch the delicate stem. The pots can

POPCORN FROM POND LILIES

"Popcorn"—quite like the real thing—can be made from the seeds of some yellow pond lilies (Nuphar polysepalum). In the fall, cut off the urn-shaped seed pod, dry it in the sun, then pull it apart to obtain the seeds. Heat the seeds just as you would popcorn and season them with salt and melted butter. Or make pond lily "popcorn balls" as follows: combine in a saucepan 2 cups sugar, 5 tablespoons molasses, 5 tablespoons water and a pinch of cream of tartar. Boil until the syrup forms a firm ball when dropped into cold water, then remove it from the heat and allow it to cool for two minutes. Add 2 tablespoons butter and 1 teaspoon vanilla extract. Stir in 2 cups popped seeds; when cool enough to handle, form into balls.

be kept together in another flat for ease in watering—again the soil must be kept moist. Seedlings develop at differing rates, according to the species. Some are strong enough to be moved to a permanent garden location in a few months. Others may need a year or longer before they can make it on their own. Early fall is a good time to move seedlings into the garden. Be sure they are kept moist and mulched during the fall.

Somewhat similar to growing wildflowers from seeds is propagating from a cutting—a piece of a plant that is snipped off the stem or root, then planted by itself to take root and become independent. This method has two advantages: it produces results faster, and it enables you to perpetuate a particular characteristic of an adult plant. A plant propagated from a cutting will be identical with its parent, while one grown from seed will bear only a family resemblance. If you happen to have a white turtlehead of an unusually pink shade, the best way to be sure of perpetuating that color is to take stem cuttings. If you use the seeds of the plant they will probably produce flowers of the ordinary color.

Cuttings from stems should be taken when new growth is firm, usually late spring or early summer, although it is wise to avoid doing so in the hot weather. They can be started in flats, but as you probably will be working with only a few plants, you may want to use individual 3-inch pots, or put several cuttings in a single larger pot. Making the cutting itself is the crucial operation. Select a 3- to 4-inch section of the stem that bears four or five leaves. This may be the end of the stem, or you may take the top for one cutting and

TO ROOT A CUTTING

A SUNKEN TUB FOR WATERLILIES

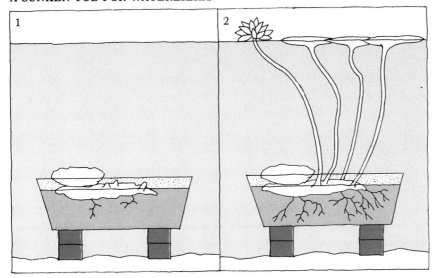

1. To prepare a place for a waterlily to grow, stack bricks on the bottom of the pool to place the plant the right distance below the water surface— 1 to 2 feet for temperate-zone lilies, 4 inches for tropical lilies. Use a container big enough to allow roots to grow; 14 inches wide and 8 inches deep is suitable for a rhizome 8 inches long and 1½ inches thick.

2. Fill the container with garden soil containing some clay to within 1½ inches of the rim. Half-bury the rhizome in the soil, growing tip up; weight it down with a flat rock. Cover the rhizome with an inch of sand or gravel, leaving the growing tip exposed.

the section below it for another. Cut with a sharp knife or razor blade. Do not use clippers: the pinching action damages the delicate cell structure inside the stem. Remove the leaves from the bottom inch of the cutting, nip off the terminal bud at the top if it is succulent and seems likely to wilt, and dip the bottom into a root-hormone powder. Then plant the cutting in the pot, taking care not to dislodge the hormone powder.

As to what mix to use for cuttings, experts differ widely, but it is safe to use coarse sand alone, vermiculite or perlite alone, or the same combination of sand and compost, leaf mold or peat moss used for seedbeds. And just as for seeds, the soil for cuttings should be moist but not soggy. A good way to insure this is to stand the pots in a tray of water and let the water seep up into the soil by capillary attraction. As soon as the top of the soil is moist to the touch, remove the pots from the water.

The cuttings will root most quickly if they are covered, as seedlings are, with plastic or glass. They should be shielded from direct sunlight until they have developed strong roots and are ready to be moved into the garden. The time needed will vary with the species and the temperature—some cuttings will root in a few months while others will take a year or longer. You can test the progress of rooting by tugging gently on the plant; if it resists being pulled, the roots are probably adequate to support the plant in the garden. In the meantime, check the moisture regularly as you would for seedlings.

If you use cuttings from roots instead of stems, the technique is slightly different. There are two variations. One method is used for plants like spotted wintergreen that have long underground stems. You can take a single long rootstock and cut it into several sections, each 3 or 4 inches long, then plant each of these directly in the garden. Each will send up a new plant. The other method is used for plants like partridgeberry with aboveground creeping stems that root every few inches. These creepers can be cut into any number of lengths so long as each section has a root formation, and the new section can also be planted directly in the garden. Root cuttings can be taken at any time of the year but are most successful when the plant is dormant.

DIVISION AND LAYERING

There remain the two propagation techniques that are easiest: dividing and layering. You can divide any plant that has a complex root structure with a number of stems or growing points in the root crown. The best time is when the plant is dormant, in the fall or before new growth starts in early spring. Simply lift the plant and gently separate the roots by hand. If the root clump is tough, you can cut it apart, even though this will injure some of the roots. When you replant the sections, set them at the same depth at which they previously grew.

Layering is most often used to propagate shrubs like rhododendrons, but it can also be applied to creeping plants. Layerings are in effect cuttings that are rooted while they are still attached to—and receiving nourishment from—the parent plant. Spring is the best time to accomplish this. Choose a branch or long stem that can be bent down far enough to touch the ground. On the underside of the stem, at the point where it touches the ground, make a shallow cut—in the case of a shrub you can simply remove some bark. Dust this cut area with root hormone. Then make a shallow hole in the ground so you can bury the branch or stem at the cut point, securing it with a stone or a forked stick. Mulch the area well. Roots will eventually form at this point, and in a year or so you will be able to cut the new plant away and transplant it to another part of your garden. Some stems and branches are long enough to be layered in several places at once, thereby inducing each one to form a new growth.

With all these ways of propagating wildflowers, you may get the feeling that the wildflowers can hardly wait to put down new roots if you will just take care of them. One New Jersey gardener tried a novel experiment. She prepared a bed of sand and simply laid the stalk of a cardinal flower on it. In no time at all it had sent forth a root at each of its branching points. She was able to cut the stalk apart to make new plants from each of the rooted sections.

SETTING WILDFLOWERS BETWEEN TREE ROOTS

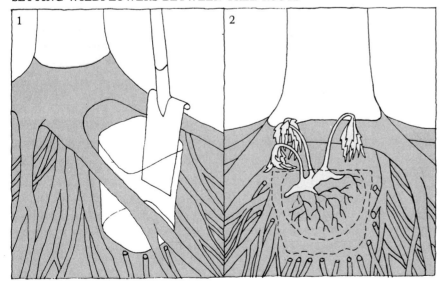

1. For a woodland plant like May apple that thrives between tree roots, dig a hole slightly larger than the root ball. Find space between large roots by trial and error. A straight-bladed spade will cut small roots; you may need an ax for bigger ones.

2. Line the bottom of the hole with an inch or two of prepared soil (page 48). Place the plant in the hole and fill it with more soil. Tamp down and water thoroughly; mulch with 2 inches of dead leaves.

Immigrants from across the sea

Many Europeans who arrived in the New World in the early 17th Century were ardent amateur botanists, and they eagerly explored the native flora. Indeed, they chronicled and sent back home so many specimens of the plants they found that today Europe is a prime source of cultivated hybrids developed from native American wildflowers. At the same time these colonists were also introducing new wildflowers into the American continent.

Some of these plant immigrants were brought across the Atlantic deliberately by homesick colonists as herbs and garden flowers. Others arrived unwittingly. With crop seeds of wheat and barley, for instance, came the seeds of field flowers that grew among these grains in Europe. More seeds made the trip in the mud on the feet of livestock, and still more traveled as stowaways in the tons of dirt used as ballast on sailing ships. Even the settlers' clothing and belongings provided hiding places for stray seeds.

Once here, many of the plant newcomers settled in with a vengeance, even crowding out the natives. In this they were aided by homesteaders. The process of clearing the woods for homes and cropland deprived the indigenous wildflowers of the moist shady forests they required to thrive; simultaneously it provided the competing aliens, accustomed to living in sunny cultivated fields, with just the conditions they needed. Over the centuries they flourished and spread, moving westward with the settlers, until today some of them are among the most familiar American wildflowers. All across the land, along roadsides and in meadows and fields, bloom buttercups and bouncing Bets and cornflowers and lady's thumbs—flowers that were never seen on the American landscape before the 17th Century.

Like their European forebears, many of these wildflower immigrants are highly edible or decorative. And though sometimes derisively labeled weeds, many of them share with their native cousins a diversity of color and form that makes them fine candidates for the wildflower garden.

Three alien wildflowers—white cinquefoil, lavender cow vetch and pink clover—form a colorful bouquet.

Five beautiful intruders

The wildflower aliens pictured here are beautiful, familiar—and annoying. To homeowners who admire a smooth, uninterrupted carpet of green around the house, the aggressive habits of these five imports far outweigh their charms. The dandelion, for example, will grow again if just a small section of its deep-burrowing taproot is left in the ground, while the creeping stems of hawkweed and yarrow defy the lawn mower and can be eradicated only by digging them out by hand or attacking them with sophisticated chemicals. Worst of all, most of these European intruders bloom prolifically and produce abundant crops of seeds with staying powers so formidable that some of them remain viable for as long as 30 years.

Orange hawkweed resolutely seeds itself from multiple heads of brilliant 1-inch flowers.

From spring until frost the yellow flower and fuzzy seed head of dandelion signal its prodigious breeding habits.

A flower in gardens, a weed on lawns, yarrow has dense underground stems that compete with grass roots for moisture.

Mouse-ear chickweed puts down roots from stem nodes and entangles itself in the turf.

Cheerful oxeye daisy has roots that are so tenacious they have to be chopped out of the ground with a knife or trowel.

The long taproot of yellow goatsbeard is cooked and eaten the same way as salsify—in cream sauce, fried or baked.

The shiny oval leaves of the watercress add a crisp, pungent taste to a salad.

A salad green and relish, garlic mustard is called sauce-alone in England because its flavor and aroma make it an all-in-one seasoning.

Wanderers from the vegetable patch

Every American school child knows how the Indians taught the Pilgrims at Plymouth to raise corn, beans and squash—native American food plants unknown in Europe. Less well known is the fact that the colonists introduced many edible plants that grew wild in Europe and quickly became naturalized here too. Greens like black mustard and sorrel; root crops like chicory and burdock; leafy cooking herbs like purslane and plantain; flavoring herbs like field marjoram and peppermint formed part of the colonist's larder in the Old World and then in the New. Many of them fell into disuse as tastes in food changed, and their culinary uses were half forgotten. But with growing interest in natural foods, edible wildings have once again come into their own.

Bright blue chicory's roots, when roasted, have long been a flavoring for coffee.

One of several mustard plants that were originally immigrants, field mustard is actually a naturalized turnip with an edible root.

Flowers to grow for their beauty

Like most English people, the early British settlers in Virginia and New England were garden lovers. Many of them brought seeds, bulbs and even cuttings of their favorite ornamental flowers. Hoping to bring a touch of beauty from the old country into their hard lives, they succeeded beyond their dreams. John Josselyn, an Englishman who lived in New England in 1638 and 1639, reported that many European species were well established there less than 20 years after the Pilgrims arrived. In time, many of these species escaped to grow wild, sometimes developing bad reputations. But as wildflowers they retain the qualities that made them cultivated flowers in 17th Century Europe and earn them a place in today's wildflower gardens.

Named for an English town, the Deptford pink has softly shaded petals.

The flowers of the curiously named viper's bugloss, pink in the bud, are bright blue when fully open, purple when dry.

Dame's rocket, an English flower, grows in clumps 1 to 3 feet high, with pink, purple or white blossoms.

St. Johnswort's frothy flowers, at home in England, were hung in windows to ward off evil spirits on St. John's Day (June 24).

An illustrated encyclopedia of wildflowers 5

If you are lucky enough to have flowers already growing wild in your neighborhood, you are off to a flying start in planning a wildflower garden: you have the best clues to the kinds of wildflowers your property will support. But if you lack this information, the encyclopedia that follows is designed to help you acquire it. Each of the 123 entries indicates where the plant grows naturally—since the re-creation of its natural environment is critical to its successful culture in the garden. Each entry lists not only the plant's geographical range, but also the type of soil in which it grows and the other conditions that surround it—whether it thrives in woodlands, meadows or bogs; in humus-rich earth or salt-filled beach sand; in the cool, dry air of high mountains or the moist atmosphere of coastal plains. Where the information is critical, the entry even pinpoints the specific kinds of plant material that surround the wildflower in its natural habitat. Some woodland wildflowers do best, for instance, in groves of beech and oak, while others depend for survival upon the organic material that has been laid down by forests of pine trees.

Curiously, many wildflowers are quite indifferent to the temperatures they grow in, but where climate is important, zones indicating the depth of winter cold are given. A climate zone map and a habitat map of the nine major North American wildflower environments appear on pages 148-149, giving further information on wildflower growing conditions.

Like all other plants, wildflowers have Latin botanical names, and they are so listed here, in alphabetical order. But the flowers are also extensively cross referenced according to their common names—sometimes more than one name. A chart on pages 150-154 shows the physical characteristics and growing conditions for each of the 123 entries, to provide at a glance a quick profile of each plant that is detailed in the encyclopedia.

Wildflowers bloom in such varied forms as the starlike gillenia (top left), the poppy-shaped Romneya (bottom), plump Dutchman's breeches (right), puffy lady's slippers (left) and shooting star (top).

SAND VERBENA
Abronia umbellata

A

ABRONIA

A. umbellata (sand verbena)

The bright pink blossoms of sand verbena are familiar spots of color through much of the year in the Southwestern desert. This ground-hugging, vinelike plant grows on creeping stems and reaches a height of 3 to 6 inches. Its thick, fleshy leaves are ½ to 1¼ inches long and its pink—and sometimes white—½-inch flowers bloom in clusters 2 inches wide. Though it is not a true verbena, this wildflower resembles garden verbena in fragrance and appearance. Sand verbena is a perennial, but it is used as an annual in gardens where winter temperatures go below freezing. It is excellent for seashore gardens, dry rock gardens and window boxes.

HOW TO GROW. Sand verbena grows in a Desert environment where winter temperatures range between 40° at night and 80° in the day. It does best in full sun and a light, well-drained, sandy soil, but it will tolerate almost any porous soil. Sow seeds indoors in the spring about six weeks before the last frost is due. Seedlings are difficult to transplant except when small, so move them first to individual 2- to 3-inch peat pots as soon as the first true leaves appear. When all danger of frost is past, move the seedlings, pots and all, into the garden. In dry areas of Zones 9 and 10, seeds may be started outdoors in late summer or early fall. In such mild climates, sand verbena will often seed itself.

ACTAEA

A. alba, also called *A. pachypoda* (white baneberry); *A. rubra* (red baneberry)

The two baneberries are woodland perennials grown in wildflower gardens for their colorful clusters of fruit, white or red, which appear at the end of red stems in the late summer or early fall. Despite their visual appeal, these berries are poisonous. The white baneberry is sometimes called "doll's eyes" because the shiny white fruit is dotted with a conspicuous black "pupil." It grows wild in the East and Midwest from Quebec to Georgia, and from Manitoba to Oklahoma and Louisiana. Red baneberry, somewhat hardier, grows as far north as Labrador. It is found in the East as far south as West Virginia; in the Midwest, as far south as Kansas and Indiana; and in the West as far south as New Mexico and Arizona. On the West Coast its range extends from British Columbia south to California.

The baneberries grow 1½ to 2 feet tall and have large, compound leaves with toothed edges. They bear lacy 2- to 3-inch clusters of tiny white flowers in the early summer that ripen into ½-inch berries. White baneberry fruit ripens about three weeks later than red baneberry.

HOW TO GROW. The baneberries grow in the following environments: Northeastern Coniferous Woodland, Deciduous Woodland, Rocky Mountain Woodland and Western Coniferous Woodland. They need shade and a soil rich in humus. White baneberry does well in a slightly acid soil with a pH of 6.0 to 7.0, while red baneberry needs a damper, more acid soil with a pH of 5.0 to 6.0. Both plants, however, are often found together in the wild. Although both can be raised from seeds sown in the fall, seedlings may take three years to produce flowers or fruit. Consequently, the best way to start baneberry is with nursery-grown rootstock, planted in spring or fall. Dig old leaves or peat moss into the soil to lighten it and improve drainage, and bury the rootstock about 1 inch deep, spacing the plants 1½ to 2 feet apart. To propagate from existing plants, divide clumps of roots in the early spring or fall. To propagate from seeds, separate them from the berry pulp as soon as the berries ripen and plant

WHITE BANEBERRY
Actaea alba

them in the fall for germination the following spring. Once baneberry is established, it seldom needs further care.

ALETRIS
A. farinosa (star grass)

Star grass is a graceful little plant with stiff, bladelike leaves up to 8 inches in length which grow in star-shaped clumps. It grows wild in fields from Maine to Florida, and among prairie grasses from Wisconsin and Minnesota as far south as Arkansas and eastern Texas. In the summer, slender leafless flower spikes rise 1½ to 2 feet high and bear ½-inch-long bell-shaped blossoms. Each flower is covered on the outside with small projections that make the blossoms look as though they were dusted with meal or coarse flour. The roots were once used medicinally to treat colic.

HOW TO GROW. Star grass is suited to the environment of the Prairie and open areas of the Northeastern Coniferous Woodland and the Deciduous Woodland. It requires a damp, sandy, acid soil with a pH of 4.5 to 5.5. It does best in full sun. Nursery-grown plants may be difficult to find but if available, can be planted any time the soil can be worked; space them 10 to 12 inches apart. Alternatively, propagate from seeds collected and sown in autumn. Star grass, once established, increases with each succeeding year so long as the soil is sufficiently acid.

ALLEGHENY FOAM FLOWER See *Tiarella*
ALUM ROOT, SMALL-FLOWERED See *Heuchera*
AMERICAN TWINLEAF See *Jeffersonia*

ANEMONE
A. canadensis (Canada anemone, meadow anemone); *A. deltoides* (three-leaf anemone)

Like their close relatives the buttercups, the anemones are a large family of hardy, adaptable perennials, growing in roadside ditches and moist, lightly shaded areas of eastern and western woodlands. The Canada anemone, one of the tallest and sturdiest species, grows wild from Labrador west to Colorado. It rises as much as 2 feet high from its creeping root and has 3-inch-wide hairy leaves resembling those of the wild geranium. A few starry white flowers, 1 to 1½ inches wide, appear on a long branching stem in late spring and early summer. The three-leaf anemone is a more delicate plant, growing 6 to 12 inches high and bearing a single 1½-inch-wide white flower. It grows wild on the western slopes of the Rocky Mountains. The flowers of both anemones have no petals; what appear to be petals are actually sepals, a leaf-like covering for the thimble-like seed heads. The seeds themselves are scattered by wind; the wide-spreading roots grow quickly, pushing up to form colonies of new plants.

HOW TO GROW. Anemones need the environment of the Northeastern Coniferous Woodland or the Rocky Mountain Woodland. They do best in light shade. The Canada anemone tolerates the severe winters of the subarctic and High Sierras; the three-leaf anemone requires a winter mulch to protect it from intense cold. Both species adapt to any soil but flourish in rich, well-drained, slightly acid soil, with a pH of 6.0 to 7.0. To prevent anemone roots from pushing out other plants, choose an isolated spot for them or grow them in a sunken open-ended gallon can. To propagate them, set root segments ½ inch deep in the spring, spacing them 6 to 12 inches apart. Cover with a mulch of leaves or pine needles to keep the soil moist. Anemones can also be propagated from seeds sown outdoors in midsummer as soon as the seeds ripen. If grown from seed they will not flower until the third year. Keep the soil moist when the flowers are in bloom, and

STAR GRASS
Aletris farinosa

CANADA ANEMONE
Anemone canadensis

For environments and climate zones, see maps, page 149.

RUE ANEMONE
Anemonella thalictroides

AMERICAN COLUMBINE
Aquilegia canadensis

unless you want anemones to multiply, cut off the faded flowers to prevent seed formation. Anemones seed themselves so vigorously that they may dominate the garden.

ANEMONELLA

A. thalictroides (rue anemone)

Although it resembles several species of the *Anemone* genus in appearance, the rue anemone is of a different genus, *Anemonella*. It is a delicate-looking perennial that grows only 5 to 9 inches tall. Its small white flowers, borne on two or more stems, are ¾ to 1 inch wide and bloom for four to six weeks in the spring. During the summer the plant becomes dormant. It is relatively easy to establish in the garden. Rue anemone grows wild in the northeast and southeast woodlands from Ontario and New England to Florida, and in midwest thickets from Minnesota to Oklahoma and Kansas.

HOW TO GROW. Rue anemone needs a Deciduous Woodland environment; it does best in light shade and a sheltered position along a garden path or in a sloping rock garden. Ideally, it should have a rich, acid soil with a pH of 5.0 to 6.0, but it can tolerate more neutral soils. To propagate, divide tuber clusters in late spring or early summer, when the plant becomes dormant; plant them 1 inch deep and 4 to 6 inches apart in the late summer or early fall and cover with a light leaf mulch or marsh hay. Rue anemone can also be propagated from seeds sown as soon as they are ripe; if seed heads are not cut off, rue anemone will sow itself. But plants grown from seed do not bloom until they are three years old.

AQUILEGIA

A. caerulea (Rocky Mountain, blue or Colorado columbine); *A. canadensis* (American or Eastern columbine); *A. chrysantha* (golden columbine); *A. formosa,* also called *A. californica* (Sitka, red or California columbine)

Columbines are perennials, found in the wild on the dry slopes and rocky ledges of woodland clearings all over the United States except along the Gulf Coast. Their distinctive nodding blossoms 1½ to 4 inches wide, dance high above deeply lobed foliage in the late spring or early summer, and have an unusual construction: their five petal-like sepals sit on top of true petals, and the back of each petal is elongated into a hollow appendage, called a spur, which contains nectar that attracts hummingbirds. Spurs vary from ½ inch to as much as 6 inches long and end in knobbed tips. The flowers are long lasting in bouquets. They are followed by five-parted fruit containing many seeds that germinate readily.

The Rocky Mountain columbine, Colorado's state flower, grows 1½ to 2½ feet tall and bears 2- to 3-inch flowers that have the overall appearance of being blue, but are actually a mixture of blue, white and yellow; this species has spurs about 2 inches long. The Eastern columbine, parent of numerous hybrids, grows 3 to 4 feet tall and has red and yellow blossoms 2 to 3 inches wide. The 4-foot-tall golden columbine, widely grown in cultivated perennial gardens, is notable for its many yellow flowers. The California columbine is a variable species ranging in height from 12 to 40 inches, and producing yellow or red-and-yellow flowers.

HOW TO GROW. The columbines grow in a Deciduous or Coniferous Woodland environment from Zones 3-10. They thrive in moist, well-drained, sandy, slightly acid soils with a pH of 6.0 to 7.0. If the soil is too rich, columbines produce lush, weak growth with few flowers and will not live long. The plants do best in light shade but will tolerate full sun if daytime temperatures seldom exceed 80°. Set out columbine nursery stock in the early spring as soon as the soil can be worked, or in the fall when the plants are dormant. Set plants 10 to 15 inches apart, with the root crowns at soil level, in the place where they are to remain; established plants are difficult to move because their roots are so long. Columbine may also be started easily from newly ripened seeds sown outdoors in early summer or sown in flats indoors during the winter for transplanting outdoors the following spring. Columbines raised from seeds blossom the second year. In zones where winter temperatures fall below freezing for long periods, cover columbine with a mulch of salt hay, straw or leaves in winter. Columbine seeds scatter in the wind and seed themselves freely near the parent plant.

ARGEMONE
A. hispida (hedgehog prickly poppy); *A. munita* (prickly poppy)

The prickly poppies are coarse, short-lived herbs usually grown as annuals. They have the typically large flowers of the poppy family. They are native to the dry mountain slopes and deserts of the West from Wyoming to central New Mexico and Southern California. These tough plants have strong stems filled with yellow sap and are called prickly poppies because their leaves and sepals end in pointed spines. They bloom in late summer. The hedgehog prickly poppy, which grows 1 to 2 feet tall, has stems covered with bristly hairs. Its large white, or occasionally purple, flowers are as much as 4 inches across. The prickly poppy grows up to 5 feet tall and has branched purplish or greenish-white stems. Its white flowers are 2 to 4 inches wide.

HOW TO GROW. The prickly poppies grow in a Desert or Semiarid Grassland environment or in open areas of a Rocky Mountain Woodland environment. They do well in full sun and light, sandy soil. Sow seeds in the spring or fall, placing them where the plants are to remain; prickly poppies are difficult to transplant. Thin seedlings to stand 9 inches apart. When prickly poppies are in a hospitable environment, they seed themselves freely and must be thinned each spring.

ARISAEMA
A. dracontium (green dragon, dragonroot); *A. triphyllum* (Jack-in-the-pulpit)

Jack-in-the-pulpit gets its name from its blossom that consists of a finger-like spadix, or "Jack," standing somberly within a green- or maroon-lined green-hooded spathe, or "pulpit"; the actual flowers are small and inconspicuous, and cluster on the Jack. In their natural damp, woodsy settings, these small, dignified plants, which bloom during late spring or early summer, are often bathed in cathedral-like streaks of light that enhance their ecclesiastical appearance. Both species grow wild in the East from New Brunswick and Quebec to South Carolina, and in the Midwest from Manitoba to Missouri and Kansas.

Green dragon, the less common of these two perennials, grows up to 3 feet high and its microscopic flowers cover a spadix that protrudes several inches beyond an unarched hood. The leaves are 4 to 6 inches long and are divided into more sections than the common Jack-in-the-pulpit, having five to 15 parts; a tightly packed cluster of orange berries covers the spadix in the late summer or fall.

The true Jack-in-the-pulpit is 1 to 3 feet tall and usually bears two long-stemmed, three-parted leaves, 4 to 6 inches long. Its shorter spadix, about 3 inches long, is enclosed within a hooded canopy of green, which is sometimes striped with red, purple, brown or white, and its flowers cluster around the Jack's base. In the late summer or fall, red berries, up to ½ inch in diameter, ripen in a packed cluster. According to legend, the Indians ate the fiery turnip-like

HEDGEHOG PRICKLY POPPY
Argemone hispida

GREEN DRAGON
Arisaema dracontium

For environments and climate zones, see maps, page 149.

GOATSBEARD
Aruncus sylvester

CANADA WILD GINGER
Asarum canadense

roots to test their courage. Both dragonroot and Jack-in-the-pulpit will sow themselves if left undisturbed.

HOW TO GROW. Jack-in-the-pulpit grows in a Deciduous Woodland environment. They do best in moist, acid soil, rich in humus, with a pH of 5.0 to 6.5 and partial shade. Without constant dampness, plants will be stunted. Start plants from seeds in the fall. Sow them thinly ¼ to ½ inch deep; almost all of the seeds will produce new plants. Transplant seedlings in late summer or early fall, when the foliage begins to turn yellow. Plants will bloom the second year after sowing. Jack-in-the-pulpit may also be propagated from root offshoots taken in the fall or very early spring.

ARUNCUS
A. sylvester, also called *A. dioicus* (goatsbeard)

Goatsbeard is a majestic perennial up to 7 feet tall, whose ornamental sprays of tiny flowers bloom briefly but spectacularly for two weeks in early summer. Its native environment is the semishade of woodland clearings in the East and Midwest from Pennsylvania and Iowa south to the Gulf Coast. In the wildflower garden it makes an imposing background plant, especially when displayed in an isolated grouping. Each flower spray contains thousands of minuscule blossoms, only ¹⁄₂₅ to ⅛ inch in diameter, which rise in loose panicles 6 to 10 inches above rather coarse but attractive, much-divided leaves. Curiously, goatsbeard plants are either male or female; one plant does not contain both sexes.

HOW TO GROW. Goatsbeard grows in a Deciduous Woodland environment. It needs a rich, moist soil and partial shade, and adapts easily to a garden environment. Buy nursery stock and set the plants 1½ to 2 feet apart in the spring. Plants can be grown from seeds, which germinate readily. Goatsbeard may also be propagated by dividing established root clumps in the spring or fall. The plants need little care as long as the soil remains moist; they will survive indefinitely if left undisturbed.

ASARUM
A. canadense (Canada wild ginger); *A. shuttleworthii,* also called *A. grandiflorum* (mottled wild ginger); *A. virgincum* (heartleaf)

These aromatic ground-hugging wildflowers make natural carpets for a wild garden planted under trees. They grow in eastern woodlands from New Brunswick to North Carolina, and in wooded areas of the Midwest from Manitoba to Missouri and Kansas. Their heart-shaped leaves, 2 to 6 inches wide, grow on 4- to 12-inch-long stems that rise in pairs from the rhizome, a fleshy, underground stem. In the spring small brown flowers appear, about 1 inch wide, in the cleft between the two stems. These dark blossoms can often be seen pushing through the soil even before the leaves have totally uncurled, and they persist until their big seeds ripen, at which point they are almost completely hidden by the foliage. The rhizomes of these plants have a spicy ginger-like aroma and taste. In fact, wild ginger was used by the Indians to flavor their foods.

The largest of these three species, Canada wild ginger, has soft, hairy leaves as much as 7 inches across. In the spring, they are sometimes brown or red, further hiding the brown flower. The smaller leaves of mottled wild ginger, about 3 inches wide, are evergreen and are spotted with white. Heartleaf also has evergreen leaves, only 2 inches wide.

HOW TO GROW. Wild ginger grows in the environments of the Northeastern Coniferous Woodland and the Deciduous Woodland; it survives winter temperatures of −40°. Mottled wild ginger and heartleaf grow in a Deciduous Woodland environment, and do best in the southern mountain regions of Virginia, Tennessee and North Carolina. All three plants thrive in shade and moist, humus-rich soil with a pH of 5.5 to 6.5. Plant in the spring or fall by burying a rhizome ½ inch deep with the tip end just reaching the soil level. Space plants 12 inches apart. Cover the ground with a mulch of oak or beech leaves, or salt hay, and do not remove this covering in the spring. Plants will seed themselves in following years and spread freely. Seeds, however, are difficult to collect by hand. Additional plants may also be obtained by dividing rhizomes of dormant plants in the spring or fall.

ASCLEPIAS
A. incarnata (swamp milkweed); *A. speciosa* (showy milkweed); *A. tuberosa* (butterfly weed)

The milkweeds, named for the milky juice of their stems (except butterfly weed, which has none), are among the most visible of summer wildflowers, a common sight along roadsides and in sunny open fields. Swamp milkweed inhabits eastern meadows from Nova Scotia to Florida and is found in bogs and along brooks in the West from Manitoba to New Mexico. Showy milkweed, a western species, inhabits moist areas of the prairies and Rocky Mountains from Manitoba and British Columbia to Texas, New Mexico, Arizona and Southern California. Butterfly weed grows in dry fields from New Hampshire to Florida, and is found on the plains of Minnesota, Colorado, Arizona and Texas. All the milkweeds are perennials and have large lance-shaped leaves that range from 2 to 8 inches in length. The leaves, like the stems, are often hairy. Swamp milkweed is 2 to 4 feet tall and bears 2-inch clusters of pink (occasionally white) flowers from May to September. Showy milkweed also grows from 2 to 4 feet high and blooms from May to September, but has slightly larger rose flowers, 3 inches across. Butterfly weed, the most popular of this family, draws multitudes of butterflies to its brilliant orange flower clusters, 1½ to 2 inches wide, in mid-to late summer. Butterfly weed grows 1 to 2 feet high and is covered with rough hairs.

Crusty seed pods appear on all three species, and pop to reveal flat brown seeds crowned with silky white hairs that carry the seeds on the wind like tiny parachutes.

HOW TO GROW. The milkweeds do well in all environments except those of the Wetlands and the Desert. They need full sun and the butterfly weed needs a well-drained sandy soil; the swamp milkweed, though it thrives on moisture in its natural habitat, will tolerate slightly dry soil. Seeds in all species may be slow to germinate, and usually do best when planted in late spring but even so will probably not bloom for a year or two. Nursery seedlings or collected plants can be transplanted while dormant in fall or spring; space the plants 2 to 3 feet apart. Butterfly weed, which has a very long taproot, is often difficult to transplant. Before transplanting any of the milkweeds, trim the jagged ends of the roots to about 4 inches. Mulch young seedlings during the first winter. Swamp milkweed and showy milkweed can also be propagated by root division of mature plants. The blooming season for all species may be prolonged if, when the first flowering starts to fade, the plant is cut back to about 6 inches. Within a few weeks new flowers will appear.

ASTER
A. linariifolius (savory-leaved aster, stiff aster); *A. novae-angliae* (New England aster); *A. novi-belgii* (New York aster); *A. puniceus* (swamp aster); *A. subspicatus*

Numbering more than 200 species, the wild asters are among the most abundant and beautiful of all autumn wild-

BUTTERFLY WEED
Asclepias tuberosa

NEW ENGLAND ASTER
Aster novae-angliae

For environments and climate zones, see maps, page 149.

GOLDFIELDS
Baeria chrysostoma hirsutula

DESERT MARIGOLD
Baileya multiradiata

flowers. The stiff aster, New England aster and New York aster are all found in eastern meadows from Newfoundland to Georgia; the New England aster also grows westward to Wyoming and New Mexico. The swamp aster is an eastern species found in marshy ground; *A. subspicatus* is native to the Northwest, from northern California to the Aleutians and east to Idaho. It is the hardiest of these five species. All five are upright, slender perennials with long, narrow stem-clasping leaves and flowers that bloom from late summer through fall. New England aster is the largest, growing as much as 6 feet tall and bearing flowers of purple, violet, pink or white, 1 to 2 inches across, with yellow centers. The stems are hairy and the leaves, 3 to 4 inches long, are sticky. The New York aster grows 3 to 4 feet tall, with flower heads of pink, rose, white or lavender, 1 to 1¼ inches across. The smooth, tooth-edged leaves are 2 to 5 inches in length. Swamp aster has red or purple stems 3 to 6 feet high and hairy, tooth-edged leaves 3 to 6 feet long. Its flowers range from purple to violet, and are 1 to 1½ inches across. Both *A. subspicatus* and stiff aster are dwarf species, growing from less than 1 foot to 1½ feet tall. Both have long narrow leaves with small flower heads of purple and violet respectively.

HOW TO GROW. Wild asters will thrive in the following environments: Northeastern Coniferous Woodland, Deciduous Woodland, Southeastern Coniferous Woodland, Rocky Mountain Woodland and Western Coniferous Woodland. Except for *A. subspicatus,* which is well-suited to the coldest regions of the North American continent, they are hardy in Zones 5-10. Sow seeds for all species in ordinary, well-drained garden soil. Set tall-growing species 2 to 2½ feet apart and shorter species 12 to 18 inches apart. All do best in full sun but will tolerate light shade. Encourage branching and strengthen the stems by snipping off the stem tips in late spring and again in early summer. Propagate additional plants by dividing root clumps in fall or spring.

AVALANCHE LILY See *Erythronium*
AVENS, LARGE-LEAF See *Geum*

B

BABY BLUE-EYES See *Nemophila*

BAERIA
B. chrysostoma hirsutula (goldfields, sunshine)

Masses of these small yellow annuals blanket the coastal cliffs of California in spring. They also appear along coastal dunes and inland valley slopes, transforming them visually into fields of gold. Goldfields grow about a foot tall with opposing pairs of leaves ½ to 1½ inches long. The bright yellow daisy-like flowers grow on slender 6-inch stems and are about 1 inch in diameter.

HOW TO GROW. Goldfields grow in a Western Coniferous Woodland environment, but they need sun. They will tolerate quite dry soil conditions, and have been found growing wild at elevations of 6,000 feet. Sow seeds in early spring in ordinary garden soil. In milder climates, similar to California's, seeds sown in fall will blossom in spring and a second crop of seeds, sown in spring, will bloom in early summer. Goldfields seeds itself, but in very dry regions these seeds will sometimes lie dormant for three or four years and then, in a year of more than average rainfall, will spring up with a profusion of flowers.

BAILEYA
B. multiradiata (desert marigold)

The desert marigold appears in early spring on rocky

slopes and mesas of the Mojave Desert and eastward across Arizona and New Mexico to the sandy plains of western Texas. This low, many-branched annual grows from 6 to 18 inches high and has woolly, gray-green leaves and stems. Numerous foot-high flower stalks bear yellow daisy-like flowers 1 to 1¾ inches in diameter, which bloom from April to October and even year-round in some favored spots. As the flowers fade, the petals one by one turn white and papery and begin to droop, making the flower look like a daisy that is made of paper.

HOW TO GROW. Desert marigold grows in a Desert environment. It does best in a rocky or sandy well-drained soil, but will also grow in heavier soil if it is not overwatered. Sow seeds in fall or spring. The plant seeds itself and thus does not need to be replanted each succeeding season. It is a good choice for the shallow soil of rock gardens.

BANEBERRY See *Actaea*

BAPTISIA
B. tinctoria (yellow false indigo, wild indigo)

Yellow false indigo is a bushy perennial, 2 to 3 feet high, that inhabits dry meadows and open woodlands of the eastern United States from Maine to Florida, and similar terrain in the Midwest from Minnesota to Louisiana. Yellow false indigo's numerous curving stems have clover-like leaves, each of which is composed of three silvery green leaflets ½ inch long. The woody stems once were used in dyeing as a substitute for true indigo, though they produced a somewhat faded blue. Small yellow flowers ½ inch long blossom on 1½- to 3-inch spikes in midsummer. As with other members of the pea family, the seeds develop inside inflated pods that can be gathered and shelled in early fall for planting then or the following spring.

HOW TO GROW. Yellow false indigo grows in Deciduous Woodland and in Northeastern and Southeastern Coniferous Woodland environments, but it needs full sun. The soil should be well drained and slightly acid with a pH of 6.0 to 7.0. Yellow false indigo withstands drought well. Sow seeds in fall or spring. Space seedlings 18 to 30 inches apart; plants will blossom when they are two to three years old. Yellow false indigo seeds itself.

BEADLILY See *Clintonia*
BEARGRASS See *Xerophyllum*
BEE BALM See *Monarda*
BELLFLOWER, ALLEGHENY See *Campanula*
BELLWORT See *Uvularia*
BERGAMOT, SWEET See *Monarda*
BERGAMOT, WILD See *Monarda*
BITTER-ROOT See *Lewisia*
BLACK-EYED SUSAN See *Rudbeckia*
BLANKETFLOWER See *Gaillardia*
BLAZING STAR See *Mentzelia*
BLEEDING HEART, FRINGED See *Dicentra*
BLOODROOT See *Sanguinaria*
BLUEBELL, CALIFORNIA See *Phacelia*
BLUEBELL, VIRGINIA See *Mertensia*
BLUEBELLS OF SCOTLAND See *Campanula*
BLUEBONNET, TEXAS See *Lupinus*
BLUE DICKS See *Brodiaea*
BLUE-EYED GRASS See *Sisyrinchium*
BLUESTEM See *Eupatorium*
BLUET See *Houstonia*
BONESET See *Eupatorium*
BOWMAN'S ROOT See *Gillenia*

YELLOW FALSE INDIGO
Baptisia tinctoria

For environments and climate zones, see maps, page 149.

BLUE DICKS
Brodiaea pulchella

WINE-CUP
Callirhoë involucrata

BRODIAEA

B. hyacinthina (white or hyacinth brodiea); *B. pulchella* (blue dicks or purplehead brodiea)

The delicate flowers and grasslike foliage of these brodieas blend into the grasses of their native habitat, the western American prairies and deserts. White brodiea grows 12 to 18 inches tall and bears clusters of 10 to 30 flowers, 1 inch long, in early summer; the flowers are pure white or white tinged with purple. Blue dicks grows 1 to 2 feet tall and bears clusters of funnel-shaped violet flowers in early spring; its flowers are less than an inch long. Both brodieas make excellent, long-lasting cut flowers. As display plants in the garden, however, they must be planted in groups of a dozen or more, because their blossoms are too dainty to be noticed except when massed.

HOW TO GROW. Brodieas grow in Prairie, Semiarid Grassland and Desert environments. They do well in full sun and a sandy, well-drained soil. Although they can be grown from seed, they will not reach flowering age for several years. More often they are propagated from their bulblike corms. Plant the corms in the fall in areas where the soil does not freeze, spacing them 3 to 5 inches apart and no deeper than 4 to 6 inches. Where late summer rainfall is abundant, put a 4-inch bed of coarse sand under the corms, to insure drainage. In areas where winter temperatures go below freezing, lift the corms in late summer after the foliage has ripened, and store them over the winter in dry sand in a cool place.

BUGBANE See *Cimicifuga*
BUNCHBERRY See *Cornus*
BUTTERFLY TULIP See *Calochortus*
BUTTERFLY WEED See *Asclepias*

C

CALIFORNIA POPPY See *Eschscholzia*

CALLIRHOË

C. involucrata (wine cup, low poppy mallow)

Wine cup is a creeping perennial, seldom growing more than 12 inches high, whose red blossoms provide masses of color across the midwestern prairies from North Dakota to Oklahoma, and on the dry grasslands of eastern Colorado and Wyoming. The hairy leaves have five notched lobes, and from June to September each flower stem bears a single 2-inch-wide flower. Wine cup's spreading habit of growth makes it a good garden plant.

HOW TO GROW. Wine cup does best in Prairie and Semiarid Grassland environments. It needs full sun and a dry, slightly acid to neutral soil with a pH of 6.0 to 7.0; good drainage is essential. Sow seeds in the fall, when they are ripe, or in the early spring. Transplant seedlings to stand 18 inches apart; mature plants are difficult to move because of the deep taproot. Plants grown from seed will produce flowers the second season. Wine cup can also be grown from nursery stock; set plants in the ground so that the tops of the roots are at ground level. In exposed locations, wine cup should be mulched for protection in the winter.

CALOCHORTUS

C. amoenus (purple globe tulip); *C. venustus* (Mariposa tulip, butterfly tulip)

Of the more than 50 species of *Calochortus*, these are typical of two main types: the purple globe tulip *(cover)* has drooping flower heads, while those of the Mariposa tulip are erect. They grow on the low slopes of the Sierra Nevada and coastal range mountains of southern California. Both have branching stems, grasslike leaves and six-petaled flowers arranged so that only the three large inside petals are visible when the flower is fully open. The purple globe tulip grows 18 to 24 inches high, with petals about 1 inch long. It blooms from spring to early summer, its pink flowers turning purple as they mature. The Mariposa tulip, with its distinctive petal markings, comes in a range of colors—white, lilac, pink, red, magenta, purple and occasionally yellow. It grows 1 to 2 feet high, with petals 1½ to 2 inches long, and blooms from late spring to midsummer.

HOW TO GROW. Both of these species need a Semiarid Grassland or Western Coniferous Woodland environment. They thrive in sun or light shade and a dry, sandy, slightly acid soil with a pH of 6.0 to 7.0. Although they withstand cold as low as −10°, they do not do well in damp eastern winters. Plant the bulblike corms in the fall, setting them 2 inches deep and 4 to 6 inches apart. Place them where other foliage will hide them when their foliage dies back in late summer—it must be allowed to wither if the rootstock is to ripen. In areas where winter temperatures fall below 10°, protect plants with a mulch of wood chips or salt hay. For additional plants, separate small side bulbs from the parent rootstock in the fall, when the plant is dormant.

CALTHA

C. palustris (marsh marigold)

The marsh marigold is one of the brightest harbingers of spring. Its golden cup-shaped flowers color the banks of streams in eastern meadowlands from Labrador to the Carolinas, and in swampy areas of the northern plains from Saskatchewan to Nebraska. But by midsummer the whole plant has disappeared. It grows 2 feet high and its 1- to 2-inch flowers spring in clusters from the tops of hollow, branching stems. The heart-shaped leaves are 2 to 3 inches across.

HOW TO GROW. Marsh marigold grows in open areas of a Northeastern Coniferous or Deciduous Woodland environment, and in a Prairie environment. It does well in full sun but will tolerate open shade, and thrives in a moist, humus-rich, acid soil with a pH of 5.0 to 7.0. During the spring blooming season, it should not be allowed to dry out but after it becomes dormant in midsummer, it will tolerate a drier soil. Sow seeds in early summer as soon as they ripen, or in the early spring. Since seed-grown plants may take two years to bloom, marsh marigolds are often started from nursery stock or from root divisions. Divide root clumps in the early summer, when the plant becomes dormant. Space clumps or nursery stock 1 foot apart, and keep the soil soggy until they become established. Protect young plants in winter with a mulch. Marsh marigolds seed themselves.

CAMASS See *Camassia*

CAMASSIA

C. leichtlinii (Leichtlin camass); *C. quamash* (common camass)

The camasses are perennials that grow from onion-like but inedible bulbs and bear spikes of starry, 1¼-inch-wide blossoms for a few weeks in early spring; their leaves are long, narrow and spearlike. Native to the Pacific Coast, they are found in wet meadows from California to British Columbia. Common camass varies in height from 2 to 3 feet, and its flowers range from white to blue. Leichtlin camass grows 2 to 3 feet tall, and has flowers of white, blue or cream. Both species make excellent long-lasting cut flowers because their flower spikes open gradually, in succession.

HOW TO GROW. Camasses grow in open meadows of a

PURPLE GLOBE TULIP
Calochortus amoenus

MARSH MARIGOLD
Caltha palustris

For environments and climate zones, see maps, page 149.

LEICHTLIN CAMASS
Camassia leichtlinii

BLUEBELLS OF SCOTLAND
Campanula rotundifolia

Western Coniferous Woodland environment. They need rich soil and do best in full sun. During the height of their growing season, the soil should be moist, even marshy; but in summer, when they are dormant, they will tolerate some drought. Plants grown from seed take three or four years to reach flowering size, so they are usually propagated from bulbs, planted in the fall or in late summer, when the foliage ripens. Plant mature bulbs 3 to 4 inches deep, younger bulbs no deeper than 2 inches, spacing them 3 to 6 inches apart.

CAMPANULA
C. divaricata (Allegheny bellflower or southern harebells); *C. rotundifolia* (bluebells of Scotland, harebells)

Both of these harebells are wild forms of the popular garden bellflower and both are perennials. Bluebells of Scotland is an adaptable plant; it can be found in eastern meadows, midwestern prairies, on the slopes of the Rockies and the California coastal mountains. It grows as far north as Alaska and Newfoundland, and as far south as West Virginia, Iowa and Texas. The less cosmopolitan Allegheny bellflower is a native of the southeastern woodlands from Virginia to Georgia. Bluebells of Scotland grows as much as 2 feet tall in the wild, but in the garden usually reaches a height of only 9 to 12 inches. The flowers, ½ to ¾ inch long, bloom in midsummer. The lower leaves are round or heart shaped, but the upper leaves are slender and almost hairlike. The Allegheny bellflower grows to 3 feet tall. Its clusters of tiny flowers bloom at the top of the plant in late summer.

HOW TO GROW. Bluebells of Scotland and Allegheny bellflowers grow in any environment except Desert and Wetland. They need a dry, well-drained soil containing sand or gravel, and do best in full sun but will tolerate light shade. Although they can be grown from seed, their germination time varies so greatly that it is usually more satisfactory to buy nursery stock. Plant in the spring or fall, setting the plants in the ground so that their rhizomes, or thickened roots, are ½ to 1 inch below the surface. Space plants 12 to 18 inches apart. To get additional plants and to prevent overcrowding, dig up and divide the clumps of roots every few years in the early spring, when the plants are dormant.

CANADA LILY See *Lilium*
CARDINAL FLOWER See *Lobelia*
CAROLINA THERMOPSIS See *Thermopsis*

CASTILLEJA
C. coccinea (Indian paint brush, painted cup); *C. flava* (yellow Indian paint brush, yellow painted cup); *C. integra* (orange paint brush, orange painted cup)

There are some 250 species of colorful wildflowers known as Indian paint brushes—the bright red bracts, which enfold their flowers, look as though they had been dipped in paint—but the three described here are the ones most commonly available from wildflower nurseries. The flowers are ½ to 1 inch wide and bloom in late spring and summer, decorating fields and open woodlands throughout North America. Indian paint brush grows from New Hampshire to Florida in the East, and from southern Manitoba to Louisiana and Oklahoma in the Midwest; yellow Indian paint brush is found in New Mexico, northern Arizona, eastern California, and in Wyoming, Idaho and Oregon; orange paint brush is native to Texas, Arizona and northern Mexico. They are all biennials, blooming in their second year. Indian paint brush, the most common species, stands 8 to 24 inches tall, and has scarlet bracts, although its flowers are pale yellow. Yellow Indian paint brush grows 4 to 6 inches high, and has leaves and stems covered with hair. Its flowers are usually red but sometimes they appear orange or yellow. Orange paint brush rises 4 to 16 inches high and bears red or pink flowers. Its smooth leaf surfaces hide hairy undersides.

HOW TO GROW. All three of these Indian paint brushes are parasites, feeding upon the roots of indigenous grasses and hence difficult to grow in a garden. Their environmental requirements differ. The two western species are Desert or Semiarid Grassland plants; they need sun and a light, dry alkaline soil. The eastern species is a Deciduous Woodland plant. It does well in either sun or light shade, will grow in damp or dry soil, and thrives in a soil containing humus. Propagate the Indian paint brushes from seed, sowing them as soon as they are ripe. But do not expect quick results. The plants are unpredictable, and even when well established do not appear regularly. They may fail to come up and then, after a long absence, emerge in large colonies.

CAULOPHYLLUM
C. thalictroides (blue cohosh)

Blue cohosh, a member of the barberry family, grows in eastern woodlands under towering maples and elms, and in moist thickets of prairie wetlands. Its natural habitat ranges from New Brunswick and Ontario south to South Carolina, and from Manitoba south to Missouri and Alabama. This sturdy perennial is valued for its bright blue berries, 1/3 inch in diameter, which appear late in the summer. Clusters of inconspicuous flowers, 1/2 inch across, bloom early in the spring. The plants grow 1 to 3 feet high and their deeply lobed leaves start halfway up each thick stem. Blue cohosh spreads rapidly from creeping roots. When planted next to red and white baneberry plants and green ferns, its blue berries provide color contrast for a woodland garden.

HOW TO GROW. Blue cohosh grows in a Deciduous Woodland environment. It needs shade and a soil ranging from very acid to neutral, with a pH of 4.5 to 7.0. Constant abundant moisture is essential. Set out nursery stock in the spring or fall, spacing plants 1½ to 2 feet apart. Make sure the roots are widely spread and that new root sprouts are about 1 inch below the surface of the soil. In order to maintain moisture, cover the bases of the plants with a permanent mulch of oak or beech leaves. Propagate by dividing clumps in the early spring or fall. Left undisturbed, blue cohosh will sow its own seeds, and can be grown from seeds planted as soon as they ripen in the fall. But they germinate erratically and the plants may take as long as four years to bloom.

CHECKERBERRY See *Gaultheria*
CHECKER LILY See *Fritillaria*

CHELONE
C. *glabra* (white turtlehead); C. *lyoni* (pink turtlehead)

The turtleheads, two wild relatives of the garden snapdragon, are named for their late-blooming flowers that look like small turtles with half-opened mouths. The plants form bushy colonies in swampy areas along streams and in wet meadows. White turtlehead can be found in the East from Newfoundland and Ontario south to Georgia, and in the Midwest from Minnesota south to Kansas and Missouri. Pink turtlehead grows in a more southerly region from Maryland and Tennessee to Florida and Mississippi. White turtlehead grows 1 to 3 feet tall; pink turtlehead averages 2 to 3 feet tall. Both have lance-shaped leaves 4 to 7 inches long, but the pink turtlehead leaves are wider. At the end of summer and in the fall, the turtleheads bear short spikes of 1- to 1½ inch flowers. In large plants of the white turtlehead

INDIAN PAINT BRUSH
Castilleja coccinea

BLUE COHOSH
Caulophyllum thalictroides

For environments and climate zones, see maps, page 149.

WHITE TURTLEHEAD
Chelone glabra

STRIPED PIPSISSEWA
Chimaphila maculata

species, the flowers are sometimes tinged with pink. Pink turtlehead blossoms are pink with yellow beards streaked with purple. Both plants are dramatic when planted near water, but they do well in any moist, wild garden as background plants.

HOW TO GROW. Both species of turtlehead thrive in a Deciduous Woodland environment. They need a moist, acid soil, pH 5.5 to 6.5, and tolerate both full sun or partial shade. In the wildflower garden they are most effective when planted in groups. Start with nursery-grown root clumps in the spring or fall, spacing plants 1½ to 2 feet apart. Spread roots open and place them approximately 1 inch below ground level. Or propagate from nursery-grown seedlings, set 18 inches apart. Cover the bases of the plants with a leaf mulch to keep in moisture. Plants can also be started from seeds sown in the fall as soon as they are ripe, but flowers will not appear until the second year. Early in the summer, pinch off the tips of the flower stalks to encourage branching and more abundant blooms later. To acquire additional plants, take stem cuttings in the summer or divide two- to three-year-old (or older) clumps in the early spring. In very damp areas, plants seed themselves, providing more plants.

CHIMAPHILA
C. maculata (striped pipsissewa, spotted pipsissewa); *C. umbellata* (common pipsissewa, prince's pine)

The tiny pipsissewas are a common sight in dry pine woods, pushing through layers of decayed needles to form a sparse evergreen ground cover. Striped pipsissewa, the less hardy of the two species, is found from Massachusetts westward to Ontario and Minnesota, and southward through the eastern woodlands to Georgia and Alabama. Common pipsissewa grows in the eastern woodlands from Canada to Georgia, and in the western woodlands from Alaska to Mexico. These small plants rise 3 to 12 inches high from spreading underground stems. Their erect aboveground stems bear whorls of leaves, 2 to 4 inches long. In the summer, faintly perfumed pink or white flowers, ½ to ⅔ inch wide, bloom in loose clusters. These are followed by decorative oval fruits which split open from top to bottom; they are used in dried arrangements. Striped pipsissewa, which flowers somewhat earlier in the season, is considered the handsomer of the two species because it has white-veined leaves. Common pipsissewa has narrower, blunt-tipped leaves of solid green. The leaves of both species have a refreshing flavor, and those of common pipsissewa are used in making root beer. Both species grow so slowly they are useful only as an accent ground cover and rarely form a dense carpet of any appreciable size.

HOW TO GROW. The pipsissewas thrive in a Northeastern, Southeastern or Western Coniferous Woodland environment. They need shade and a dry, very acid soil with a pH of 4.0 to 5.0. Planted under pine trees or other conifers, they require no special soil preparation, but in other locations the ground should be enriched with leaf mold. Pipsissewas do not transplant well, and are best propagated from stem cuttings taken in summer and rooted in sand and peat moss. Set out rooted cuttings in the late spring, spacing plants 6 to 8 inches apart. Plants can also be propagated by division of the underground stems.

CHINESE HOUSES See *Collinsia*
CHOCOLATE LILY See *Fritillaria*

CIMICIFUGA
C. americana (American bugbane); *C. racemosa* (cohosh bugbane, black cohosh, black snakeroot, fairy candles)

These wildflowers are known as bugbanes because insects are repelled by their rank-smelling flowers, but the delicate tapering shape of their flower spires has also earned them the name fairy candles. Both American bugbane and cohosh bugbane grow naturally in partially shaded clearings adjacent to woodlands.

American bugbane is native to the southeastern woodlands but it grows as far north as Pennsylvania and it has also been found as far west as Wisconsin. The hardier cohosh bugbane inhabits northeastern woodlands in Maine and Ontario, but grows south to Georgia and has also been found in the Ozark Mountains and in Wisconsin. Both plants come into bloom in late summer. American bugbane is the smaller of these two perennials, growing only 2 to 4 feet high; cohosh bugbane, the more majestic species, towers 5 to 8 feet tall, and its flower spikes are often 2 feet long. Sometimes, indeed, they even reach a length of 3 feet. Cohosh bugbane's wandlike seed heads are attractive in dry arrangements. Because of their height and coarse foliage, bugbanes make excellent background plants.

HOW TO GROW. Both bugbanes are suited to the environment of a Deciduous Woodland or a Southeastern Coniferous Woodland. They require partial shade; too much sunlight causes the tall spires of the cohosh bugbane to become crooked. Both species require a rich, moist soil that has been deeply mulched with compost or leaf mold. American bugbane grows best in slightly acid to neutral soil, with a pH of 5.5 to 6.5, while cohosh bugbane needs a more acid soil with a pH of 5.0 to 6.0. Start plants from nursery-grown rootstock in the spring or fall, burying the roots 1 to 1½ inches below ground in the place where the plants are to remain; space rootstocks 12 inches apart. Alternatively, set out nursery-grown seedlings while dormant in early spring or fall, or sow seeds in the fall as soon as they are ripe. Often seedlings do not flower until the third or fourth year. During dry weather, keep the soil very wet, making sure moisture penetrates to the deep roots.

CLARKIA
C. amoena (farewell-to-spring); *C. elegans* (rose clarkia)

Named for the explorer Captain William Clark of the famous Lewis and Clark expedition, the clarkias inhabit dry open slopes in the forests of the Northwest, from California north to British Columbia. Both species are annuals 2 to 3 feet tall and bear delicate blossoms abundantly. The large satiny farewell-to-spring blossoms, 2 to 4 inches wide, are white, pink, red or lilac. They bloom from early to midsummer and are followed by tapering seed pods filled with many small brown seeds. The smaller rose clarkia blossoms are ¾ to 1 inch wide in shades of pink through purple. They appear at intervals along erect stems in early summer, and are followed by curved seed pods covered with tiny hairs. Both species have been hybridized for garden use into double-blossomed and dwarf forms.

HOW TO GROW. Both clarkias thrive in a Western Coniferous Woodland environment. They need a light, sandy soil and do well in full sun or partial shade. Seeds germinate best in cool weather; in the West, they should be sown in the fall during the early part of the rainy season; in the East, in the early spring as soon as the ground can be worked. Sow seeds where plants are to remain because both clarkias are difficult to transplant. Thin seedlings to stand 9 inches apart. When plants are about 6 inches high, pinch back the tops to encourage branching. Water the plants moderately, keeping the soil moist but not soggy until they begin to flower; then water less frequently.

COHOSH BUGBANE
Cimicifuga racemosa

FAREWELL-TO-SPRING
Clarkia amoena

For environments and climate zones, see maps, page 149.

VIRGINIA SPRING BEAUTY
Claytonia virginica

YELLOW CLINTONIA
Clintonia borealis

CLAYTONIA
C. virginica (Virginia spring beauty)

Spring beauty is a tiny perennial wildflower that carpets the eastern woodlands in the spring from Newfoundland to Georgia, and also grows in Rocky Mountain woodlands in Colorado. Dainty pink or white blossoms, ½ inch across, rise from 4- to 6-inch wiry stems. The plant has a tuberous root and grasslike leaves. Spring beauty blooms early and lasts several weeks, but the plant all but disappears in the summer. In the garden it should be given a place where its dainty flowers can be seen at close range.

HOW TO GROW. Spring beauty is suited to a Deciduous Woodland or Rocky Mountain Woodland environment. It needs soil rich in humus with plenty of moisture, but it will grow under drier conditions as long as the ground is kept moist during the flowering period before the trees leaf out. It adapts to acid or neutral soils, and to shade or semi-shade. Plant nursery-grown corms in the fall, setting them 2 to 3 inches deep singly or in groups spaced 4 to 6 inches apart. To hide barren spots when spring beauty plants become dormant, intersperse them with ferns. Spring beauty will sow itself but the seeds are difficult to collect for planting elsewhere because of the plant's diminutive size.

CLINTONIA
C. borealis (yellow clintonia, blue beadlily); *C. umbellulata* (speckled beadlily)

Yellow clintonia is a northerly plant, growing in eastern woodlands from Newfoundland to North Carolina, and northern woods from Manitoba south to Indiana. Speckled beadlily inhabits eastern woodlands and wetlands from New York to Georgia. Both are dainty perennials with shiny, broad leaves, 2 to 3 inches wide and 4 to 12 inches long, that remain green well into the fall. The tiny nodding bells of fragrant beadlily blossoms are borne in loose umbrella-shaped clusters in late spring. Marble-sized berries appear in the late summer.

Yellow clintonia is sometimes known as the cornlily because it has greenish-yellow blossoms, ½ to ¾ inch wide. The plant grows 6 to 12 inches tall. Speckled beadlily's smaller but more numerous white flowers are only ¹/₅ to ¹/₃ inch long and are spotted with brown; the berries are almost black. Both the foliage and the flower stems are covered with woolly hairs and the plants are seldom more than 6 inches tall. The beadlilies make attractive velvety ground covers in shady areas.

HOW TO GROW. Both species of beadlilies are difficult to domesticate. They must have an environment—Deciduous Woodland or Northeastern Coniferous Woodland—that closely approximates the conditions under which they are found in the wild. They cannot tolerate heat and cannot survive hot, humid summers. Both need shade and a moist, humus-rich, relatively acid soil. Yellow clintonia does best in a soil with a pH of 4.5 to 5.5; speckled beadlily takes a less acid soil of pH 6.0 to 7.0. Plant in the fall, setting the thick rootstock—the rhizomes—½ to 1 inch deep in a horizontal position so that the tip just reaches ground level. Cover with a generous mulch of decayed oak leaves mixed with marsh hay. It is possible to start beadlilies from seeds removed from the berry pulp and sown as soon as they are ripe—but they may take as long as 12 years to produce three or four leaves. Generally, beadlilies do not transplant well, although rooted plants moved in the spring with large chunks of sod sometimes reestablish themselves successfully. Additional plants can be propagated by dividing the rhizomes of established plants in the fall.

COBRA LILY See *Darlingtonia*
COHOSH See *Caulophyllum*
COHOSH BUGBANE See *Cimicifuga*

COLLINSIA

C. heterophylla, also called *C. bicolor* (collinsia, Chinese houses, pagoda collinsia, innocence)

With their clustered flowers, rising in tiers like an oriental pagoda and shading in color from white through rose and lilac to deep purple, collinsias are very decorative. These hardy annuals abound on California mountain slopes and open woods. Their flowers, which bloom in midsummer, resemble the snapdragon. They are about 1 inch across and grow on flower stalks 1 to 2 feet high. The leaves are arranged in pairs, each leaf being ½ to 2½ inches long. Collinsias do well as rock garden plants and are excellent flowers for cutting.

HOW TO GROW. Collinsias grow in light shade or sun in almost any well-drained soil. Although they do not tolerate heat, they do best where summer night temperatures remain above 65°. Sow seeds in the fall, or in the spring as soon as the ground is warm; thin seedlings to stand 12 inches apart.

COLUMBINE See *Aquilegia*
CONEFLOWER See *Echinacea*

COPTIS

C. groenlandica (common goldthread); *C. trifolia* (Alaska goldthread)

The dark leaves of the goldthreads form natural evergreen carpets in rich acid bogs and moist woodlands as far north as the Arctic Circle. Common goldthread grows from Greenland south through the eastern woodlands to North Carolina and Tennessee, and west to Indiana and Iowa; Alaska goldthread inhabits the rainy slopes of the coastal range in Washington and British Columbia north to Alaska. The plant's wiry stems and divided leaves look like those of wild strawberries, but the two are not related. The goldthreads are named for their tangled yellow threadlike roots that creep just beneath the ground surface. These perennials grow only 4 to 6 inches tall and bear ½-inch-wide white flowers in early summer.

HOW TO GROW. The goldthreads grow in the environment of the Northeastern Coniferous Woodland, the Deciduous Woodland and the Western Coniferous Woodland. They do well in very acid soil, with a pH of 4.0 to 5.0, and in boglike conditions that are rich in humus. Both species grow in sun in far northern areas but do better in shade and will quickly cover the ground if they are given a winter blanket of decayed leaves. They do not tolerate summer temperatures above 80°. Set nursery plants in the ground in the spring or fall, spacing them 6 to 12 inches apart. In the winter, cover them with a mulch of oak leaves, which should be partially removed in the spring. Goldthreads can be propagated easily by dividing plant clumps in the spring. Seeds, if obtainable (they are difficult to find), should be sown as soon as they are ripe and kept moist until they germinate. Flowers usually appear the following year.

CORAL BELLS See *Heuchera*

COREOPSIS

C. lanceolata (lance coreopsis); *C. maritima* (Pacific coreopsis, sea dahlia)

The daisy-like coreopsis family, a genus of some 100 species, grows wild along roadsides and in grassy fields throughout the temperate zones of North America. The two species

COLLINSIA
Collinsia heterophylla

ALASKA GOLDTHREAD
Coptis trifolia

For environments and climate zones, see maps, page 149.

LANCE COREOPSIS
Coreopsis lanceolata

BUNCHBERRY
Cornus canadensis

listed here are perennials with bright yellow flowers and lance-shaped leaves. Lance coreopsis, native to the East, grows 1 to 2 feet tall and bears 2-inch blossoms on long, thin stems in the summer. Pacific coreopsis, a native of the southern California coast, does well in seaside gardens where winter temperatures do not fall below 20°. It grows 1 to 3 feet tall and its flowers, about 3 inches across with 1-inch-wide orange centers, are borne on hollow stems in autumn. Both last many weeks as cut flowers.

HOW TO GROW. Coreopsis will grow in dry fields and on hillsides of a Deciduous Woodland environment and in Semi-arid Grasslands. It does well in any ordinary dry, well-drained, sandy or rocky soil and thrives in full sun; it is among the easiest of wildflowers to grow. Sow seeds in the spring where plants are to remain, and thin seedlings to stand 8 to 12 inches apart. For additional plants, divide coreopsis clumps in the spring or fall after two or three years of flowering. Plants can also be grown from seeds harvested in the fall and sown immediately or in the early spring.

CORNUS
C. canadensis (bunchberry)

Despite its miniature size, the low-growing bunchberry, only 3 to 5 inches tall, is related to the flowering dogwood tree. It is a native of cool, wet northern woodlands from Alaska to Greenland; in the West it ranges to the mountains of northern California, in the East, to the mountains of West Virginia. The plant's dogwood-like flowers, less than an inch in diameter, appear in the early summer and are made up not of petals but of four white bracts surrounding a tiny true flower. In the fall, each bunchberry produces a cluster of bright red ¼-inch berries at the end of the stem. Bunchberry spreads rapidly by means of creeping underground stems that travel through the forest leaf mold to form new colonies.

HOW TO GROW. Bunchberry thrives in Northeastern and Western Coniferous Woodland and Deciduous Woodland environments. It needs a cold boglike soil, preferably one rich in acid sphagnum moss with a pH of 4.0 to 5.0. Although it does best in shade, it will adapt to filtered light if the soil is kept cool and moist with a covering of old leaves or pine needles. Plant nursery-grown plants in spring or fall, in groups of two or three spaced about a foot apart. Bunchberry may also be grown from seeds separated from their pulp as soon as the berries are ripe and sown ¼ inch deep in a mixture of three parts sand to one part sphagnum moss. Bunchberry seeds may take two or three years to germinate.

COW PARSNIP See *Heracleum*
CRANBERRY, MOUNTAIN See *Vaccinium*
CUCUMBER ROOT See *Medeola*

CYPRIPEDIUM
C. acaule (pink lady's slipper, pink moccasin flower); *C. arietinum* (ramshead lady's slipper); *C. calceolus* (yellow lady's slipper); *C. californicum* (California lady's slipper); *C. candidum* (white lady's slipper); *C. reginae* (showy lady's slipper)

These native-born American orchids get their romantic name from the unusual pouch shape of the lower petal of each flower, which resembles a lady's slipper or moccasin. The other petals and sepals are variously colored and shaped, combining with the pouches to make exceedingly ornamental and curious blooms. The flowers appear in late spring or summer, according to the species. Lady's slippers are found in moist woodlands and bogs, but each species has a slightly different geographical range and requires its own special growing conditions if it is to be domesticated success-fully. Pink lady's slipper can be found growing wild from Newfoundland south to Alabama and from Manitoba south to Minnesota and Indiana. Ramshead lady's slipper grows in the region of Quebec and New York, and in Manitoba and Minnesota. Yellow lady's slipper's natural habitat runs from Newfoundland south through the Appalachian Mountains to Alabama, and it is also found in the Rockies, while California lady's slipper is a native of the western coastal range from California to Oregon. White lady's slipper grows in the eastern and midwestern woodlands from New York to Minnesota and is found as far south as the Ozarks in Missouri. Showy lady's slipper ranges across the northern part of the continent from Newfoundland west to North Dakota and extends as far south as Georgia in the East and Missouri in the Midwest.

Pink lady's slipper, one of the most beautiful of the species, blooms in the summer and produces a single flower on each stem; the conspicuous pouch is usually pink with red veins, but is occasionally white. The flower stalk rises to a height of 8 to 20 inches, and there are two large leaves at ground level, 4 to 8 inches long. Ramshead lady's slipper, a rare species, blooms in the late spring and is named for its curiously shaped red-veined white flower whose lip, or pouch, tapers downward to a point and resembles a goat's muzzle. The flower stalk is 8 to 16 inches tall, the stiff leaves 7 to 10 inches long. The yellow lady's slipper, one of the easier species to grow, appears in two forms. The small-flowered *parviflorum* variety has flowers with bright yellow lips streaked with purple and bronze-brown petals; the lips of the larger-flowered *pubescens* variety are pale yellow and its petals are streaked with green, purple and brown. Both varieties are usually 18 to 24 inches tall, though *pubescens* occasionally reaches a height of 3 feet. On both plants the flower stalks carry one to three blossoms.

The California lady's slipper bears six to 12 small yellow-and-white flowers, 1 to 1¼ inches across, on a single stalk 1 to 2 feet high; it blooms in late spring. Another seldom-seen species is the white lady's slipper, which grows only 6 to 12 inches tall and produces only one blossom per stem. Showy lady's slipper is the tallest and most decorative of the *cypripediums,* growing 1½ to 3 feet tall. Both the leaves and stems are covered with soft white down, and the flowers, borne as many as three to a stem, are 1½ to 2 inches across, and are either pure white or white flushed with rose.

HOW TO GROW. As a group, lady's slippers need the shade of a Northeastern or Western Coniferous Woodland or a Deciduous Woodland environment. They also require moist, acid soil. But each species in addition will only thrive in the particular micro-environment to which it is accustomed. It is dependent upon fungi that exist in its natural setting—a fact that can make lady's slipper very frustrating for the wild-flower gardener. Pink lady's slipper thrives on very acid soil with a pH of 4.0 to 5.0, and grows best in deep leaf mold. It is almost impossible to domesticate except near areas where it is already growing wild. Ramshead lady's slipper grows in swamps and damp, mossy woods—preferably pine woods. Both versions of the yellow lady's slipper grow in boggy, deciduous woods, with the larger variety thriving in drier soils as well. The growing conditions needed by California lady's slipper are so specialized that it grows well only in its native habitat, rarely surviving elsewhere for more than three years. White lady's slipper, contrary to the general rule, grows best in alkaline bogs and swamps and is usually found in limestone-rich areas with a soil pH between 6.5 and 7.5, while showy lady's slipper does best in wet acid swamps and bogs, like those found in Coniferous Woodlands.

SHOWY LADY'S SLIPPER
Cypripedium reginae

For environments and climate zones, see maps, page 149.

CALIFORNIA PITCHER PLANT
Darlingtonia californica

CARDINAL LARKSPUR
Delphinium cardinale

The seeds of lady's slipper, like those of other orchids, are dustlike, and seed propagation is very difficult. Mature plants increase by forming new root buds and shoots. Start lady's slippers in the fall from nursery plants. Set rhizomes of all except showy lady's slipper 1 to 1½ inches deep; the shallow-growing roots of the latter should be only ½ inch from the surface. Space plants 1 to 2 feet apart and water them generously. To retain moisture, mulch plants lightly with dead leaves or pine needles. Lady's slippers should not be moved; the older the plant, the better the bloom.

D

DARLINGTONIA

D. californica (California pitcher plant, cobra lily)

No one could doubt the California pitcher plant's family connection with the exotic pitcher plant of the East. This voracious native of bogs and marshes in the Cascade Mountains has twisting, tubular leaves, 3 to 30 inches long, in which insects are trapped, drowned and digested. These leaves end in a downward-curving hood from which projects a forked tonguelike appendage. Light filtering through the dappled surface of the hood and a special honey secreted by glands within the leaves entice unsuspecting insects into the plant's hollow interior, where victims are kept from escaping by a downward-pointing lining of hairs. In the spring and early summer, the California pitcher plant bears a single purplish flower, 2 inches wide, on a tall, leafless stem.

HOW TO GROW. Though its native environment is the Western Coniferous Woodland, the California pitcher plant has been cultivated successfully in the Northeastern Coniferous Woodland environment of New England—but there it needs a protective winter mulch of leaves. It thrives in a cool, shaded bog but will also grow in a mixture of equal parts of peat moss and sand, provided it is kept very moist. Set nursery-grown plants in such a mixture or in a bog, spacing them 6 to 12 inches apart and keeping the base of each plant slightly above ground level. Or sow seeds in sphagnum moss in 6-inch pots, for transfer to the garden when the plants are one year old. Insect collecting begins when the plant produces its pitcher-like leaves in its second year. It does not bloom until the third to fifth year.

DELPHINIUM

D. cardinale (cardinal larkspur, scarlet larkspur); *D. decorum* (yellow-tinge larkspur, blue larkspur); *D. menziesi* (Menzies larkspur, low blue larkspur); *D. parryi* (Parry larkspur, violet woods larkspur)

The stately spires of the wild delphiniums, up to 7 feet tall, are a breathtaking sight among the tall grasses of West Coast woodland meadows from California to southwestern Oregon and, in the case of Menzies larkspur, as far north as Alaska. These handsome perennials are called larkspurs because the flower spur—a hollow extension at the back of each blossom—suggests a lark in flight. The long stalks of blossoms usually appear in shades of blue to purple, although there are white and red larkspurs, too. They bloom profusely in the late spring and summer. Cattle grazing on meadows containing larkspur have died from eating these plants.

The cardinal larkspur is a rare red species, growing 3 to 7 feet tall and bearing 1- to 1½-inch-long flowers. The yellow-tinge larkspur, a smaller species, ranges from 4 to 18 inches tall and has ½- to ¾-inch blue to purple flowers whose upper petals shade to white or yellow. Menzies larkspur averages 6 to 18 inches tall and has deep blue flowers with white or pale blue upper petals and spurs; the flowers are ½ to ¾ inch long. The Parry larkspur generally grows no more than a foot tall, although it sometimes reaches 3 feet; it has small blue flowers with upper petals of white or yellow.

HOW TO GROW. All wild delphiniums do best in glades and along streams of a Western Coniferous Woodland environment. They need full sun during the day, cool dry nights and a moist, sandy soil rich in humus. Plant nursery-grown stock in the early spring, spacing plants 12 to 24 inches apart, depending on their eventual size. Make sure the crown of the roots is 1 to 2 inches beneath the surface of the ground. Propagate delphiniums from newly ripened seeds, if possible, because fresh seeds germinate better than older ones. They can be planted outdoors in midsummer. Alternatively, start them indoors in peat pots in the early spring for transfer outdoors in summer; they will flower the following spring, and may flower the first fall. Tall varieties may need staking so their towering spires do not break in the wind.

DESERT MARIGOLD See *Baileya*

DICENTRA

D. canadensis (squirrel corn); *D. cucullaria* (Dutchman's breeches); *D. eximia* (fringed bleeding heart)

These small, delicate plants are wild relatives of the cultivated bleeding heart. They are found in the filtered light and humus-rich soil of deciduous woodlands. Squirrel corn's native habitat includes eastern Canada and the eastern United States south to North Carolina and Tennessee; in the Midwest it is found from Minnesota to Missouri. Dutchman's breeches flourishes from eastern North Dakota south to Kansas, and eastward to the Atlantic; it is also found in Washington, northeast Oregon and Idaho. Fringed or plumed bleeding heart grows in the Appalachians from New York to Tennessee and Georgia; it is the easiest of the three species to cultivate. All three wild dicentras are perennials and all have fernlike leaves, arching stems and drooping flowers which they bear from mid- to late spring. The leaves of squirrel corn and Dutchman's breeches die down in summer, but those of fringed bleeding heart remain green. Squirrel corn grows from a small kernel-shaped corm that squirrels and chipmunks like to eat. It reaches a height of 6 to 10 inches, has smooth blue-gray foliage and bears ½-inch-long, fragrant, greenish-white flowers, touched with pink. The fragile white blossoms of Dutchman's breeches, ½ to ⅔ inch long, separate into two spurs and resemble baggy trousers hanging upside down. These early blooming plants, which grow 6 to 10 inches tall, tend to multiply into large groups. Fringed bleeding heart grows in bushy clumps that are 12 to 20 inches tall, and its ½-inch rose-colored flowers bloom intermittently throughout the summer until the first frost.

HOW TO GROW. All three dicentras do best in a Deciduous Woodland environment. They need the filtered sunlight and light shade of early spring. Squirrel corn and Dutchman's breeches do best in a rich slightly acid to neutral soil with a pH of 6.5 to 7.0. If the soil is too acid the plants produce leaves but no flowers. Fringed bleeding heart tolerates full sun and needs a more acid soil with a pH of 5.0 to 6.0. Although all three can be propagated from seeds sown as soon as they are ripe, they do better if raised from rootstock. Plant in the fall, setting the fleshy roots of Dutchman's breeches 1 to 1½ inches deep and 4 to 6 inches apart; plant squirrel corn corms 2 inches deep in groups of three or more. (A covering of wire mesh will discourage rodents.) Set roots of fringed bleeding heart about 1 inch deep and 2 feet apart. Cover all with a winter mulch of leaf mold or marsh hay.

All three species will seed freely, but it takes several years for the seedlings to develop. Fringed bleeding heart should

DUTCHMAN'S BREECHES
Dicentra cucullaria

For environments and climate zones, see maps, page 149.

HAIRY FAIRY BELLS
Disporum lanuginosum

COMMON SHOOTING STAR
Dodecatheon meadia

be divided every two or three years to encourage flowering, but treat the roots with care as they are very brittle.

DISPORUM

D. lanuginosum (hairy fairy bells); *D. trachycarpum* (wartberry fairy bells)

The fragile-looking blossoms of these dainty perennials sway to and fro in the slightest spring breeze as if they were being gently tugged. They are found in mountain woodlands, both east and west. Hairy fairy bells grows wild from Ontario through Ohio and New York, south to Georgia and Alabama. Wartberry fairy bells grows from Manitoba to British Columbia and south to Oregon, northern California and Colorado. The flowers of both species are ⅓ to ¾ inch long, and appear singly or in clusters of two or three in the late spring, followed in the summer by bright red berries.

Hairy fairy bells grows 16 to 30 inches tall, and has blossoms about 1 inch long; its leaves and stems are covered with tiny hairs. The somewhat shorter western species averages 1 to 2 feet tall and bears greenish-white flowers, ½ inch long. Both plants are most effective when seen from below, and are attractive planted on a bank above a woodland path.

HOW TO GROW. Both species of fairy bells do well in any Woodland environment, Deciduous or Coniferous. They need partial shade and a moist, acid to neutral soil with a pH of 5.0 to 7.0, rich in leaf mold or peat moss. Set rhizomes in the ground in the spring, burying them 1 to 2 inches deep in a horizontal position; space plants 12 to 24 inches apart. Or sow seeds in the fall as soon as they are ripe and can be separated from the berry pulp. Keep the soil moist until the seeds germinate. For additional plants, divide rootstocks of established plants in the spring or fall.

DODECATHEON

D. amethystinum (jewel shooting star); *D. clevelandii* (Cleveland shooting star); *D. meadia* (common shooting star)

During the spring, the shooting stars decorate fertile prairies and woodland glades with sprays of glistening jewel-tinted blossoms. The jewel shooting star, a midwestern species, is found in the valleys along the Mississippi River and its tributaries from Wisconsin to Missouri, but its range extends into Pennsylvania river valleys, too. The Cleveland shooting star grows on the West Coast, especially in Southern California. The common shooting star, also a midwestern species, grows from Manitoba south to Louisiana, eastward into Pennsylvania and westward into Texas. In all of the species the flower petals sweep backward, exposing beaklike anthers that look as though they are plummeting earthward. (Shooting stars have also been called mad violet, prairie pointer, rooster head, mosquito bill and bird bill.) The oblong leaves form low rosettes of foliage around a single flower stem, and in the summer after the plant has flowered this foliage completely disappears. The species vary in height and color, and in the configuration of their seed pods.

Jewel shooting star is a small plant, seldom more than 12 inches high, with blossoms the color of amethyst stones. The delicate seed capsule that follows the flowers is ⅓ inch long. The Cleveland shooting star has flower stems 12 to 18 inches high, with up to 10 flowers per stem; the blossoms are purple with a yellow base. The common shooting star is 10 to 15 inches tall, with a shower of 1-inch-long flowers, 10 to 20 to a stem, in tones of pink, rose, lilac, purple and white. Each is followed by a ½-inch cuplike seed pod.

HOW TO GROW. The shooting stars do well in a Prairie environment or in open areas of a Deciduous Woodland. They need a humus-rich soil of slightly acid to neutral content, pH 6.5 to 7.2, and will grow in full sun or partial shade. During their period of bloom, they need moisture, but when dormant they can withstand drought. Plant in the fall, burying rootstock ½ inch deep, spacing plants 10 to 16 inches apart, and interspersing them with later-blooming flowers so that the shooting stars' midsummer dormancy will be hidden. Cover them with a mulch of old leaves. Shooting stars can also be raised from seeds sown in the fall, but seedlings are weak the first few years and often do not survive. Additional plants may be propagated by dividing the rootstocks in the fall, making sure each new section contains a bud.

DOGTOOTH VIOLET See *Erythronium*
DOUGLAS MEADOW FOAM See *Limnanthes*
DRAGONROOT See *Arisaema*

DROSERA

D. rotundifolia (roundleaf sundew)

The sundew, like the pitcher plants, is an insectivorous wildflower but its range is a continent wide: it is found in peat bogs and swamps throughout North America. The plant entangles insects in sticky hairs that cover the surface of its small, round leaves, ¾ to 2 inches wide. Having captured their prey, the leaves curl inward and excrete an acid that digests the prey, then unfold again. In the summer, curving flower stalks unroll to a height of 2 to 14 inches and bear small pink or white flowers ¼ to 1½ inches across. The viscous wet hairs on the leaves glisten in the sun so they seem to be covered with dew. In a bog garden, these perennials spread rapidly to form a natural carpet.

HOW TO GROW. The sundew grows in all environments except those of the Desert and Semiarid Grassland. It needs full sun and a muddy, very acid soil rich in peat moss or sphagnum moss, with a pH of 4.0 to 5.0. Set nursery plants so they rest just on the surface of the ground; the roots will reach down for the moisture they need. Propagate additional plants by root division or from seeds. To guarantee sufficient moisture for seedlings, plant the seeds in a pot that is set into a dish kept filled with water. Osmosis will keep the surface soil damp. Given a nearly natural environment, sundew will also reproduce itself readily from seed.

DUTCHMAN'S BREECHES See *Dicentra*

E

ECHINACEA

E. angustifolia (narrow-leaved coneflower, black Samson coneflower), *E. purpurea* (purple coneflower)

Beginning in early summer and continuing well into fall, masses of tall coneflowers can be seen in the dry, sunny fields of the Midwest and South. Narrow-leaved coneflower grows from Saskatchewan to Texas, and it is also found in Tennessee. Purple coneflower is found in an area circumscribed by Michigan, Ohio, Georgia, Louisiana, Oklahoma and Iowa. These long-lived perennials have stiff, branching stems that end in solitary flowers that resemble the black-eyed Susan in shape, except that their petals curve backward. Each flower center contains a prickly rising dome. Narrow-leaved coneflower, the smaller of these two species, grows from 4 to 20 inches high with long narrow leaves and purple-pink flowers ⁴/₅ to 1³/₅ inches wide. The larger purple coneflower is about 3 feet tall and has purple-red flower heads 3 to 4 inches across. Both coneflowers are excellent plants for dry borders.

HOW TO GROW. The coneflowers grow best in a Prairie environment, in dry soil supplemented with leaf mold. They

ROUNDLEAF SUNDEW
Drosera rotundifolia

PURPLE CONEFLOWER
Echinacea purpurea

For environments and climate zones, see maps, page 149.

TRAILING ARBUTUS
Epigaea repens

FIREWEED
Epilobium angustifolium

need full sunlight or very light shade. They are propagated from seeds sown outdoors in the late spring or early fall or may be started indoors in flats in a mixture of soil, peat moss and sand for transplanting outside in the spring. Plants may also be propagated from root cuttings or clump divisions in the spring or fall. Set plants 18 to 24 inches apart.

EPIGAEA
E. repens (trailing arbutus, mayflower)

A traditional harbinger of spring in deciduous and coniferous woodlands of the East, the tiny pink or white flowers of trailing arbutus exude a telltale fragrance from under their protective covering of leaf mold long before most wildflowers have shown any sign of life. This dwarf evergreen is found in forests of oak and pine from Newfoundland through the Appalachians to Florida and Alabama, but its range extends west through Kentucky to Iowa and it is also found in Saskatchewan. The plant's leathery leaves, 1 to 3 inches long, form dense spreading mats of foliage on branches 6 to 12 inches long. The flowers—less than 1 inch long—cluster at the ends of the branches and are followed by the fruit, small white berries, which are eaten by ants, snails and birds. Trailing arbutus is so widely loved—and indiscriminately removed from its natural setting—that in some states it is protected by law.

HOW TO GROW. Trailing arbutus grows best in a Deciduous Woodland environment—in semishade and in humus-rich, well-drained acid soil with a pH of 4.0 to 5.0. While in spring bloom, it needs sunlight, but it must be protected from hot summer sun—as it is in nature by the emerging leaves of trees. Start plants from nursery stock in the spring or fall, and mulch with a mixture of evergreen needles and leaves of birch, oak or maple. Propagate by stem layering, or from seed—but seedlings may take three years to flower.

EPILOBIUM
E. angustifolium (fireweed)

Fireweed is a summer-flowering perennial that springs up along streams, in wet, sunny meadowlands and often in newly burned-over woods. It grows wild across the northern latitudes of the continent from Greenland to Alaska, and its range extends south to North Carolina, Indiana, Kansas, New Mexico and California. In the West, beekeepers prize it as a source of honey, and it is a natural forage plant for deer and elk. The plant has willow-like leaves, 2 to 6 inches long, growing alternately up a 2- to 8-foot-tall stem that ends in a spike of purple or magenta flowers, each about 1 inch across. The flowers are followed in the fall by velvety seed pods up to 2 inches long; the seeds are covered with fine hair that makes them windborne. Fireweed spreads rapidly on far-reaching underground runners and can be a nuisance.

HOW TO GROW. Fireweed grows in the open areas of any Deciduous or Coniferous Woodland environment. It does well in mountain meadows as high as the tree line, and along streams and lakes in the valleys. It needs a moist, slightly acid soil with a pH of 6.0 to 7.0, and full sun. Propagation is from seeds sown in the spring or fall, or from root division in the spring or fall.

ERIOGONUM
E. crocatum (wild buckwheat, sulfur flower)

Wild buckwheat, a plant especially attractive to bees, is a low-growing perennial that inhabits the dry, sunny slopes of the Santa Monica mountains from Southern California into the Baja California peninsula. Its oval leaves, 1 to 1½ inches long, are so woolly they appear almost white, and its dense clusters of sulfur-yellow flowers, ½ to 1½ inches across, spring at right angles from 8-inch-tall stems. Wild buckwheat is in blossom from spring until midsummer.

HOW TO GROW. Wild buckwheat does best in a Semiarid Grassland environment. It needs full sun and a dry, porous, well-drained soil. It is particularly suited to a sunny, well-drained rock garden. It is difficult to raise successfully east of the Mississippi because of wet winter weather. Shield the plants from rain and snow by covering them in the fall with a pane of glass raised above the foliage on bricks or stakes. Propagate from seed sown early in the spring, or by dividing existing plants in the fall. (This plant may be listed in your region as an endangered species; check with your local conservation office.)

ERYTHRONIUM

E. albidum (white fawn lily); *E. americanum* (common fawn lily, yellow adder's-tongue, dog-tooth violet, trout-lily); *E. grandiflorum* (lamb's tongue fawn lily); *E. montanum* (avalanche lily, avalanche fawn lily); *E. revolutum* (mahogany fawn lily)

The fawn lily, known as the dog-tooth violet in the East, is a spring-flowering woodland plant that appears in various forms in cool deciduous forests over most of the northern United States and Canada. The white fawn lily grows wild from Ontario to Minnesota, south to Kentucky, Arkansas and Oklahoma but is rare in the East; the common fawn lily inhabits moist woods from Nova Scotia west to Minnesota and south through the Appalachians to Florida and Alabama. The lamb's tongue fawn lily, avalanche lily and mahogany fawn lily are all native to the Pacific Coast, the lamb's tongue fawn lily growing from California to British Columbia, the avalanche in the high mountains of Oregon and Washington, and the mahogany in California and Oregon.

Fawn lilies rise from slender deep-buried corms, and their flowers are rather like miniature day lilies except that the petals usually sweep backward. The white fawn lily has narrow leaves and white flowers 1½ inches long that grow singly on flower stalks 6 to 9 inches high. The common fawn lily has mottled leaves—green with purple-brown and white markings; its yellow flowers, 1½ inches long, appear as solitary blossoms at the top of 4- to 10-inch stalks. Lamb's tongue fawn lily reaches a height of 1 to 2 feet and its flower stalks hold three to five bright yellow flowers, 2 inches long. The avalanche fawn lily's flowers are white with an orange base and grow singly or in groups of two or three on 18-inch-long stalks. The blossoms of the mahogany fawn lily are deep purple at maturity—but when newly opened are white, lightly flushed with pink. Its leaves are mottled with light brown. Fawn lily foliage dies down in midsummer.

HOW TO GROW. Fawn lilies grow best in a Deciduous Woodland environment. They need light shade and a moist humus-rich acid soil with a pH of 5.0 to 6.0. Plant the corms in the summer or fall, spacing them 4 to 6 inches apart and covering them with enough soil so that the top is 3 to 5 inches below the surface of the ground. (Common fawn lily will flower sooner if planted 6 inches deep.) Mulch with coarse peat moss or chopped leaves every two or three years in the fall. Fawn lilies, left undisturbed, will perpetuate themselves and last indefinitely. For additional plants of white or common fawn lilies, propagate in summer or fall from the small offset bulbs that develop around larger ones, replanting immediately so the bulbs do not dry out. It is best to purchase the corms of the western species; if they are propagated from seeds, they may require up to five or more years to reach flowering size.

WILD BUCKWHEAT
Eriogonum crocatum

COMMON FAWN LILY
Erythronium americanum

For environments and climate zones, see maps, page 149.

CALIFORNIA POPPY
Eschscholzia californica

MISTFLOWER
Eupatorium coelestinum

ESCHSCHOLZIA
E. californica (California poppy)

The state flower of California, where it blooms continuously from February through September, the California poppy grows in open dry grasslands along the Pacific Coast from Southern California to Washington. It is a perennial, about a foot tall, bearing wide cup-shaped blossoms 2 to 3 inches across, in shades of bright yellow to deep orange. The flowers, which rise above mounds of feathery blue-green foliage, open when the sun strikes them and close when the sun sets.

HOW TO GROW. California poppies grow best in a Semiarid Grassland environment. They need full sun and a sandy, well-drained soil. Although technically perennials and grown as such in Zones 8-10, they are also cultivated as annuals as far north as Zone 3. In Zones 3-7 sow seeds in the fall or very early in the spring, as soon as the soil can be prepared. Sow seeds where they are to grow, as they are difficult to transplant. Space plants 6 inches apart. In Zones 8-10 the California poppy often seeds itself and reappears each year.

ESCOBITO See *Orthocarpus*

EUPATORIUM
E. coelestinum (mistflower, blue boneset); *E. perfoliatum* (boneset, thoroughwort); *E. purpureum* (bluestem, sweet Joe Pye weed)

In the late summer and early fall, the massed colors of the bonesets—blue, white, pale purple—brighten the edges of streams and wet meadows from the East to the Midwest. All are perennials. Mistflower, with its 3- to 4-inch clusters of ageratum-like flowers, is found growing along streams from New Jersey south to Florida and the Caribbean islands, and in the Mississippi basin. It grows from 1½ to 3 feet tall and spreads rapidly on underground stems, so rapidly, in fact, that it is best used only in large gardens. Boneset reaches a height of 2 to 4 feet and has curious leaves, 4 inches long, which join each other in pairs at the base, so that the stem of the plant seems to pass through their center. The flat-topped flower heads are composed of tiny flowers that grow in clusters of 10 to 20 blossoms, about ½ inch across. Its natural habitat is swampy ground and low-lying fields from Nova Scotia and Quebec south to Florida; in the Midwest it is found from Minnesota to Louisiana and in Oklahoma. Bluestem, often known as sweet Joe Pye weed, grows from 2 to 9 feet tall, and is found throughout New England, south to Florida, and in the Midwest in Minnesota, Nebraska and Oklahoma. Its 4-inch foliage surrounds the stem in whorls of two to five leaves, and its flowers form domed clusters 4 inches across. When bruised, the plant smells of vanilla.

HOW TO GROW. The bonesets grow in open areas of a Deciduous Woodland environment and in a Prairie environment. They do well in sun or light shade and in well-drained garden soil, but they need constant moisture; if grown in dry soil they will be stunted and may not survive. Mulch the plants with leaves to conserve moisture. They are most easily started from nursery stock. Plant mistflower in the spring; boneset and bluestem in the spring or fall. Space mistflower and boneset 1 foot apart; bluestem 2 feet apart. These species can be propagated by clump division in the spring, but the roots are densely matted and difficult to separate. Both mistflower and bluestem can, in addition, be started from seeds, planted in the spring or fall, and will seed themselves. Boneset, however, almost never seeds itself, and is seldom grown from seed successfully.

EVENING PRIMROSE, HOOKER See *Oenothera*

F

FAIRY BELLS, HAIRY See *Disporum*
FAIRY CANDLES See *Cimicifuga*
FALSE SOLOMON'S SEAL See *Smilacina*
FAREWELL-TO-SPRING See *Clarkia*
FAWNLILY See *Erythronium*
FEATHER SOLOMON PLUME See *Smilacina*
FIREWEED See *Epilobium*
FOAM FLOWER, ALLEGHENY See *Tiarella*

FRAGARIA

F. virginiana (Virginia strawberry, wild strawberry)

Better known for its fruit than for its flowers, the Virginia strawberry, a member of the rose family, can be found in eastern meadows from Labrador to Georgia and in prairie grasslands from Alberta to Oklahoma. Like its cultivated cousin, the Virginia strawberry is a low-growing perennial that spreads by sending out slender aboveground runners bearing miniature new plants. Strawberry plants bear oval serrated leaves divided into groups of three leaflets. The golden-centered, five-petaled white flowers, about ½ to ¾ inch across, grow on separate short stalks and blossom in spring in delicate clusters. The fruit is smaller and more conical than that of cultivated strawberries (many of which were hybridized from *F. virginiana*) but often sweeter.

HOW TO GROW. Virginia strawberries grow among grasses in open, sunny fields in Deciduous Woodland and Prairie environments. They do best in a well-drained humus-filled soil with a pH of 5.5 to 6.5. To move plants to another area, transplant newly rooted runners in late summer or early fall. Set each plant so that half of the crown, where the stems rise from the roots, is below ground. Virginia strawberries are of the easiest possible culture and yield delectable fruit.

FRINGED BLEEDING HEART See *Dicentra*
FRINGED GENTIAN See *Gentiana*

FRITILLARIA

F. biflora (chocolate lily, black fritillary); *F. lanceolata* (checker lily, riceroot fritillary); *F. pudica* (yellow fritillary)

Hardly has the snow melted on grassy wooded slopes across western North America when the fritillaries burst into bloom. Depending on the species, these colorful perennials bear one to seven nodding flowers on top of slender stems that grow from bulblike corms. The chocolate lily, found in the coastal range of California, grows about 1½ feet tall and has dark brown bell-shaped flowers streaked with green and purple. The checker lily, tallest of the three, can reach a height of 3 feet, but its mottled bowl-shaped blossoms—a mixture of purple, yellow and green—blend into the colors of the plant's surroundings and are easy to miss in the wild. The yellow fritillary, growing only 4 to 12 inches tall, produces a fragrant, vivid yellow-orange blossom that turns red with age. In the wildflower garden the fritillaries make a gay display of spring color when planted in clusters along borders or edgings, but they can also be scattered randomly among rough field grasses.

HOW TO GROW. Fritillaries grow best in a Western Coniferous Woodland or Rocky Mountain Woodland environment. They require a well-drained neutral soil, with a pH of 6.0 to 7.5, and a spot that is shaded from the sun during the hottest part of the day. Plant corms in summer or fall, spacing them 3 to 4 inches apart and covering them with 3 to 4 inches of soil. Fritillaries are best left undisturbed, but if propagation is desired, dig up the bulbs. In early summer, after the foliage dies, separate the small bulbs that surround

VIRGINIA STRAWBERRY
Fragaria virginiana

CHOCOLATE LILY
Fritillaria biflora

For environments and climate zones, see maps, page 149.

BLANKETFLOWER
Gaillardia aristata

GALAX
Galax aphylla

the larger ones; replant immediately. The new plants will yield flowers in four to six years.

FRITILLARY See *Fritillaria*
FUCHSIA, CALIFORNIA See *Zauschneria*

 G

GAILLARDIA

G. aristata, also called *G. grandiflora* (blanketflower, common perennial gaillardia)

Several species of blanketflower are perennials or annuals native to the hills, plains and prairies of the West from British Columbia and Saskatchewan south to New Mexico, Arizona and Texas. The perennial species, *G. aristata,* bears disc-shaped flowers 2½ to 4 inches across on slender stems 8 to 24 inches tall, which usually stand erect. The plant is extremely drought- and heat-resistant, making it a dependable source of cut flowers throughout the summer.

HOW TO GROW. Blanketflowers grow in a Prairie environment or in open areas of a Rocky Mountain Woodland environment. They do best in well-drained soil and full sun. In clay soils, lacking humus, the leaves will grow at the expense of the flowers and the plants are likely to die in winter. Sow seeds in the spring when there is no longer any danger of frost. They will germinate in seven to 10 days and blossom the same year. Or start seeds indoors four to six weeks before the expected date of the last frost. Space seedlings 10 to 12 inches apart in the garden. Additional plants can be propagated by dividing and resetting the clumps in spring. After two or three years plants become overcrowded and should in any case be divided.

GALAX

G. aphylla (galax)

Galax is an evergreen perennial ground cover native to the southern Appalachian Mountains. It spreads by means of a thick mat of runners. The wiry leaf stems are 4 to 6 inches long, but during the summer its spikes of tiny white flowers are carried on 12- to 18-inch stalks well above the foliage. Toothed, leathery leaves are a lustrous green in summer, then turn bronze in late fall or winter. Although native to the Southeast, galax is hardy enough for northern climates through Zone 6 if given acid soil and shade. It makes an impressive spring display when grown as a colony.

HOW TO GROW. Galax grows best in a moist, acid Deciduous Woodland environment. It produces its most vivid colors in sun (the leaves stay green in shade) and requires constant moisture and soil rich in leaf mold or peat with a pH of 5.0 to 5.5. To propagate, divide the thick, pinkish rhizomes in spring or fall, making sure each has a bud. Plant segments horizontally, about 1 inch deep, spacing them 6 to 12 inches apart. Mulch with 6 to 8 inches of leaf mold or pine needles in Zones 5 and 6.

GAULTHERIA

G. procumbens (checkerberry wintergreen, spicy wintergreen, checkerberry)

Checkerberry wintergreen, an aromatic evergreen ground cover, is a relative of bearberry and trailing arbutus that grows in the open woodlands of the eastern United States and Canada as far south as Georgia and Alabama, as well as in Manitoba and Minnesota. The plant's creeping woody stems, 2 to 6 inches tall, bear clusters of thick, leathery 1- to 2-inch-long leaves at their tips. In the spring, these leaves emerge as red shoots, soon followed by shiny green foliage that turns slightly bronze in the fall. During the summer, bell-shaped blossoms, ¼ to ½ inch long, appear where the leaves meet the stem. The flowers are followed by mealy, mint-flavored edible berries, ¼ to ½ inch wide, that last until spring. The berries, enjoyed by children and birds alike, make checkerberry wintergreen a desirable ground cover despite its sparse growth. The leaves can be dried and used to brew wintergreen tea.

HOW TO GROW. Checkerberry wintergreen is found in a Northeastern or Southeastern Coniferous Woodland environment or in a Deciduous Woodland environment. It does best in partial shade and well-drained, humus-rich soil with a pH of 4.0 to 5.0. It is one of the more difficult wildflowers to establish because it gets its food from minute fungi that must be present in the soil. The least difficult way to raise checkerberry wintergreen is to set out nursery plants that are rooted in sod. Space plants 1 to 2 feet apart and mulch them with leaf mold or pine needles. Until plants are established keep the soil very moist. Checkerberry wintergreen can also be propagated, less successfully, from cuttings and rhizomes in the spring or fall; propagation from seed is least satisfactory, as seeds are unreliable and very slow to germinate.

GAY-FEATHER See *Liatris*
GENTIAN See *Gentiana*

GENTIANA

G. andrewsii (Andrews gentian, closed gentian, blind gentian); *G. crinita* (fringed gentian)

The intensely blue fall-blooming gentian is one of the most beautiful of American wildflowers. Both species grow in wet meadows and moist open woodlands, but their range is somewhat different. Andrews gentian is found across Canada from Quebec to Saskatchewan, and south through the Appalachians to Georgia; it also grows in Nebraska and Arkansas. Fringed gentian is native across North America from Maine to Manitoba, and south through the Appalachians to Georgia; it also grows in Ohio, Indiana and northern Iowa.

Andrews gentian is a perennial with closed, bottle-shaped flowers that are borne in candelabra-like clusters where the upper leaves meet the stems. Although most blossoms are deep blue, rare white flowers occasionally appear. This species grows 1 to 3 feet tall. Fringed gentian, a biennial, is known for its distinctive 2-inch-long fringed blossoms, which grow in solitary elegance at the tips of short, branching stems. Later-blooming than Andrews gentian, these four-petaled flowers open only in the sun. Their leaves are lighter than those of Andrews gentian and the plants grow 1 to 2 feet tall.

HOW TO GROW. Both species of gentian grow in Northeastern and Southeastern Coniferous Woodland environments and in Deciduous Woodlands. Andrews gentian adapts to partial shade or full sun and grows well in a moist, slightly acid to neutral soil with a pH of 6.0 or below. Purchase nursery-grown plants in the fall. Place the roots so their tops are about 1 inch below the surface of the ground and space plants 8 to 12 inches apart. This species can also be started from seeds sown in flats in the fall as soon as they are ripe and transplanted to the garden the following spring. But plants grown from seed do not bloom until their third year. Once established, Andrews gentian can be propagated by dividing old plants. Generally they require no special care.

The biennial fringed gentian, one of the most difficult wildflowers to grow, can only be started from seed. Sow the tiny seeds outdoors in peat pots or flats in the fall, pressing them into the soil. Keep the soil moist at all times until the seedlings begin to appear. Then cover the pots or flats with

CHECKERBERRY WINTERGREEN
Gaultheria procumbens

ANDREWS GENTIAN
Gentiana andrewsii

For environments and climate zones, see maps, page 149.

SPOTTED GERANIUM
Geranium maculatum

PRAIRIE SMOKE
Geum triflorum

burlap or evergreen boughs to protect them over the winter; remove this covering the following spring. During the first year, seedlings grow very slowly but should be watered regularly. Before the second winter, cover the tender plants with a light mulch of salt hay. In spring of the second year, transplant the seedlings from their pots or flats to a damp, meadow-like site. With good luck, the fringed gentian will flower in the fall and produce seeds for other colonies at the end of its two-year life cycle.

GERANIUM

G. maculatum (spotted geranium, wild geranium); *G. robertianum* (herb Robert)

The wild geraniums are but distantly related to the common garden geranium, but their deeply cut foliage somewhat resembles that of the cultivated varieties. They are found along roadsides and in open woods and meadows throughout the East and Midwest. Both species grow 1 to 2 feet tall and bear five-petaled flowers that are followed by long, tapered seed pods. When the seeds are ripe, these pods burst open, scattering their contents. The spotted geranium, a perennial, grows from Maine to Manitoba, and south to Georgia, Tennessee, Arkansas and Oklahoma. Its flowers, ½ to 1 inch wide, appear in the spring and early summer. Herb Robert, an annual, is found from Newfoundland to Manitoba, and south to Maryland, West Virginia, Indiana and Nebraska. It has somewhat hairy stems and bears pink-to-red flowers, ½ inch wide, that bloom in pairs throughout the summer and into the fall. When the fernlike leaves of herb Robert are crushed, they give off a musky odor.

HOW TO GROW. Both the spotted geranium and herb Robert grow in a Northeastern or Southeastern Coniferous Woodland environment or in a Deciduous Woodland environment. They adapt to sun or light shade and do best in a sheltered position where they are protected from the wind. Both species thrive in slightly acid to neutral soil, with a pH of 6.0 to 7.0. To grow spotted geraniums, set nursery plants in the gound in the early spring or fall, spacing them 10 to 15 inches apart. Cover the bed with a light mulch of leaves to keep the soil moist. Plants can also be started from rhizomes, set 1 inch deep, or from seeds sown as soon as they are ripe. Seedlings do not bloom until the second or third year. Grow herb Robert from seeds collected and sown as soon as they are ripe, in the early fall.

GEUM

G. macrophyllum, also called *G. japonicum* (large-leaf geum, large-leaf avens); *G. triflorum* (prairie smoke, old man's whiskers)

During the spring and summer, fields, prairies and open woods of North America seem filled with geums, perennial wildflowers that spread with a network of runners, forming horseshoe-shaped configurations. Large-leaf geum is found from Labrador to Alaska and south to New York, Michigan, Idaho and California. It grows 1 to 3 feet tall and is named for the large round serrated leaf that terminates its leaf stalk. It bears five-petaled yellow blossoms ¼ inch across. Prairie smoke is found from Ontario to British Columbia, south to Illinois, Iowa, New Mexico and California. It grows 6 to 12 inches tall, has deeply cut leaves and bears drooping ½-inch-long cream-to-pink flowers. The entire plant is covered with silky hairs and is notable for its interesting plumed fruit, shown here in enlarged size, which appears after the flowers fade and remains on the plant for several weeks.

HOW TO GROW. Geums grow in Prairie, Rocky Mountain Woodland, Deciduous Woodland and Northeastern Coniferous Woodland environments. They need sun and thrive in a well-drained, sandy soil with a pH of 6.0 to 7.0. Set out nursery plants in the spring or fall, spacing them 12 to 24 inches apart. Plants spread rapidly. Although they may also be grown from seeds, few are likely to germinate and they are often eaten by goldfinches. For additional plants, divide the underground stems in the late summer.

GILIA

G. capitata (blue thimble flower, globe gilia); *G. rubra,* also called *G. coronoptifolia* or *Ipomopsis rubra* (red gilia, standing-cypress, Texas plume, Spanish larkspur)

These annuals dot the dry slopes of western mountains with myriad flowers during the late spring and summer. The two species listed above do not resemble each other except for their long-stemmed, long-lasting blossoms, excellent as cut flowers for bouquets. Blue thimble flower is found from Southern California to British Columbia and Idaho. It grows 1 to 2 feet tall and bears ¼- to ½-inch white-to-violet blossoms in dense globular flower heads. Red gilia, a biennial usually grown as an annual, has escaped from its native habitat in Texas and Oklahoma, and is now found growing wild in North Carolina, Florida and Mississippi, as well as in Michigan and New England. It has feathery, threadlike inch-long leaves on stems as tall as 6 feet and bears long spikes of tubular red flowers spotted inside with pale yellow. Both species look best in a massed planting.

HOW TO GROW. Both species of gilia do best in a Semiarid Grassland environment. Red gilia also will grow in a Prairie environment and in open areas elsewhere. The gilias thrive in full sun and a dry, sandy soil with a pH of 6.0 to 7.0. They are easily grown from seeds sown where the plants are to remain. Sow seeds in the fall or in the spring. Thin plants to stand about a foot apart. To keep tall stems upright, put small branching twigs next to the half-grown plants; they will provide support and soon be hidden by foliage.

GILLENIA

G. trifoliata (bowman's root)

Bowman's root is a 2- to 3-foot-tall woodland perennial found growing in thickets and open spaces of Ontario, Michigan and New York, south to Georgia and Missouri. It has thin, branching flower stalks and three-part leaves. Its small pink-to-red flowers, ½ to 1 inch long, bloom in loose clusters during the early summer.

HOW TO GROW. Bowman's root, a wildflower relatively easy to grow, needs a Deciduous Woodland environment or a Northeastern or Southeastern Coniferous Woodland environment. It does best in partial shade but will tolerate sun and thrives on a humus-rich, somewhat damp acid soil with a pH of 5.0 to 6.0. To grow bowman's root, set out nursery plants in the spring, spacing them 12 to 24 inches apart; cover the bed with a light mulch to preserve moisture. Or start from seeds sown in the fall; these will bloom in the second year. For additional plants, divide established roots in the early spring. Bowman's root looks best planted in a colony.

GINSENG, AMERICAN See *Panax*
GLOBE GILIA See *Gilia*
GOATSBEARD See *Aruncus*
GOLDEN CUP See *Hunnemannia*
GOLDEN-EYED GRASS See *Sisyrinchium*
GOLDENROD See *Solidago*
GOLDEN SEAL See *Hydrastis*
GOLDFIELDS See *Baeria*
GOLDTHREAD See *Coptis*

BLUE THIMBLE FLOWER
Gilia capitata

BOWMAN'S ROOT
Gillenia trifoliata

For environments and climate zones, see maps, page 149.

DOWNY RATTLESNAKE PLANTAIN
Goodyera pubescens

SHORE GRINDELIA
Grindelia robusta

GOODYERA

G. pubescens (downy rattlesnake plantain); *G. tesselata* (checkered rattlesnake plantain)

These members of the orchid family bear little superficial resemblance to their more famous cousins; they are grown for distinctive white-veined, evergreen foliage that looks like rattlesnake skin. The rattlesnake plantains are woodland perennials that hug the ground as their creeping roots spread out under pines and oaks. From summer to early fall, they bear spikes of many tiny $1/8$- to $1/5$-inch-long white flowers that, if examined with a magnifying glass, resemble more common orchids. Downy rattlesnake plantain is found primarily in dry upland areas from Newfoundland and Quebec to Minnesota, south to Georgia, Alabama and Arkansas. Its 6- to 18-inch flower stalks are covered with soft hairs. The handsome leaves are 3 or more inches long. Checkered rattlesnake plantain, the less common species, grows throughout Canada and south through the Appalachians to North Carolina and Tennessee; it is also found in the mountains of Minnesota, New Mexico and Arizona. It too grows best in dry areas. The vein markings on its 2-inch-long leaves are less distinct and its 14-inch-long stems are more prostrate. Both perennials do well in rock gardens.

HOW TO GROW. Both rattlesnake plantains grow in Northeastern Coniferous and Deciduous Woodland environments. Downy rattlesnake plantain also grows in a Southeastern Coniferous Woodland environment; and checkered rattlesnake plantain also grows in a Rocky Mountain Woodland environment. Both plants do best in a well-drained mixture of pine needles and acid soil with a pH of 5.0 to 6.0, in partial shade. Set out nursery plants in the spring, spacing them 3 to 6 inches apart. Protect them over the winter with a light mulch of leaves. Rattlesnake plantains can be propagated by dividing the plants so that each section contains a rosette of foliage and accompanying roots. This is best done in early fall so that the new plants will have time to become established before winter.

GREAT BLUE LOBELIA See *Lobelia*
GREEN DRAGON See *Arisaema*

GRINDELIA

G. robusta (shore grindelia)

Native to dry fields and salt marshes from Santa Barbara County to Baja California, shore grindelias grow 2 to 4 feet high and have wide, daisy-like yellow flowers, $1\frac{1}{2}$ to 2 inches across, with as many as 45 petals. Each flower head is contained in long curling bracts, and the stem is clasped by leaves that extend up to 7 inches in length. Shore grindelia blooms from early spring into fall. The leaves, stems and flowers of this perennial contain a sticky white resin that often oozes out onto buds or broken foliage.

HOW TO GROW. Shore grindelia grows in a Desert environment. It thrives in full sun and a dry, sandy soil with a pH of 7.0 to 8.0. It cannot tolerate wet, cold winters. Seeds sown in the fall will produce plants that will flower the next spring.

H

HAIRY FAIRY BELLS See *Disporum*
HAREBELLS, SOUTHERN See *Campanula*
HEARTLEAF See *Asarum*
HEDGEHOG PRICKLY POPPY See *Argemone*

HELENIUM

H. autumnale (common sneezeweed); *H. bigelovii* (Bigelow sneezeweed)

From midsummer well into the fall, the large golden flowers of the sneezeweeds (occasionally reddish brown) can be seen along roadsides and among the tall grasses of wet meadows and marshes throughout North America. These sturdy perennials grow 1 to 5 feet high and bear multipetaled flowers resembling those of the sunflower except that the ends of the petals are toothed. The 1- to 1½-inch flowers appear several at a time at the top of branching stems. Common sneezeweed, the most widespread of the two species, grows across Canada from Quebec to British Columbia, and south through the Appalachians to Florida; it is also found in Arizona. Bigelow sneezeweed, a western species, is found in the Sierra Nevada mountains from Southern California to southern Oregon. Somewhat shorter than common sneezeweed, it averages 1 to 3 feet in height, but has slightly larger flower heads, 1½ to 2½ inches across; the center of the flower is brown.

HOW TO GROW. The sneezeweeds grow in the Deciduous and the Northeastern, Southeastern and Western Coniferous Woodland environments. Plants require full sun and do best in low, wet, open sites, such as marshes and meadows, although they adapt to moist garden soil. They need a pH of 5.5 to 6.5. Propagate by division of roots in the spring or from seeds sown in the spring or fall. Nursery-grown plants are widely available. Plants started from seed will bloom in the second year; plants obtained from a nursery will bear flowers the first fall. If it is left undisturbed in the garden, sneezeweed will reseed itself.

HELIANTHUS
H. decapetalus (golden thin-leaved sunflower)

A wild relative of the cultivated sunflower, the golden thin-leaved sunflower is a clump-forming perennial of sunny open woods and stream embankments from Maine to Minnesota and southward to North Carolina, Kentucky and Missouri. It grows from 2 to over 5 feet tall with numerous yellow flowers, 2 to 3 inches wide, that bloom at the tops of thin, branching stems from late summer into the fall. From this native species gardeners can select double-flowered forms; among the most popular is *H. decapetalus multiflorus*, sometimes called golden glow. The double forms rarely produce seeds, but like the original species, spread rapidly from underground creeping roots, establishing new colonies in a short time and, if they are not kept under control, can soon take over a clearing.

HOW TO GROW. The golden thin-leaved sunflower grows in Northeastern Coniferous Woodland and Deciduous Woodland environments. It does best in moist soil of pH 5.5 to 7.0, with full sun. Propagate by dividing root clumps in the spring or by sowing seeds in the fall or early spring, covering them with ½ inch of soil. Thin or transplant seedlings to stand about 1 foot apart.

HELIOTROPE, WILD See *Phacelia*

HEPATICA
H. acutiloba (sharp-lobed hepatica); *H. americana,* also called *H. triloba* (round-lobed hepatica)

The charming little hepatica is one of the very early flowers of spring from Nova Scotia to Manitoba southward to northern Florida and Missouri. Natives of rocky hillsides and dry woods, these perennials grow only 4 to 6 inches tall. In the spring, fuzzy flower stems arise from the center of the clump of the previous year's foliage and bear single ½- to 1-inch-wide blue, white, purple and, rarely, pink blossoms. After the flowers have faded, the old foliage dies down and

COMMON SNEEZEWEED
Helenium autumnale

GOLDEN THIN-LEAVED SUNFLOWER
Helianthus decapetalus

For environments and climate zones, see maps, page 149.

ROUND-LOBED HEPATICA
Hepatica americana

COW PARSNIP
Heracleum maximum

new leaves appear; these leaves mature and remain green until the following spring.

Round-lobed hepatica is the more common species; sharp-lobed hepatica resembles it but has oval, sharply pointed leaf lobes and usually bears slightly larger flowers. Both species can be found growing in colonies in the wild. In the garden, they do well tucked into a lightly shaded rock garden or planted on a sloping hillside where they form clumps.

HOW TO GROW. The hepaticas grow in the Northeastern and Southeastern Coniferous Woodland and the Deciduous Woodland environments. Round-lobed hepatica grows in soil with a pH of 5.0 to 6.0, but sharp-lobed hepatica does better in less acid soil with a pH of 6.0 to 7.0. Both need some direct sunlight for flowering. In the early spring or the fall, buy nursery plants and set them in the garden 8 to 12 inches apart. Just before the first frost, cover the plants with a light mulch of leaves and remove most of it the following spring. For additional plants, divide root clumps in the fall, keeping two or three plants in each clump. But do not expect quick results; hepatica roots grow slowly. Sow seeds as soon as they are ripe. Although hepaticas will sow themselves, this process can be helped by covering the plants with a light layer of marsh hay sprinkled with water to protect the seeds from chipmunks. After two or three years, the plants will be well established and may need to be thinned or transplanted.

HERACLEUM

H. maximum, also called *H. lanatum* (cow parsnip)

The cow parsnip, a giant among wildflowers, rises to a height of 3 to 8 feet and looks like an unlikely cross between a maple tree and a parsnip. It is found in moist, sunny or partially shaded places along creeks and streams from Labrador to Alaska, south to Georgia, Indiana, Kansas and New Mexico. Cow parsnip is a perennial with coarse, deeply lobed leaves and towering flower stalks that, in midsummer, bear 6- to 10-inch flat-topped clusters made up of numerous tiny white flowers.

HOW TO GROW. Cow parsnip grows best in a Wetland environment but adapts easily to any moist, rich soil. It thrives in sun or partial shade if it is supplied with plenty of moisture. Sow seeds as soon as they are ripe in the fall, or propagate new plants by dividing root clumps in the spring. Cow parsnip will grow with little attention and, if the flower clusters are not cut off before they go to seed, the plant will seed itself, establishing large colonies wherever it has sufficient dampness. It will do well in a bog garden or in damp, shady areas beside a stream.

HERB ROBERT See *Geranium*

HEUCHERA

H. micrantha (small-flowered alumroot); *H. sanguinea* (coral bells)

The wandlike heucheras are found on rocky ledges in the mountains of the West and Southwest. Their slender flower stalks culminate in loose panicles of hanging bell-shaped blossoms that bloom from late spring until midsummer; the stalks rise above clumps of large geranium-like leaves. Small-flowered alumroot, which is found in the Sierra Nevada and Cascade ranges to British Columbia, reaches up to 3 feet tall and bears white or pink flowers. Coral bells, native to the mountains of southern Arizona and northern New Mexico, grows 1 to 2 feet tall and bears red blossoms. Both of these perennials make attractive border plants for shady spots, and are long lasting as cut flowers.

HOW TO GROW. Small-flowered alumroot grows best in a

Western Coniferous Woodland environment, coral bells in a Rocky Mountain Woodland environment. But both species adapt readily to almost any slightly acid to neutral garden soil, pH 6.0 to 7.0, and do well in either full sun or partial shade. Plant nursery stock in the spring or fall, setting plants 10 to 15 inches apart with the tops of the roots just at the soil level. To propagate additional plants, divide established plants in the spring. Both of these species may also be grown from seeds sown as they are ripe in late summer, or in early spring.

HIBISCUS

H. californicus (California rose mallow); *H. moscheutos,* also called *H. palustris* (rose mallow)

Tall natives of riverbanks, swamps and salt marshes, the rose mallows are noted for their huge pink or white flowers with deep red centers, which bloom from midsummer until fall. Like the flowers of their relative, the garden hollyhock, they open one at a time all through the summer. Rose mallow, native to the southern states from Maryland to the Gulf Coast and westward to Missouri and Indiana, grows 3 to 8 feet tall and bears flowers 4 to 7 inches wide. California rose mallow, found in the central valleys of that state, bears flowers 4 to 8 inches in diameter on stalks 3 to 7 feet high. Both plants are perennials.

HOW TO GROW. The rose mallows do best in a Wetland environment within their respective geographical ranges, but they will also adapt to almost any moist garden soil, especially if it is enriched by the addition of compost or peat moss. Both species thrive in full sun. The fastest way to start rose mallows is to plant nursery seedlings, spacing them 3 feet apart with the tops of the roots 3 to 4 inches below the ground. Rose mallows also can be grown from seeds planted in the early spring, but plants produce few flowers in the first year. To propagate additional plants, divide roots of established plants in the spring or take stem cuttings in the summer. Left undisturbed, rose mallows will sow themselves readily; young plants can easily be moved from the wild into the garden to provide dependable bloom late in the growing season. (California rose mallow may be declared an endangered species, however; in that state check with the local conservation office.)

HOUSTONIA

H. caerulea (bluet)

During the spring, colonies of dainty bluets twinkle across the meadows, open fields and woodland floor throughout most of the eastern United States and southern Canada. Like tiny four-pointed stars, the ½-inch-wide blue-to-white blossoms with bright yellow centers are borne atop branching stems that range from 2 to 8 inches tall. When they are not in flower, their leaves, only ½ inch high, form dense tufts of green carpeting.

Bluets are perennials, with root stalks that creep to establish new colonies.

HOW TO GROW. This species is suited to the Northeastern and Southeastern Coniferous and the Deciduous Woodland environments. Bluets do well in full sun or light shade and moist soil with an acid to neutral pH of 5.5 to 7.0. Plants can be grown easily from seeds sown in early spring or in the fall. Scratch the soil and scatter the seeds where you want the plants to bloom. Once bluets are established, you can also propagate them by dividing the clumps of green tufts in the spring before or after flowering. They also reseed themselves, and may escape from the wild garden to become a

CORAL BELLS
Heuchera sanguinea

ROSE MALLOW
Hibiscus moscheutos

For environments and climate zones, see maps, page 149.

BLUET
Houstonia caerulea

MEXICAN TULIP POPPY
Hunnemannia fumariaefolia

nuisance in a carefully tended lawn. Occasionally nursery-grown plants are available.

HUMMINGBIRD FLOWER See *Zauschneria*

HUNNEMANNIA

H. fumariaefolia (Mexican tulip poppy, golden cup)

The Mexican tulip poppy escaped from cultivation to survive wild in the dry, hot deserts of Southern California. Its lustrous 2½- to 3-inch-wide yellow flowers bloom from mid-summer to fall. Although its finely cut foliage and its flowers resemble those of the cultivated California poppy, the Mexican tulip poppy is a taller plant, usually 2 to 3 feet tall. It is an excellent border plant for the garden and provides a constant supply of flowers until frost.

HOW TO GROW. The golden tulip poppy is a perennial in the hot Desert environment but can be grown as an annual in other environments where there is full sun and dry soil with a pH of 7.0 to 8.0. Sow seeds outdoors where plants are to grow after the night temperatures remain above 50°. Thin seedlings to 8 to 10 inches apart when they are about 6 inches tall. Keep the soil barely moist; do not overwater.

HYDRASTIS

H. canadensis (golden seal, orange-root)

A native wildflower in New England, the Midwest, and in the South to Tennessee and Arkansas, this plant has been pushed almost to extinction in its natural environment by collectors seeking its roots, which contain a substance used in remedies to stop bleeding. Golden seal has deeply veined leaves 4 to 8 inches wide and raspberry-like fruits that replace inconspicuous flowers in the late summer or fall. During the spring, one large leaf rises from the fleshy, orange root, followed by a hairy stem that grows 6 to 24 inches tall. Soon two more leaves appear near the top of the stem and a short flower stem grows between them.

HOW TO GROW. Golden seal is suited to the Northeastern and Southeastern Coniferous and the Deciduous Woodland environments. It needs partial to full shade and moist, humus-rich soil with a pH of 5.0 to 6.0. Start plants in early spring or fall by burying several rhizomes ½ to 1 inch deep and 6 to 10 inches apart. Plants also may be started from seeds sown in the fall as soon as they are ripe, but germination may take a year or more. Seeds should be sown atop a prepared bed and covered with a 1-inch layer of leaf mold. Keep the seedbed moist but not soggy.

HYPOXIS

H. hirsuta (common golden star grass, hairy star grass)

The tiny blossoms of common golden star grass decorate dry fields and prairies over much of the continent east of the Rockies during early summer. The leaves of this perennial look like blades of grass that grow 6 to 12 inches tall from a small bulblike underground root, a corm. The entire plant—stem, flower, buds and leaves—is covered with minute hairs.

HOW TO GROW. Common golden star grass grows in the Northeastern and Southeastern Coniferous Woodland, the Deciduous Woodland and the Prairie environments. Plants need full sun and do well in rich soils as well as sandy loam with a pH of 6.0 to 7.0. Although plants survive dry conditions in their native habitat, they do best in the garden if the soil is kept moist but not soggy. Start plants in the spring or fall, burying corms about 1½ inches deep in groups a few inches apart. In Zones 3-6, protect them with a mulch. Propagate additional plants by collecting the small corms that grow around the parent plant. Seeds are difficult to collect, and if used they should be sown in the fall. Common golden star grass will multiply itself by producing offsets from its corms.

I

INDIAN CUCUMBER ROOT See *Medeola*
INDIAN PAINT BRUSH See *Castilleja*
INDIGO, YELLOW FALSE See *Baptisia*
INDIGO, WILD See *Baptisia*
INNOCENCE See *Collinsia*

IRIS

I. cristata (crested iris); *I. douglasiana* (Douglas iris, mountain iris); *I. verna* (vernal iris); *I. versicolor* (blue flag iris)

Wild irises are perennials that grow in swamps, wet meadows and moist woods throughout North America. Like their cultivated relatives, they are easily identified by their flat, sword-shaped leaves and distinctive flowers. Each blossom consists of three erect petals and three larger outer petal-like sepals, usually the same color as the petals, which ordinarily curve downward from the base of the flower and are marked with crests of a contrasting color. The striking flowers bloom from spring through early summer in a very wide range of colors, often in combinations—and are aptly named after the Greek goddess of the rainbow.

The crested iris is a dwarf species, growing primarily in the southeastern United States, with 2-inch-wide purple or white flowers that have a conspicuous, fringed white crest. These nearly stemless plants grow 3 to 8 inches tall with leaves up to 12 inches long. The Douglas iris, native to California and southwestern Oregon, grows 6 to 30 inches tall and bears cream to red-purple flowers. Vernal iris, a dwarf species only 6 inches tall, has early-blooming violet flowers with a yellow or orange lengthwise band on each sepal and ½-inch-wide, foot-long leaves that often become black and leathery as they age. This species is found in the Southeast, and is sometimes considered one of the more difficult to grow in the garden. The most familiar wild iris, the blue flag is, unlike its tiny relatives, a robust plant 2 to 3 feet tall, similar to the cultivated iris. The thick, bladelike foliage forms dense masses, and the erect flowers, 3 inches wide, make a colorful summer display in the northeastern and north central states. (Do not confuse this plant with the similar-looking but unrelated sweet flag, because the blue flag root is poisonous.)

HOW TO GROW. The crested iris grows in the Deciduous Woodland environment. This species will spread to form a ground cover and grows well in sun or high open shade in soil with a pH of 6.0 to 7.0. The Douglas iris grows in the Western Coniferous Woodland environment. It does well in full sun or light shade in well-drained soil with a pH of about 7.0. The vernal iris is suited to the Deciduous and the Southeastern Coniferous Woodland environments. It does best in open shade and moist, sandy soil with a pH below 5.0. The blue flag grows in the Northeastern Coniferous Woodland environment. It needs full sun and moist soil with a pH of 6.0 to 7.0.

Irises are best grown from divisions of roots or rhizomes; plants started from seed can take up to three years to bloom. In the spring or fall, place roots or rhizomes 6 to 12 inches apart barely below the surface of the ground so that the tip is just at soil level. Keep the ground moist. To propagate irises from seeds, sow the seeds in moist peat moss in flats in the fall. When seedlings appear the following spring, transplant them to a protected nursery bed and grow them there for a year before moving them to a permanent location. All spe-

GOLDEN SEAL
Hydrastis canadensis

COMMON GOLDEN STAR GRASS
Hypoxis hirsuta

For environments and climate zones, see maps, page 149.

BLUE FLAG IRIS
Iris versicolor

AMERICAN TWINLEAF
Jeffersonia diphylla

cies but the vernal irises reseed themselves readily if left undisturbed in congenial surroundings.

J

JACK-IN-THE-PULPIT See *Arisaema*
JACOB'S-LADDER, CREEPING See *Polemonium*

JEFFERSONIA

J. diphylla (American twinleaf)

This woodland perennial is found from New York to Ontario, Wisconsin and Iowa and south to Maryland and Alabama. It has two unique features—its leaves are divided into twin winglike sections and its seed capsule has a hinged lid that pops open when the seeds are ripe. In the spring before the foliage is fully developed, a single flower appears atop a leafless, 8- to 10-inch-tall stem and is extremely short lived. After the flower has faded, the leaf stems continue to grow, in some cases to 3 feet, and ultimately tower over and hide the seed capsule. This extraordinary wildflower is an unusual accent near ferns or in a shady rock garden.

HOW TO GROW. The American twinleaf is suited to the Northern Coniferous and the Deciduous Woodland environments. It does best in partial to open shade and moist, humus-rich soil with a pH of 5.5 to 7.0. Set plants 6 to 8 inches apart in the spring or fall. Plants can be grown from seeds sown as soon as they are ripe, but they are slow to flower. Propagate additional plants by dividing in the fall. In cold climates provide protection for the plants by applying a mulch of leaves over them in fall.

JOE PYE WEED, SWEET See *Eupatorium*

L

LADY'S SLIPPER See *Cypripedium*
LAMB'S TONGUE FAWNLILY See *Erythronium*
LANCE COREOPSIS See *Coreopsis*
LARKSPUR See *Delphinium*
LARKSPUR, SPANISH See *Gilia*
LEOPARD LILY See *Lilium*

LAYIA

L. platyglossa (yellow daisy tidy tips)

Yellow daisy tidy tips is an annual native of the coast of Southern California. The flowers, 1 to 1½ inches wide, bloom in the spring and early summer. Although the petals generally are two-colored, some may be all yellow or all white. The leaves, 1½ to 3 inches long and hairy, alternate along a stem 4 to 12 inches tall.

HOW TO GROW. Yellow daisy tidy tips is suited to the Semi-arid Grassland and Western Coniferous Woodland environments. It grows well in light, sandy or humus-rich soil with a pH of about 7.0. Sow seeds during the fall or early spring on the surface of prepared soil where the plants are to remain; thin the seedlings to stand 12 inches apart.

LEWISIA

L. cotyledon (Siskiyou lewisia); *L. rediviva* (bitter-root)

Named for Captain Meriwether Lewis of the Lewis and Clark expedition, the sturdy lewisias are Western mountain perennials, adapted to poor soil. Bitter-root is the Montana state flower. It is found in rocky crevices or gravel river bars from California to Oregon and Washington and eastward through the Rockies to Colorado and Montana. In the early fall, it produces slender, succulent leaves, 1 to 4 inches long, that remain green all winter. The leaves disappear when the flowers are in full bloom in early spring. Startlingly delicate, the pink flowers are 1 to 2 inches across, and perch on short stems 1 to 2 inches high. A fleshy taproot stores up moisture needed for the plant's survival. In summer the bitter-root is dormant, but it revives in the fall and produces new leaves.

Siskiyou lewisia is not as widely spread, growing mostly in northwestern California and southwestern Oregon. It too grows from a fleshy root, but produces broad, oval leaves, 2 to 4 inches long, and compact bunches of small flowers, white with pink-veined petals, which stand up above the leaves on stems 4 to 12 inches high. The flowers appear in late spring.

HOW TO GROW. Both lewisias grow in a Rocky Mountain Woodland environment. They adapt to any area where the soil is poor, rocky or sandy, with good drainage, only a trace of humus, and a pH of 5.5 to 6.5. Bitter-root requires moisture during the time the plant has foliage and flowers, and intense dry heat during the summer dormancy period.

Plants and seeds of both species are available from nurseries. Because the seeds require a period of several months of cold weather before they will germinate, it is best to sow the seeds in the fall, barely covering them with sandy soil. If they are to be planted in the spring, keep the seeds refrigerated over winter to ensure germination in the spring. Transplant seedlings to individual containers and grow in the protection of a cold frame for at least one full season, preferably two, before setting into the garden. Siskiyou lewisia can also be propagated from offset shoots growing from the base of the plant. The best time for transplanting is in the early fall, while the plants are still dormant.

LIATRIS

L. pycnostachya (Kansas gay-feather, cattail gay-feather); *L. scariosa* (tall gay-feather); *L. spicata* (spike gay-feather)

The gay-feathers are perennials, growing along roadsides and in fields throughout the eastern and midwestern United States. They have spiky stalks, 2 to 5 feet tall, covered with leaves resembling blades of grass. In August and September they produce bright, feathery flowers along the upper part of the stalks. These may be lavender purple, rose pink or occasionally white. They are unique among flowers in that the top blossoms of each stalk open first, whereas most plants open their lower buds first.

The species interbreed readily in the wild, thus producing plants with variable characteristics that are often difficult to classify. Kansas gay-feather, 4 to 5 feet high, has downy leaves; its stalks are more densely covered with foliage and flowers than the other species. It also blooms longer, from July to October, and is found in damp woodland clearings and on prairies from Wisconsin and Minnesota to northern Texas. Tall gay-feather, 2 to 4 feet high, has larger, fewer leaves and flowers than the other two species and its flowers spring from a dry, scaly base. It is found in dry forest clearings from Pennsylvania to northern Florida, and also grows in the Midwest from South Dakota to Texas. Spike gay-feather, 3 to 5 feet tall, has flowers that emerge from a somewhat sticky purple-tinged base. It grows in wet places from Ontario south to Florida in the East, and from Michigan to Louisiana in the Midwest.

HOW TO GROW. Gay-feathers grow in Deciduous Woodland and Prairie environments, and do best in slightly sandy soil of 6.0 to 7.0 pH and poor to medium fertility. Except for spike gay-feather, which tolerates moist conditions at the edge of marshes or bogs, the plants are drought resistant as well, and thrive in dry, well-drained soil. All three species need full sun.

Buy nursery-grown plants and set them in the ground in the spring or fall, at intervals of 12 to 18 inches. The usual

YELLOW DAISY TIDY TIPS
Layia platyglossa

BITTER-ROOT
Lewisia rediviva

For environments and climate zones, see maps, page 149.

KANSAS GAY-FEATHER
Liatris pycnostachya

WOOD LILY
Lilium philadelphicum

method of propagation is by division of the clumps in the spring or fall. Gay-feathers can also be grown from seeds, but they germinate slowly, often taking a year. Transplant the seedlings to a nursery bed for one growing season, then move them to their permanent location.

LILIUM

L. canadense (Canada lily); *L. pardalinum* (leopard lily); *L. philadelphicum* (wood lily); *L. superbum* (Turk's-cap lily)

Some 20 species of lily grow wild in the United States, of which these four are typical. All four are slender-stalked, relatively tall plants that bear most of their leaves in whorls or circular groups along the stems, and produce trumpet-shaped flowers whose brightly colored petals are usually dotted with dark spots.

The Canada lily is found in damp meadows and thickets nearly everywhere in the East, from Quebec to Alabama, and in Minnesota and Indiana. The stem, 2 to 6 feet tall, is topped in June and July with 2-inch pendulous yellow or occasionally orange or red flowers.

The leopard lily is a West Coast species that grows along streams and around springs in the mountains of northern California and southern Oregon. Its bright orange-red petals, spotted with purple, are deeply reflexed, exposing a paler speckled interior. The 3-inch flowers appear in May and June at the top of stalks that vary from 1 to 7 feet tall.

The wood lily, an inhabitant of drier areas, is usually found in woodland clearings. Its native habitat ranges from Maine to North Carolina, and it is found as far west as Nebraska, New Mexico and British Columbia. Its darkly freckled orange, red-orange or yellow flowers, 3 to 4 inches wide, face upward at the top of a stalk 2 to 3 feet high and bloom from early to late summer.

The Turk's-cap lily grows 3 to 8 feet tall, and bears as many as 50 purple-spotted 2½- to 3-inch nodding orange flowers that usually appear in pairs from midsummer until early fall. The Turk's-cap lily is native to wet meadows and low-lying areas over the eastern part of the continent, from New Brunswick and Minnesota in the North to Florida and Alabama in the South.

HOW TO GROW. These lilies require the environment of the Northeastern, Southeastern or Western Coniferous Wood-lands, Deciduous Woodland or Prairie. They do best in sun or light shade and—with the exception of the wood lily—moist growing conditions. A strongly acid soil, with a pH of 5.0 to 6.0, is best for the wood lily, but for the others a moderately acid to neutral soil, pH 6.0 to 7.0, is most compatible. Wild lilies are usually grown from purchased bulbs because seed-grown plants take four or five years to flower. Plant bulbs in fall when they are dormant, or in very early spring, setting them 8 to 12 inches apart and 4 to 5 inches deep. Random planting gives a natural appearance.

To propagate from established plants, dig up bulbs in the fall, taking care to preserve the feeder roots at their bottom. Peel off some of the outer scales; up to a third of the bulb can be peeled away safely. Then replant the bulbs. Dust the scales with a fungicide such as captan and place them in a plastic bag full of damp vermiculite or perlite. Seal the bag and keep at room temperature for two months. The scales will develop into tiny bulbs with short roots and tiny leaf shoots. Refrigerate the bag, or pot the little bulbs and place them in a cold frame for two more months. Set out in the open garden in the spring. They should reach flowering size in three or four years. Lilies can also be grown easily from seeds sown in spring or fall, but they require several years to reach maturity.

LILY See *Lilium*
LILY, AVALANCHE See *Erythronium*
LILY, CANADA See *Lilium*
LILY, CHECKER See *Fritillaria*
LILY, CHOCOLATE See *Fritillaria*
LILY, LEOPARD See *Lilium*
LILY, TURK'S-CAP See *Lilium*
LILY, WOOD See *Lilium*

LIMNANTHES

L. douglasi (Douglas meadow foam)

Meadow foam grows wild in damp areas near ponds or bogs. It is native to the coastal ranges of California and southern Oregon, and to the foothills of the Sierra Nevada. In spring this annual bears delicate-appearing fragrant flowers, 1 inch wide, that perch singly on stems growing from the upper leaf axils. The flower color varies from solid white to cream with white tips to white with rosy veins. The compound leaves are made up of from five to 13 leaflets with serrated edges, smooth and slightly succulent. The height of the plant varies from 4 to 20 inches, and it has a spreading, sprawling habit of growth.

HOW TO GROW. Meadow foam grows best in a Western Coniferous Woodland environment. It grows in sunny meadows, and needs a constantly moist soil with a pH of 5.5 to 6.5. To propagate, sow seeds at random in the spring or fall.

Water whenever necessary to maintain constant moisture. Meadow foam, once established, seeds itself each year.

LOBELIA

L. cardinalis (cardinal flower); *L. syphilitica* (great blue lobelia)

These two lobelias are tall perennials with upright flower spikes that grow in swampy areas and beside brooks throughout the eastern half of the continent, from Maine to Manitoba in the North, south into Florida, Louisiana and Texas. Generally 1 to 4 feet high, some lobelias have been known to grow as tall as 6 feet. Both species have thin, tapering leaves with serrated edges. Their blossoms resemble tiny orchids: a tube with five lobes at the end, two above forming "ears," three below forming a drooping lower lip. The red blossoms of the cardinal flowers are slender and about 2 inches long; they appear from midsummer until fall. The more robust blossoms of the great blue lobelia appear in midsummer; they are shorter and more compact, and range from bright blue through violet, with white markings on the lower lobes. Occasionally both species produce white flowers, and the great blue lobelia also occurs in a burgundy variety, but these color aberrations cannot be reproduced from seed and must be propagated by root division.

The root system of both species is shallow and fibrous, and spreads very rapidly.

HOW TO GROW. Lobelias need a Wetland environment. They tolerate sun or light shade and grow best in a humus-rich soil with a pH of 5.5 to 7.0.

Sow seeds in the spring or, preferably, in the fall in a flat that contains equal parts leaf mold and coarse sand. Keep moist. Transplant the seedlings in the late spring to stand 8 to 12 inches apart. Other methods of propagation are from stem cuttings taken in midsummer before the blossoms appear, and from root division in the spring or fall. Or start plants from nursery stock.

Mulch newly planted lobelias in the fall with leaves to keep them from being pushed from the soil by alternate freezing and thawing and also during dry periods in the summer to conserve moisture.

DOUGLAS MEADOW FOAM
Limnanthes douglasi

CARDINAL FLOWER
Lobelia cardinalis

For environments and climate zones, see maps, page 149.

SKY LUPINE
Lupinus nanus

CUCUMBER ROOT
Medeola virginica

LUPINE See *Lupinus*

LUPINUS

L. hartwegi (Hartweg lupine); *L. nanus* (sky lupine); *L. texensis,* also called *L. subcarnosus* (Texas bluebonnet)

The lupines listed here are western annuals and are hard to differentiate because they interbreed, producing offspring with a range of variations in the height of foliage and the colors of flowers. They are members of the pea family, and the flowers resemble pea blossoms, growing in spikes at the top of erect stalks. The compound leaves, made up of elongated leaflets radiating from a central point, branch out from the stalk below the flowers.

Hartweg lupine, a native of Mexico, has crept northward into the southwestern United States. It grows 2 to 3 feet tall with flowers covering as much as a foot of the stalk from midsummer into early autumn. When the blossoms open they are blue speckled with white but turn red as they age. The leaves are made up of seven to nine very hairy leaflets. The sky lupine blooms in early summer on the grassy slopes of California coastal ranges. A dwarf version of Hartweg lupine, it grows only 4 to 20 inches high, bearing blue flowers speckled with white or yellowish spots; the flowers darken with age. Downy hair covers the upper surface of the leaves, which have six to eight leaflets. The flowers cluster rather sparsely along the upper 2 to 10 inches of the stem. Texas bluebonnet grows over the eastern half of that state in dry, sandy fields, averages 1 to 2 feet in height and has five-leaflet compound leaves covered on both sides with hair. In spring and early summer, deep blue blossoms spotted with white cluster thickly on the upper portions of the stalk.

HOW TO GROW. Lupines grow in the Semiarid Grassland environment. They need sun and a well-drained, moderately fertile soil with a neutral pH of about 7.0. Sow the seeds in early spring as soon as the ground can be worked. Keep the soil moist until seedlings appear, or, to speed germination, put seeds in a jar, pour warm water over them and allow them to soak for 24 hours before planting. Lupines are notoriously difficult to transplant; if transplanting is necessary, move them with a clump of soil while they are still seedlings. Once a stand is established they seed themselves.

M

MALLOW, LOW POPPY See *Callirhoë*
MALLOW, ROSE See *Hibiscus*
MANDRAKE See *Podophyllum*
MARIGOLD, DESERT See *Baileya*
MARIGOLD, MARSH See *Caltha*
MARIPOSA TULIP See *Calochortus*
MARSH MARIGOLD See *Caltha*
MAY APPLE, COMMON See *Podophyllum*
MAYFLOWER, See *Epigaea*
MEADOW BEAUTY, COMMON See *Rhexia*
MEADOW FOAM, DOUGLAS See *Limnanthes*
MEADOW RUE See *Thalictrum*

MEDEOLA

M. virginica (cucumber root, Indian cucumber root)

A white tuberous root gives the cucumber root, a delicate woodland perennial, its name; it is usually found in the rich, damp humus of forest floors in the eastern half of North America, from Quebec to Minnesota in the North, south to Florida and Louisiana. The young plant grows 6 to 12 inches high before producing a radiating cluster or whorl of oval leaves. The stem continues to grow above this leaf cluster another 6 to 12 inches, ending with a smaller leaf cluster and, in May and June, two to nine tiny yellow-green drooping flowers with long orange stamens. When the flowers mature in the fall, the resulting dark purple berries, ¼ to ½ inch across, sit upright on the stem and the foliage takes on a purple hue, very beautiful against the evergreen ferns that are the plant's common companions.

HOW TO GROW. Cucumber root needs a Northeastern or Southeastern Coniferous Woodland environment or a Deciduous Woodland environment. It thrives on a moist, rich, moderately acid soil, with a pH of 5.5 to 6.5, and in deep to moderate shade. Plant the dormant tubers in the spring or fall, setting them 1 to 2 inches deep and about 6 inches apart. Additional plants may be propagated by division of tuberous roots and by seeds sown in the fall; seedlings take several years to reach flowering size.

MENTZELIA
M. laevicaulis (blazing star, blazing star mentzelia); *M. lindleyi,* also called *Bartonia aurea* (Lindley blazing star, Lindley mentzelia)

The blazing stars, natives of the western desert and coastal ranges, are named for their five-petaled flowers, arranged in the shape of a star, which surround a burst of stamens, numerous, threadlike and almost as long as the petals. The leaves and stems of the plants are slightly sticky to the touch because they are covered with fine, barbed hairs.

Blazing star, a short-lived perennial, grows 2 to 3½ feet tall and produces pale yellow flowers 2½ to 5 inches across. Its leaves are narrow, 2 to 8 inches long, and have wavy edges. It blooms from summer until fall, and is found in sagebrush country from Wyoming to California.

Lindley blazing star, an annual, blooms from spring until early summer, mostly in California. It is 1 to 4 feet tall, with blossoms 1½ to 2½ inches across and leaves 2 to 3 inches long. The waxy petals, gold with a red splotch at the base, are oval, coming to points at the tips. The flowers grow in groups of two or three at the top of a branched stem. They open in the evening, close about noon the following day, and are very fragrant.

HOW TO GROW. Both species of blazing star grow best in a Desert or Semiarid Grassland environment. They need full sun and a sandy, well-drained soil with a pH of 7.0 to 8.0. Soil heavy with clay can cause them to rot. Moisture is necessary until the plants begin to bloom, at which time they must have very dry conditions. Sow seeds for Lindley blazing star in the late fall or early winter, and in the plants' permanent location, because they generally do not transplant well. Lindley blazing star will reseed itself each year. Sow seeds for the perennial blazing star in early summer in flats or trays, then transplant the seedlings to pots in the fall and place in a sheltered area outdoors for the winter. Transplant to permanent beds in the spring.

MERRYBELLS See *Uvularia*

MERTENSIA
M. virginica (Virginia bluebell)

Although native to Virginia, Virginia bluebell also blooms across the eastern United States in meadows, beside streams and in moist woodlands. During the spring blooming season, its clusters of pink buds turn into the inch-long trumpet-shaped blue flowers much sought after by bees. The flowers dangle at the ends of 1- to 2-foot stems that are often branched. The foliage, emerging as pink shoots, turns silvery green upon maturity and dies down in midsummer, so Virginia bluebells should be mixed with other plants that retain

LINDLEY BLAZING STAR
Mentzelia lindleyi

VIRGINIA BLUEBELL
Mertensia virginica

For environments and climate zones, see maps, page 149.

BUSH MONKEY FLOWER
Mimulus aurantiacus

PARTRIDGEBERRY
Mitchella repens

their foliage to ensure that the space they occupy is not bare from midsummer onward.

HOW TO GROW. Virginia bluebell grows well in an open Deciduous Woodland environment. It prefers partial shade, but will grow in full sun. Plants prefer soil with a pH of 5.5 to 6.5 and must be kept moist in spring, but they tolerate dryness in summer while they are dormant. To propagate, divide the young brown fleshy roots (not old black ones) anytime between early summer, when the plant becomes dormant, and the freezing of the ground. Plant root segments with the tops 1 inch deep and 1½ feet apart. Seeds sown in summer, fall or spring will produce seedlings large enough to flower the third year. The plant increases rapidly by itself in damp, humus-filled soil. Virginia bluebell is one of the easiest wildflowers to grow in the eastern part of the country, and one of the most pleasing.

MEXICAN TULIP POPPY See *Hunnemannia*
MILKWEED See *Asclepias*

MIMULUS
M. aurantiacus, also called *M. glutinosus* and *Diplacus aurantiacus* (bush monkey flower)

Bush monkey flower is a shrubby perennial native of the West Coast south of San Francisco. It grows 2 to 4 feet tall and bears 2- to 4-inch-long orange, buff or salmon flowers on slender stems from early spring through summer.

HOW TO GROW. Bush monkey flower is suited to the Semi-arid Grassland environment. It requires full sunlight and dry, well-drained soil with a pH of 7.0 to 8.0. Sow seeds outdoors in the fall to obtain plants that will flower the following summer, scattering the seeds on the surface of the soil, then covering them with a sprinkling of soil. The plants will reseed; new plants can also be started from stem cuttings— taken from new growth in spring and early summer.

MISTFLOWER See *Eupatorium*

MITCHELLA
M. repens (partridgeberry)

An evergreen creeper native to the moist, shady woods of eastern North America, partridgeberry is decorated with red berries all winter and bears white or pink fringed flowers through the summer. The tiny ⅜-inch rounded leaves are shiny and the fragrant ½-inch flowers are waxy; both grow in pairs. After the flowering season, each pair of flowers forms a single edible berry. Partridgeberry forms colonies and provides year-round mats of rich green 2- to 4-inch-high foliage dotted with flowers or fruit. It is an ideal plant for shady rock or wild gardens. It is traditionally planted in dish gardens at Christmastime.

HOW TO GROW. Partridgeberry grows best in a Deciduous or Coniferous Woodland environment in light to deep shade and moderately moist soil rich in leaf mold with a pH of 5.5 to 6.5. Propagate in spring by dividing clumps of partridgeberry, or take cuttings in the summer. Start them in pots filled with equal parts of damp peat moss, sand, leaf mold or compost and woods soil. Seeds, planted in the fall, also produce plants, but do so very slowly.

MOCCASIN FLOWER, PINK See *Cypripedium*

MONARDA
M. didyma (bee balm, Oswego tea, sweet bergamot); *M. fistulosa* (wild bergamot)

During summer and early fall these flamboyant perennials, with their clumps of colorful blossoms up to 5 feet tall, lure butterflies and hummingbirds as well as bees. Bee balm, which bears red flowers 2 to 3 inches in diameter, grows in moist meadows and along stream banks throughout the eastern United States as far south as Georgia. Wild bergamot, with lilac or sometimes white blossoms of a similar size, grows in dry fields and along roads throughout the United States and southern Canada. These species are members of the mint family and have fragrant leaves.

HOW TO GROW. The monardas grow best in full sun or light shade. Bee balm needs a Deciduous Woodland environment and moist soil with a pH of 5.5 to 6.5. Wild bergamot needs a Prairie environment and sandy soil with a pH of 6.5 to 7.5. Plant nursery stock of either species 12 to 18 inches apart in the spring, setting the rhizomes, or fleshy roots, horizontally 1 inch deep with the tip pointed toward the surface. Or sow seeds in spring or fall. Both species will grow most vigorously if the clumps are divided and replanted each spring. After two or three years, the centers of the clumps become bare, and then the plants must be dug up and separated in the fall; the young outer portions can be replanted, but the aging centers should be discarded. In borders, cut bergamot back after it blooms to keep the plant compact and encourage the growth of more flowers.

MONKEY FLOWER See *Mimulus*
MOUNTAIN CRANBERRY See *Vaccinium*
MULLEIN, FLANNEL See *Verbascum*
MULLEIN, MOTH See *Verbascum*

N

NEMOPHILA

N. maculata (spotted nemophila); *N. menziesi* (baby-blue-eyes)

The nemophilas grow wild in California and are cultivated as annuals in coastal and mountainous areas where night temperatures in summer can be expected to drop below 65°. Spotted nemophila grows 6 to 12 inches tall in mounds bearing saucer-shaped 1- to 2-inch-wide flowers with a dark purple spot at the outer tip of each of its five white petals. Baby-blue-eyes has spreading stems 10 to 20 inches long that grow close to the ground. Its clear blue flowers are 1 to 1½ inches across with white centers.

HOW TO GROW. The nemophilas grow best in a Western Coniferous Woodland environment. They require full sun and a sandy, well-drained soil with a pH of 6.0. Sow seeds in late spring for summer blooms. Plant them in masses where you want the flowers to grow, and thin the seedlings to stand 9 to 12 inches apart. For spring blooms in Zones 9 and 10, sow the seeds in the fall.

NYMPHAEA

N. odorata (American waterlily, sweet waterlily)

All over North America, ponds and slow-moving streams are perfumed in summer by the incredibly fragrant 3- to 6-inch-wide blossoms of the wild waterlily. The aquatic plant's thick, broad leaves, known as lily pads, are 4 to 12 inches in diameter. They float gracefully on the water, rising on 1- to 2½-foot stems from a tuberous horizontal root. The many-petaled flowers, usually white but sometimes pale pink, are borne on leafless stems and sit upon the surface of the water. The blossoms open only in the morning sun, close at noon, and last for three or four days. A hardy perennial, the American waterlily spreads rapidly and often threatens to clog a small pond if it is not thinned occasionally.

HOW TO GROW. The American waterlily needs a Wetland

BEE BALM
Monarda didyma

BABY-BLUE-EYES
Nemophila menziesi

For environments and climate zones, see maps, page 149.

AMERICAN WATERLILY
Nymphaea odorata

environment with an acid pH of 4.0 to 5.0. It thrives on full sun, warm water and deep, rich mud in quiet ponds and slow-moving streams. The easiest and fastest way to start the waterlily is to plant nursery stock in the spring or fall, pinning down the tuberous roots in the mud until they take hold. But waterlilies may also be grown from seeds collected in the fall from the seed pods that ripen below the water. Encase seeds in small globs of clay and drop them into water 1 to 2 feet deep; or sow seeds in containers of muddy water to be transferred outdoors as seedlings the following spring.

O

OCONEE BELLS See *Shortia*

OENOTHERA
O. fruticosa (common sundrop); *O. hookeri* (Hooker evening primrose)

The flowers of sundrop open during the day, those of Hooker evening primrose during the evening. Neither is a true primrose. Both are natives of sunny fields and both produce four-petaled, cup-shaped flowers that will bloom throughout the summer. Common sundrop, native to the eastern half of the continent, is found from Nova Scotia south to Florida and Alabama and west to Indiana and Missouri. This day-blooming perennial grows 1 to 3 feet tall and bears clusters of yellow flowers 1 to 2 inches wide. The leaves are narrow and pointed, 1 to 2½ inches long. Hooker evening primrose, a biennial, grows 3 to 8 feet high with flowers 1 to 2 inches across, which are yellow when newly opened but turn orange or red as the blossoms age. It is a Western species, growing in the Rocky Mountains and along the Pacific Coast from California north to Washington.

HOW TO GROW. Common sundrop grows in open areas of a Northeastern or Southeastern Coniferous Woodland environment or a Deciduous Woodland environment. It needs full sun and does best in a dry, sandy, well-drained soil with a pH of 5.5 to 6.5. Hooker evening primrose grows in a Rocky Mountain Woodland or Western Coniferous Woodland environment. It needs full sun and a moist soil with a pH of about 7.0. Grow common sundrop and Hooker evening primrose from nursery stock planted in the spring, 12 to 15 inches apart. Or propagate from seed sown in the spring in the East, in the fall in the West.

OLD MAN'S WHISKERS See *Geum*

OPUNTIA
O. compressa (compressed prickly-pear cactus); *O. fragilis*, also called *O. brachyarthra* (fragile prickly-pear cactus); *O. polycantha*, also called *O. missouriensis* (many-spined prickly-pear cactus)

There is little doubt that the prickly pears are members of the cactus family. Their pear-shaped, jointed stems, called pads, are covered with long needle-like spines. Brilliant flowers bloom along the edges of the pads in midsummer and are followed by fleshy fruits, usually red or yellow. These hardy perennials have no real leaves; their fat green stems serve both as leaves and water-storage organs to tide the plant over dry seasons. Compressed prickly-pear cactus, the most eastern species, is found in the Central Plains states from Minnesota to Oklahoma, in Ontario, and from Massachusetts south to Alabama. It grows only 8 to 10 inches high, and its pads are generally prostrate, making a prickly ground carpet. The bright yellow flowers are 2 to 3 inches wide. Fragile prickly-pear cactus is found in the Midwest and Southwest from Wisconsin south to Texas and Arizona, and from British

COMMON SUNDROP
Oenothera fruticosa

Columbia to northern California. The plants are 3 to 8 inches tall and have pads about 2 inches long. They form low mats that sometimes reach 4 feet in diameter. The flowers are green-yellow, 1 to 2 inches across. Many-spined prickly-pear cactus, a native of the southern and northwestern plains, grows from North Dakota to Texas and Arizona, and from Washington to northern California. Its swollen stems are 2 to 6 inches long and spread to form mats as much as 1 foot high and several yards wide. The lemon-yellow flowers are 2 to 2½ inches in diameter.

HOW TO GROW. Like all cacti, the prickly pears do well in a Desert or Semiarid Grassland environment. They need full sun and a poor, neutral, well-drained soil with a pH of 6.5 to 7.5. The prickly pears listed here are not much affected by temperature; they withstand heat of more than 100° and cold as low as −40°. The easiest way to propagate them is by detaching pads and putting them into sandy soil; roots form quickly and plants will soon become established. Prickly pears can also be easily grown from seeds that have been collected from the fruits.

ORANGE-ROOT See *Hydrastis*

ORTHOCARPUS
O. copelandii (Copeland's owl's clover); *O. purpurascens* (owl's clover, Escobito, pink paintbrush)

Some 18 species of owl's clover grow on the dry hillsides and meadows of the mountains of California and Oregon. All are annuals that bear flowers in spikes interspersed with conspicuous flower leaves, called bracts. The individual flowers are curiously formed: they have a pointed beaklike upper lip and a swollen lower lip that resembles a tiny sack or cluster of sacks. The two lips are often different colors.

The summer-flowering Copeland's owl's clover, a native of the coastal range in northern California and southern Oregon, grows 4 to 14 inches high and bears rather sparse flower heads made up of lavender and white flowers about ½ inch long. The spring-flowering owl's clover grows in California in the coastal range and the foothills of the Sierras. Its dense multicolored flower head, made up of 1-inch-long flowers, sits atop a stem 4 to 16 inches high. The deeply cut, almost threadlike leaves are ½ to 2 inches long.

HOW TO GROW. Both species of owl's clover require a Western Coniferous Woodland environment. They thrive in full sun and a dry, sandy soil with a pH of about 7.0. Sow seeds in early fall for flowers the following year, and keep the soil moist during the period of germination. Owl's clover seeds itself each year.

OSWEGO TEA See *Monarda*
OWL'S CLOVER See *Orthocarpus*

OXALIS
O. acetosella (common wood-sorrel); *O. violacea* (violet wood-sorrel)

The fragile-looking wood-sorrels are natives of the cool, moist woods. These small plants bear inch-wide flowers on 3- to 5-inch threadlike stems during the spring and early summer. Like the flower stems, the three-part leaves grow directly from a creeping root. The delicate foliage folds up each night, then reopens the next day. Common wood-sorrel, native from Quebec to the southern Blue Ridge Mountains and as far west as Saskatchewan, is one of several plants called shamrock. It grows up to 6 inches tall and bears single white flowers. Violet wood-sorrel, named for the color of its blossoms, is found throughout the eastern and midwestern

COMPRESSED PRICKLY-PEAR CACTUS
Opuntia compressa

OWL'S CLOVER
Orthocarpus purpurascens

For environments and climate zones, see maps, page 149.

COMMON WOOD-SORREL
Oxalis acetosella

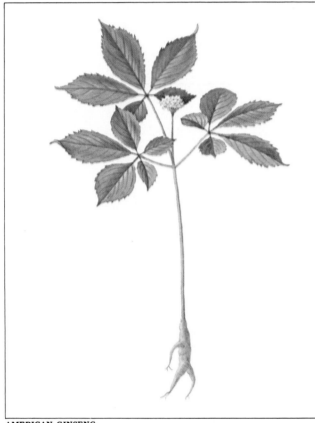

AMERICAN GINSENG
Panax quinquefolius

states in drier soil and bears its flowers in clusters atop 4- to 6-inch stalks.

HOW TO GROW. Both species are suited to Northeastern Coniferous, Southeastern Coniferous and Deciduous Woodland and Prairie environments. Both do well in shade, but common wood-sorrel requires cool, moist, humus-rich soil with a pH of 4.0 to 5.0, while violet wood-sorrel needs drier, less acid soil with a pH of 6.0 to 6.5. Common wood-sorrel is the more difficult plant to grow. Set out nursery plants at any season. Plants can be propagated by dividing established rootstocks in the spring.

P

PAGODA COLLINSIA See *Collinsia*
PAINT BRUSH, INDIAN See *Castilleja*
PAINTBRUSH, PINK See *Orthocarpus*
PAINTED CUP See *Castilleja*

PANAX
P. quinquefolius (American ginseng)

An ancient and persistent belief in the health-giving and aphrodisiac powers of ginseng root has led to excessive harvesting of the wild plant until it is now threatened with extinction. It once grew abundantly in cool, shady, hardwood forests from Quebec to Manitoba, southward through mountainous areas to Louisiana and Georgia, and westward to Missouri. The treasured aromatic root resembles a small parsnip that forks as it matures. The plant grows 6 to 18 inches tall, usually bearing three leaves, each with three to five leaflets 2 to 5 inches long. A 1-inch cluster of six to 20 light green flowers blooms in early summer. Even more eye-catching than the pale flower is the fruit, a bright red autumn berry about ½ inch in diameter.

HOW TO GROW. American ginseng thrives in a Deciduous Woodland environment. It needs a moist, well-drained, slightly acid, humus-rich soil with a pH of 4.5 to 6.0. Because the plants are scarce in the wild and seeds are slow to germinate (about 18 months), start with nursery plants one to two years old. In late fall or early spring, set plants 5 to 8 inches apart with eyes of rootstocks 2 to 3 inches deep and facing up; avoid bending the roots. Put a permanent 4-inch mulch of hardwood leaves over the roots.

PARTRIDGEBERRY See *Mitchella*

PEDICULARIS
P. canadensis (early wood betony)

Early wood betony is widespread in eastern North America, growing in dry, open upland woods from Maine and Quebec west to Manitoba and south to Florida; it is also found in Texas. With its deeply indented feathery leaves 3 to 5 inches long, this woodland perennial is sometimes mistaken for a fern. Plants grow 6 to 18 inches tall; in late spring and early summer, each stem bears a 2-inch-long flower spike with a cluster of leaflike bracts at its base. The tubular blossoms are yellow tinged with brown or red.

HOW TO GROW. Early wood betony grows in a Northeastern or Southeastern Coniferous Woodland environment or in a Deciduous Woodland environment. Because it is partially parasitic on roots of other plants and the specific host plants are unknown, early wood betony may be difficult to grow in a wildflower garden. With luck, it may be possible to introduce humus-rich woodland soil containing the appropriate host into your garden; it should have a pH of 5.5 to 6.5. Purchase nursery plants to set in this soil in the spring before the flowers appear or in the fall after the flowers fade. Plant in full sun or partial shade. Apply a permanent 2- to 4-inch leaf mulch around the plant.

PENSTEMON
P. barbatus (beardlip penstemon); *P. cordifolius* (vine penstemon, honeysuckle penstemon); *P. palmeri* (Palmer's penstemon); *P. spectabilis* (showy penstemon)

These four penstemons are natives of the western prairies and mountains. They are members of a large genus, comprising approximately 230 different species that are sometimes called beard-tongues because of the hairy stamens projecting from their tubular blossoms. All four are summer-flowering perennials, although some are short-lived outside their native environments and must be treated as annuals when cultivated. They are all tall, making them excellent border plants, and are good flowers for cutting.

Beardlip penstemon grows in the Rocky Mountains and is noted for its flaming red blossoms, which look like small exploding firecrackers. They grow along the top 9½ inches of a stalk that rises 1 to 6 feet tall. Vine penstemon, a native of Southern California, is a loosely branched plant, usually about 4 feet high but sometimes reaching as high as 8 feet. Its foliage is shaped like a narrow heart, up to 2 inches long. The flowers, which bloom in clusters along one side of the stem, are red or infrequently yellow, 1 to 1½ inches long, with pronounced lips. Palmer's penstemon, found in the Mojave Desert, grows up to 4 feet tall and bears spikes of fragrant white flowers tinged with pink or lilac, along the top 8 to 24 inches of the stem. The flowers are 1 inch or more long, and resemble those of the snapdragon. The showy penstemon, whose habitat is Southern California, is named for its spectacular profusion of flowers. More than a hundred of them, 1 to 1½ inches long, bloom in a variety of colors from blue to violet and pink in conical clusters as much as half the height of the plant, which ranges up to 4 feet.

HOW TO GROW. The penstemons grow in Semiarid Grassland and Desert environments. They do best in full sun but will tolerate light shade, and thrive in a sandy, well-drained soil with a pH of 7.0 to 8.0. They need little water during the summer and have difficulty surviving moist eastern winters. Sow seeds in the fall or early spring where plants are to remain; plants from fall-sown seeds will bloom the following summer. Or set out nursery plants 12 to 18 inches apart. Penstemons blossom on new growth, so they should be pruned back close to the ground each spring to encourage new shoots. The vine penstemon blooms in early summer and then becomes dormant; it is sometimes treated as an annual. Penstemons may need to be replaced every two or three years when grown under cultivation, although they seed themselves freely when grown under conditions approximating those to which they are accustomed in the wild.

PHACELIA
P. campanularia (California bluebell); *P. grandiflora* (bee phacelia); *P. tanacetifolia* (wild heliotrope, tansy phacelia)

These appealing western wildflowers come in different shapes and sizes but they all bear striking flowers during the spring. They are all found principally in California, although wild heliotrope grows in Arizona as well. California bluebell bears clusters of bell-shaped blossoms ¾ to 1 inch long: it is a fragile-looking plant growing only 8 to 9 inches high. The rare bee phacelia rises to a height of 1 to 3 feet and has large saucer-shaped blossoms, 1 to 2 inches across, in shades of blue to rose. Its oval, toothed leaves are 3 to 4 inches long. Wild heliotrope blooms in dense clusters of fringed lavender flowers on plants 1 to 2 feet high; its feather-like leaves grow

EARLY WOOD BETONY
Pedicularis canadensis

SHOWY PENSTEMON
Penstemon spectabilis

For environments and climate zones, see maps, page 149.

BEE PHACELIA
Phacelia grandiflora

WILD SWEET WILLIAM
Phlox divaricata

up to 8 inches long. All the phacelias are annuals that do well in gardens but are not suitable for cutting. The plants are covered with glands that exude a rust-brown liquid when touched: it causes many people to break out in a rash.

HOW TO GROW. The phacelias grow in a Semiarid Grassland environment. They need full sun, hot, dry days and cool nights. California bluebell grows well in poor, sandy, dry soil, while bee phacelia and wild heliotrope do better in soil with some moisture; both do best with a pH of 7.0 to 8.0. In Zones 3-8 sow seeds outdoors in the spring after the danger of frost is past. In Zones 9 and 10, sow them in the early fall for flowers the following spring. Scatter seeds at random, raking them in lightly, or sow in rows ⅛ inch deep. Thin seedlings of California bluebell to stand 6 to 8 inches apart; space the others 12 to 14 inches apart. In very hot climates, where summer temperatures are 80° to 90° for long periods, flowers will bloom only in the spring; elsewhere they may blossom for as long as 10 to 14 weeks.

PHLOX
P. divaricata (wild sweet William, wild blue phlox); *P. stolonifera* (creeping phlox)

Wild relatives of the popular garden phlox, the native phloxes splash the open woods and meadows with their blue-to-purple colors. Both the upright wild sweet William and the prostrate creeping phlox are spring-blooming perennials. Wild sweet William is found from Quebec to Minnesota, south to Florida, Nebraska and Texas. Creeping phlox grows in the East from Pennsylvania and Ohio to Georgia. Wild sweet William usually grows 8 to 18 inches tall, occasionally reaching 3 feet, and bears loose masses of blue flowers, each less than an inch wide. This species is an excellent plant for a wildflower border.

Creeping phlox is a low-growing ground cover, ranging in height from 6 to 12 inches. Its leaves are almost round, about 1½ inches across, and grow in pairs along fast-spreading stems that cling to rocky terrain in moist woodlands. Their blossoms are about 1 inch across and grow in loose clusters; in their natural habitat they are mostly purple or violet but pink forms occasionally appear.

HOW TO GROW. Wild sweet William and creeping phlox grow in a Deciduous Woodland environment. Both species do well in moist, humus-rich moderately acid to neutral soil with a pH of 6.0 to 7.0. They need partial shade or filtered sunlight. Nursery plants can be set outdoors in the spring or fall. Space wild sweet William 8 to 12 inches apart; tuck creeping phlox into the rock garden or plant 6 to 12 inches apart under trees, for a ground cover. Both species can be propagated by taking stem cuttings in early summer, but the easiest way to get additional plants is by dividing them in late spring after they have flowered, and replanting them. These species will also multiply by sowing their own seeds and will spread into large clumps in a short time.

PINK PAINTBRUSH See *Orthocarpus*
PIPSISSEWA See *Chimaphila*
PITCHER PLANT See *Sarracenia*
PITCHER PLANT, CALIFORNIA See *Darlingtonia*
PLANTAIN, RATTLESNAKE See *Goodyera*

PODOPHYLLUM
P. peltatum (common May apple, mandrake)

In the spring, the common May apples unfold their large leaves like a series of small umbrellas, to carpet moist woodlands and shady roadsides from Quebec to Minnesota, south to Florida, Louisiana and Texas. Taller than most ground covers, these unusual plants are 12 to 18 inches high. When they first appear, their leaves are tightly rolled, and they remain rolled until the plant has reached almost its full height. Then a single leaf opens, or a pair of leaves, almost a foot across, shading a solitary, waxy-white flower, 1 to 2 inches wide, which appears in the fork between the two leaves. The plants are called common May apple after the 1- to 2-inch yellow fruit that replaces the blossoms in late summer. The seeds inside the "apples" are poisonous, as are the plant's roots and leaves. Common May apples are perennials and spread rapidly on thick rhizomes to form large colonies, which may need to be confined. They are excellent plants for camouflaging the yellowing foliage of spring-blooming bulbs, although they also die back by midsummer.

HOW TO GROW. Common May apples need a Deciduous Woodland, Northeastern Coniferous Woodland or Southeastern Coniferous Woodland environment. They do well in light shade under trees in moist soil enriched with leaf mold, of moderate to neutral acidity, with a pH of 5.5 to 6.5. In the fall, bury rhizomes 1 to 1½ inches deep with the tip end pointing upward. Or sow seeds in the fall, as soon as they ripen. Common May apples often seed themselves, and the seedlings can be transplanted at any time. Additional plants can also be propagated by dividing the roots of established plants in the fall.

POLEMONIUM
P. reptans (creeping Jacob's ladder)

Despite its common name, this perennial native of eastern and midwestern woodlands and meadows does not really creep, but grows in sprawling mounds about a foot wide and high. Its fernlike leaves with five to 15 paired leaflets grow from stems 8 to 16 inches tall, and remain green until the first frost. From late spring until midsummer, it bears inch-wide loose clusters of dainty, bell-shaped blue flowers at the tips of the stems.

HOW TO GROW. Creeping Jacob's ladder is suited to the Northeastern and Southeastern Coniferous and the Deciduous Woodland environments. It grows best in humus-rich, well-drained soil with a pH of 6.0 to 7.0, and can tolerate full sun or partial shade. In the spring or fall, set out nursery-grown plants 12 to 18 inches apart. Propagate by dividing established clumps in spring or by sowing seeds outdoors in the fall. If creeping Jacob's ladder is left undisturbed, it spreads by self-sown seeds.

POLYGONATUM
P. biflorum (small Solomon's seal); P. commutatum (great Solomon's seal, giant Solomon's seal)

These perennials, natives of forests and roadsides throughout the East and as far west as Manitoba, North Dakota and Texas, are admired for the blue berries that dangle from arching, unbranched stems in the late summer or early fall. The pale, greenish-white, bell-shaped flowers, ½ to 1 inch long, borne in clusters beneath the leaf joints, bloom in the late spring. Small Solomon's seal grows 1 to 3 feet tall and usually bears clusters of one to three flowers, while great Solomon's seal reaches 2 to 6 feet in height and produces up to 10 flowers in each cluster.

HOW TO GROW. Solomon's seal is suited to Northeastern Coniferous, Southeastern Coniferous and Deciduous Woodland and the Prairie environments. Plants do well in partial to deep shade and humus-rich soil with a pH of 4.5 to 5.5 for small Solomon's seal and a pH of 5.0 to 7.0 for great Solomon's seal. The larger species, which frequently grows along streams, requires very moist soil, while the smaller does well

COMMON MAY APPLE
Podophyllum peltatum

CREEPING JACOB'S-LADDER
Polemonium reptans

For environments and climate zones, see maps, page 149.

SMALL SOLOMON'S SEAL
Polygonatum biflorum

COMMON MEADOW BEAUTY
Rhexia virginica

under drier conditions. In the spring or in the fall when the plant is dormant, plant rhizomes 1 to 2 inches deep and 12 inches apart with the tips of the growing shoots just below the surface of the soil. Plants can also be raised from seeds sown in the fall, but they take two to four years to flower. Multiply Solomon's seal by dividing the stout, branching rhizome in the spring. Established plants spread by rhizomes, and also reseed themselves.

POPPY, CALIFORNIA See *Eschscholzia*
POPPY, CALIFORNIA TREE See *Romneya*
POPPY, MATILIJA See *Romneya*
POPPY, PRICKLY See *Argemone*
PRAIRIE SMOKE See *Geum*
PRICKLY-PEAR CACTUS See *Opuntia*
PRICKLY POPPY See *Argemone*
PRIMROSE, HOOKER EVENING See *Oenothera*
PRINCE'S PINE See *Chimaphila*
PURPLE GLOBE TULIP See *Calochortus*

R

RATTLESNAKE PLANTAIN See *Goodyera*

RHEXIA

R. virginica (common meadow beauty)

The common meadow beauty is a perennial native to meadows and bogs of the United States and southern Canada as far west as Louisiana and Ontario. Its inch-wide pink flowers, which bloom in clusters in mid- to late summer, were once described by Thoreau as "perfect little cream pitchers" because their seed capsule at the base of the flower develops into an urn-shaped receptacle. The stalkless, hairy-edged leaves grow in pairs on a smooth 2-foot-tall stem marked with four vertical ridges that make it look square.

HOW TO GROW. The common meadow beauty is suited to a Wetland environment. It grows from a tuberous root and, unlike other species of this genus, has no runners. It needs soil with a pH of 4.0 to 5.0 and full sun or partial shade. Plant the tuber-like rhizomes in the spring or fall, 1 to 2 inches deep and about 12 inches apart. Sow seeds in the fall as soon as they are ripe in a mixture of 1 part sand and 4 parts peat; they will germinate the following spring. Propagate more plants by dividing the roots in the spring or fall. The common meadow beauty reseeds itself and eventually forms large clumps.

ROMNEYA

R. coulteri (Matilija poppy, California tree poppy)

The fragrant white blossoms of Matilija poppy, 4 to 8 inches wide, look like billowing, pleated crepe paper with distinctive, bristly, yellow centers. They virtually cover the plant, a perennial 3 to 7 feet tall, during early summer in canyons and dry stream beds in southwestern California. Although each flower lasts only two to four days, these decorative blossoms make distinctive bouquets if cut just before the buds open and if the stem ends are seared.

HOW TO GROW. The Matilija poppy does best in Zones 8-10 of the Semiarid Grassland environment, but can also be grown in Zones 6 and 7 if it receives proper drainage and is covered over the winter with a thick mulch of salt hay. Like many other western wildflowers, it thrives in well-drained soils with a pH of 6.0 to 7.0. It needs little water and full sun. Because the underground roots spread rapidly, it is best to set nursery plants 3 to 4 feet apart in the spring in the East and in the fall in the West. In the early fall, cut back established plants to 6 inches high to stimulate new growth the following spring. Plants started from seeds sown in the spring bear flowers in two to three years. To speed germination, sow the seeds in flats, scattering them over the surface of the fine, sandy peat, and cover them with straw or pine needles. Burn this mulch before watering the seeds. The plants can be propagated by removing and planting sucker shoots and by root cuttings in a mixture of 2/5 loam, 1/5 sand, 1/5 peat and 1/5 leaf mold. The plants should be left undisturbed indefinitely; they reseed themselves.

ROSE CLARKIA See *Clarkia*
ROSE MALLOW See *Hibiscus*
ROSY TWISTED STALK See *Streptopus*

RUDBECKIA
R. hirta (black-eyed Susan)

One of the most familiar of the wildflowers is the black-eyed Susan. A biennial that came originally from the western prairies, its daisy-like rays of golden petals with brown, cone-shaped centers can be seen today throughout much of the continent, from Nova Scotia south to Florida and west to Colorado and Texas. The black-eyed Susan grows 1 to 3 feet tall and its 2- to 4-inch-wide flowers bloom from mid- to late summer. The plant's coarse leaves grow on stiff stems, and both the foliage and stems are covered with rough hairs. They are excellent cut flowers, but by the end of summer black-eyed Susans are often infested with red spider mites and aphids. Nevertheless, this is one wildflower that survives under cultivation as well as it does in the wild. If flowers are cut soon after blooming, the plant sometimes can be made to flower a third year.

HOW TO GROW. Black-eyed Susans grow in a Prairie environment. They thrive in almost any soil in full sun, although they will tolerate some shade. Sow seeds as soon as they are ripe, in the late summer or early fall. Plants will flower in their second year and, like all biennials, die after the seeds ripen. Black-eyed Susans reseed themselves and reappear each year in profusion, so much so that in some places they are a pest. They can be transplanted but not divided.

RUE ANEMONE See *Anemonella*

S

SAGE, BLUE See *Salvia*
SAGE, CLEVELAND'S See *Salvia*

SALVIA
S. azurea (blue sage); *S. clevelandii* (Cleveland's sage)

The wild sages are fragrant-leaved perennials, native to western prairies and grasslands, and prized in the garden for their tall stalks of brilliant blue flowers. Blue sage, a common southwestern species, grows on the prairies from Missouri and Arkansas to Nebraska and Texas, but it has been cultivated as far east as New England. It is 2 to 5 feet tall, and its thin stems are topped by multiple spikes of full-lipped blue flowers, ½ inch wide, during the late summer and early fall. The slender leaves are from 2 to 4 inches long. Cleveland's sage, a Southern California species, is a shrub 3 to 4 feet high, with very aromatic leaves ranging in length from ¾ to 1½ inches. Unlike blue sage, the dark blue flower heads are set far apart and bloom throughout the summer.

HOW TO GROW. Blue sage and Cleveland's sage need a Prairie or Semiarid Grassland environment. Both species do well in full sun and a well-drained soil with a pH of 7.0 to 8.0, but blue sage requires a more fertile soil than Cleveland's sage, which survives in poor, dry soil. Propagate both

MATILIJA POPPY
Romneya coulteri

BLACK-EYED SUSAN
Rudbeckia hirta

For environments and climate zones, see maps, page 149.

BLUE SAGE
Salvia azurea

BLOODROOT
Sanguinaria canadensis

species from seeds, sown as soon as they are ripe; seed-grown plants will flower in the second year. For quicker results, buy nursery plants and set them 15 to 18 inches apart. Additional plants may be propagated from stem cuttings taken in the early summer, but cuttings are often difficult to root. If left undisturbed, these sages will grow indefinitely.

SAND VERBENA See *Abronia*

SANGUINARIA

S. canadensis (bloodroot)

Bloodroot is named for its blood-red sap, but despite this chilling name it is a fragile-looking white wildflower. Each spring this hardy perennial pushes through the ground to carpet mossy riverbanks and stream edges in the eastern half of North America from Quebec to Manitoba, south to Florida, Alabama and Oklahoma. Like a protective hand, each plant's single leaf appears first, tightly clasped around the 6- to 9-inch flower stem. The stem is capped in the early spring by a solitary star-shaped flower, 1½ to 2 inches wide, which folds up every night and lasts but a week. As the flowers wither, the large, deeply lobed leaves unfurl to form an unbroken mat of attractive foliage that dies down completely late in the summer. Bloodroot grows easily and spreads rapidly to form a lush patch of color in the woodland garden within a few years.

HOW TO GROW. Bloodroot needs a Deciduous Woodland environment. Although it grows in shade, the blossoms need sunlight in the spring. It does best in a moist, humus-rich soil but will adapt to soils ranging from moderately acid to nearly neutral with a pH 5.5 to 6.5. It should be protected from strong wind and drying summer sun. The easiest and fastest way to grow bloodroot is to plant a rhizome, or fleshy root. Set the rhizomes in the ground in the fall, spacing them 6 inches apart and burying them ½ to 1 inch deep, with the bud end pointing upward. Cover the surface of the ground with a mulch of decayed leaves. Bloodroot can also be grown from seeds sown in late summer, as soon as they are ripe, but seedlings do not bloom until the second or third year. Sow the seeds in a cold frame in a mixture of half leaf mold and half sand, topped with milled sphagnum moss. They will germinate in the spring. Transfer seedlings to their permanent location when their single leaf is an inch across. For additional plants, dig up and divide the rhizomes in the fall. Plants begun from root divisions frequently bloom the following year. Left undisturbed, bloodroot will seed itself.

SARRACENIA

S. flava (trumpet pitcher plant, yellow pitcher plant); *S. purpurea* (common pitcher plant)

Pitcher plants augment their soil-derived diet by devouring insects they catch in their furled, pitcher-shaped leaves. They lure their victims into these hollow tubes and drown them in leaf pools filled with slimy secretions and rain water. Downward-facing hairs inside the leaves keep the insects from escaping before they are digested.

The trumpet species, native to bogs from Virginia south to Georgia and Florida, has long, funnel-shaped leaves, 16 to 20 inches high, that look like narrow pipe-organ trumpets. The flowers of the trumpet species are yellow, 2 to 4 inches wide, and have a pungent smell; they bloom atop 1- to 2-foot stems in the late spring or early summer. The common pitcher plant, more widespread, grows in acid peat bogs from Labrador to Minnesota in the North, as far south as northern Florida and Alabama. Its mottled leaves are 4 to 10 inches long and have a pitcher-like lip at one side. During midsummer, a single nodding red blossom about 2 inches wide appears at the end of a 1-foot stem.

HOW TO GROW. The pitcher plants need a Wetland environment. They thrive in sunny swamps, and do best in soil rich in peat or sphagnum moss, with a pH of 4.5 to 5.5. The fastest way to establish pitcher plants is from nursery stock. Set the plants in a bog so that their roots reach down to the moisture but the top of the roots rests at water level. Pitcher plants can also be grown from seeds sown as soon as they are ripe in a mixture of equal parts of sand and peat moss. Seeds germinate in about a month, but plants grown from seed take three to five years to flower. Stand each pot in a dish of water and enclose both dish and pot in a plastic bag so that seeds do not dry out. When the seedlings are well established, set them outdoors in the bog. Pitcher plants can also be propagated by dividing them in the spring.

SAXIFRAGA

S. virginiensis (Virginia saxifrage, early saxifrage)

Dainty little clusters of star-shaped flowers peer out from rocky cliffs and ledges in the early spring to mark the presence of Virginia saxifrage, a perennial native to woodland clearings from Quebec to Manitoba and Minnesota and south to Georgia and Oklahoma. The branching flower stems of the plant rise 12 to 18 inches above a rosette of low-growing leaves, 1 to 3 inches long, and both stems and leaves are nearly covered with downy hairs. It is one of the first wildflowers to bloom in the spring and can be tucked into a wall crevice or planted in a rock garden.

HOW TO GROW. Virginia saxifrage must have a Deciduous Woodland environment. It does well in sun or partial shade, needs a rocky or loamy soil with a pH of 6.0 to 7.0 and is tolerant of both wet and dry growing conditions. It does not do well, however, in the humid conditions of coastal plains. Set out nursery stock in the spring, tucking plants into pockets of soil between stones or spacing them 8 to 10 inches apart. Plants can be propagated from seed sown at any time or from divisions in spring. Virginia saxifrage reseeds itself readily if left undisturbed.

SEA DAHLIA See *Coreopsis*

SEDUM

S. acre (goldmoss sedum); *S. ternatum* (mountain sedum)

These two succulent ground covers belong to a large family of more than 300 perennials known as the sedums or stonecrops. Their thick, juicy leaves grow on creeping stems that may cover large areas. Goldmoss sedum, ½ to 2 inches high, makes matlike carpets in dry, sandy or rocky soil from Quebec to Washington and south to North Carolina and Illinois. Clusters of its dark yellow flowers bloom on short stems in the early summer. It has small, spicy-tasting leaves, only ⅛ to ¼ inch long.

Mountain sedum, a taller species ranging from 3 to 6 inches high, grows in mountain rocks from New York west to Michigan and Illinois and south to Georgia and Tennessee. Its tiny white flowers, only ⅓ inch wide, form loose clusters in the late spring.

HOW TO GROW. Goldmoss sedum and mountain sedum grow in a Deciduous Woodland environment. They do well in full sun or light shade and tolerate even the poorest soils if there is good drainage. They do best with a pH of 6.0 to 7.0. Set out plants any time of the year as long as the soil is workable. Space them 9 to 12 inches apart or tuck plants between rocks. Sedum can also be started from seeds sown at any time. Additional plants can be propagated by dividing

COMMON PITCHER PLANT
Sarracenia purpurea

VIRGINIA SAXIFRAGE
Saxifraga virginiensis

For environments and climate zones, see maps, page 149.

MOUNTAIN SEDUM
Sedum ternatum

OCONEE BELLS
Shortia galacifolia

old ones. Both species will reseed themselves and spread rapidly on creeping runners that send up new shoots and leaves as they move along.

SHOOTING STAR See *Dodecatheon*
SHORE GRINDELIA See *Grindelia*

SHORTIA
S. galacifolia (Oconee bells)

A native of the woodlands of the Smoky Mountains of North Carolina, Oconee bells grow 2 to 6 inches tall from a cluster of shiny, bright green leaves at the base; the leaves are leathery and about 2 inches across. The bare stalks terminate in nodding, bell-shaped flowers, about an inch across, varying in color from white to pale pink, and occasionally to a true pink. The stems have a reddish cast, and the leaves also turn red in winter, producing a bright patch of unexpected color.

HOW TO GROW. Oconee bells grow in a Deciduous Woodland environment. They are hardy even in climates colder than their native North Carolina, which has led to their wide cultivation in New England. They do best in a well-drained, slightly acid soil, with a pH of 5.5 to 6.5, and thrive on a soil that has been enriched with leaf mold or a combination of peat and sand. Plant in shade or semishade to preserve a cool, moist environment.

Propagate from seeds sown at random in the fall, or, for faster results, from stem cuttings or root cuttings. Root the stem cuttings in a sand-and-peat mixture in late summer, and set out in the fall. Divide roots by cutting root rhizomes from an established plant in the fall. Handle gently when transplanting. (This plant may be declared an endangered species in your area; check with your local conservation office.)

SISKIYOU LEWISIA See *Lewisia*

SISYRINCHIUM
S. angustifolium (common blue-eyed grass); *S. bellum* (western blue-eyed grass); *S. californicum* (golden-eyed grass)

Blue-eyed grass, the common name of *Sisyrinchium,* is indicative of its appearance. This dainty perennial looks like blades of grass with tiny starlike flowers attached. It grows naturally in damp meadows or pebbly embankments and roadsides in virtually all of the United States.

The stem of blue-eyed grass seems to merge with the leaf, for both are flat, sharp-edged and narrow, about ¼ inch wide. At the point where they meet, the flowers angle out from the stalk in small winglike clusters. They bloom over a long period in spring and summer, but each blossom lasts only a few hours or a day, and does not open at all on cloudy days. Each blossom is about 1 inch wide and has six petals. The fruit is a small round pod, ¼ inch in diameter, which blackens as it dries.

Summer-flowering common blue-eyed grass grows from 4 to 20 inches tall and is generally found east of the Rockies. Western blue-eyed grass, up to 2 feet tall, bears spring-blooming flowers in shades of blue and purple. Golden-eyed grass, 6 to 16 inches tall, blooms in early summer and has yellow flowers with petals more rounded than those of the other two species. Western blue-eyed and golden-eyed grass grow from British Columbia southward along the Pacific Coast to central California.

HOW TO GROW. Blue-eyed grass grows in almost any environment except the Wetlands or Desert. It requires sun and thrives in moist, well-drained, slightly acid soil with a pH of 6.0 to 7.0. Because it is easily confused with real grasses when it is not in bloom, it should be planted in clusters for easy identification.

Sow seeds in late summer when they are ripe. However, plants started from root divisions will produce flowers more quickly. Set root clumps in the ground in the spring or fall, spacing them 6 to 12 inches apart and covering the base of the plant with ¼ to ½ inch of soil. The coarse fibrous roots of blue-eyed grass form dense clumps. Blue-eyed grass transplants easily and will reseed itself.

SMILACINA
S. racemosa (feather Solomon plume, false Solomon's seal)

Feather Solomon plume, a woodland plant, can be found naturally under shrubs and low trees in virtually all parts of North America except Florida. It is a hardy perennial, standing 1 to 3 feet high, with large, slender, oval leaves, 3 to 9 inches long and more than 2 inches wide, alternating on either side of a slightly arching stem. The leaves are prominently veined with hairy edges and downy undersides. The stem zigzags from leaf to leaf, ending in a feathery cluster of flowers 1 to 6 inches long. Each cluster is made up of many small branches covered with tiny white or creamy blossoms no more than ¼ inch wide. The flowers bloom in the spring, followed in midsummer by brown- or purple-speckled white berries that turn red as they mature in the fall.

HOW TO GROW. Feather Solomon plume grows in any environment except that of the Wetlands or Desert. It does best in light shade and a moderately acid, well-drained rich soil that is moist but not wet with a pH of 5.5 to 6.5. Propagate from seeds separated from the pulp and planted in the fall, as soon as they are ripe. But be patient: the seeds require two years to germinate and five years to bloom. For quicker results, plant nursery stock or propagate from root divisions. Cut the fleshy root, or rhizome, so that each section contains one or more of the newly formed eyes from which new shoots emerge. Set in the ground in the spring or fall in the location where it will grow permanently; feather Solomon plume often does not bloom the first year after transplanting. Plant the rhizome so that the top of the new shoot is just below the surface of the soil, spacing the plants 10 to 12 inches apart to allow for the creeping root growth. Mulch well to preserve moisture.

SNAKEROOT, BLACK See *Cimicifuga*
SNEEZEWEED See *Helenium*

SOLIDAGO
S. californica (California goldenrod); *S. canadensis* (Canada goldenrod)

These two members of the far-flung goldenrod family are both perennials. California goldenrod is a West Coast plant that grows from Oregon to Mexico. It can be found most abundantly in moist ravines and in the rich sediments of stream banks, but it also survives in dry, poor soils. Canada goldenrod grows in variable forms across most of the eastern half of the United States and southern Canada.

California goldenrod rises from a rosette of leaves at its base, and reaches a height of 5 to 9 feet. The basal leaves are about 1 inch wide and up to 5 inches long; those that alternate along the stem are generally about half as large. The stems and foliage vary in appearance, with some specimens appearing downy and gray-green while others are clear green and smooth. The edges of the leaves are frequently notched. Tiny fluffy golden flowers, about ⅕ inch across, appear in the fall, growing in long clusters that form a natural bouquet on the upper part of the plant. The shape of the

COMMON BLUE-EYED GRASS
Sisyrinchium angustifolium

FEATHER SOLOMON PLUME
Smilacina racemosa

For environments and climate zones, see maps, page 149.

CALIFORNIA GOLDENROD
Solidago californica

ROSY TWISTED STALK
Streptopus roseus

clusters is sometimes narrow and erect, sometimes open and arching. Canada goldenrod has rough-textured dull green leaves on stems about 5 feet tall. It blooms in the late summer and early fall, in a one-sided, vertical cluster of tightly packed, shaggy, golden yellow flowers only ¼ inch across.

HOW TO GROW. California goldenrod grows in a Western Coniferous Woodland environment. It does best in moist, rich soil, but adapts readily to less than optimum conditions such as drought and poor or heavy soil. The only element it must have in abundance is sun. Canada goldenrod grows in a Northeastern Coniferous Woodland and Deciduous Woodland environment. It is a meadow plant that does well in full sun in neutral to moderately acid soil, from 5.5 to 7.0 pH.

Sow seeds in the fall and cover very lightly (no more than ¹/₁₆ inch) by sprinkling soil over the area or by watering gently to push the seeds down into the earth. Or start plants from divisions of clumps in the spring or fall. Set plants at the same depth as they previously grew, or a little deeper, and about 2 feet apart. Whether started from seeds or root divisions, keep plants moist until they are established.

SOLOMON'S SEAL See *Polygonatum*
SOLOMON'S SEAL, FALSE See *Smilacina*
SPANISH LARKSPUR See *Gilia*
SPIDERWORT, VIRGINIA See *Tradescantia*
SPRING BEAUTY, VIRGINIA See *Claytonia*
SQUIRREL CORN See *Dicentra*
STANDING-CYPRESS See *Gilia*
STAR GRASS See *Aletris*
STAR GRASS, COMMON GOLDEN See *Hypoxis*
STAR GRASS, HAIRY See *Hypoxis*
STRAWBERRY, VIRGINIA See *Fragaria*
STRAWBERRY, WILD See *Fragaria*

STREPTOPUS

S. roseus (rosy twisted stalk)

The tiny blossoms of the rosy twisted stalk are almost concealed by the foliage, and as a consequence the plant is more often grown for its leaves. It grows naturally in deep, cool woodlands or in shady areas around the edge of swamps, and is found in Canada, the eastern United States as far south as Georgia, the Midwest to Wisconsin, and the northern Pacific states.

The stalk is covered with sparse, bristly hairs and grows 1 to 2 feet high in a zigzag shape, with alternating leaves along its length. The leaves are thin, almost translucent, and vary from oval at the bottom of the plant to slender and elongated near the top; the bottom leaves are 2 to 4 inches long. The flowers, appearing in spring and early summer, grow on short, bowed stems that sprout from the joint where the leaf joins the stem. Ranging from pink to purple in color, they look like ½-inch-long trumpets. In late July the flowers are followed by bright red berries, about ⅓ inch across.

HOW TO GROW. Rosy twisted stalk grows best in the environments of Northeastern and Western Coniferous Woodlands and Deciduous Woodlands. It does well in deep to light shade, in a moist, well-drained, humus-rich soil that is neutral to slightly acid, with a pH of 6.0 to 7.0. It is essential that it be kept cool in summer; mulching will help.

Propagate from rhizomes set out in early spring or fall when the plant is dormant. Plant the rhizomes 1 inch deep and spread the fibrous feeder roots carefully. Or propagate from seeds separated from the berry pulp as they ripen. Sow the seeds immediately; they will, however, require several years to bloom. Keep the plant well mulched. In time a small stand of rosy twisted stalk will develop into a colony.

SULFUR FLOWER See *Eriogonum*
SUNDEW, ROUNDLEAF See *Drosera*
SUNDROP, COMMON See *Oenothera*
SUNFLOWER, GOLDEN THIN-LEAVED See *Helianthus*
SWEET JOE PYE WEED See *Eupatorium*
SWEET WILLIAM, WILD See *Phlox*

T

TEXAS BLUEBONNET See *Lupinus*
TEXAS PLUME See *Gilia*

THALICTRUM

T. dioicum (early meadow rue); *T. polycarpum* (Sierra meadow rue)

The graceful meadow rues are perennials found in the eastern half of North America and on the West Coast. Their feathery flowers have no petals and obtain their color from tiny threadlike stamens less than ¼ inch long that extend like tassels from the sepals (the small green casing that encloses the bud). The flowers appear in drooping bunches from spring through early summer, often beneath the leaves. The leaves' dainty appearance results from their compound structure; each is only 1 inch wide and is made up of three small, round, scalloped leaflets.

The early meadow rue is found chiefly in dry eastern woodlands and shady ravines from Labrador to Georgia, but its range extends as far west and south as North Dakota, Kansas, Missouri and Alabama. It varies in height from 8 to 30 inches, and is grown more for its handsome foliage than for its misty purple flowers that appear in midspring. The taller Sierra meadow rue, 16 to 40 inches in height, grows in moist woodlands from California to Oregon. Its flowers have white to pale pink stamens and pale purple sepals.

HOW TO GROW. Early meadow rue grows in the Northeastern and Southeastern Coniferous Woodland environment and the Deciduous Woodland environment. The Sierra meadow rue grows in the Western Coniferous Woodland environment. Both do best in humus-rich, slightly acid soil with a pH of 6.0 to 7.0, and need light shade and fairly dry soil.

After flowering, the fibrous root structure of both species produces offshoots at the base of the plant that become new plants the following season; these can be cut away to establish new plantings. Plant root clumps in the spring or fall, spacing them 1 to 2 feet apart, with the base of the plant at soil level. Mulch to keep the soil moist. Meadow rue can also be grown from seed, but usually requires two years to bloom.

THERMOPSIS

T. caroliniana (Carolina thermopsis)

The Carolina thermopsis, a perennial wildflower, is found on sandy hillsides in full sun, originally in North Carolina, although it now grows in many areas of the eastern United States. It is a tall, bushy plant 3 to 5 feet high, with dense yellow flower spikes, 10 to 12 inches long, that bloom in early summer. Each individual flower springs erectly from the stem, is about 1 inch long and resembles a pea blossom.

The leaves are made up of several oval leaflets that are smooth on top, downy underneath, and about 1 inch wide and 2 to 3 inches long.

HOW TO GROW. The Carolina thermopsis grows in a Deciduous Woodland environment. It needs full sun and a sandy, well-drained, humus-rich soil with a pH of 6.0 to 7.0. It is deep-rooted, very hardy, and tolerates drought well. Propagate from seeds as soon as they ripen in midsummer. Seedling plants begin to bloom the second season, and reach full size in four or five years.

EARLY MEADOW RUE
Thalictrum dioicum

CAROLINA THERMOPSIS
Thermopsis caroliniana

For environments and climate zones, see maps, page 149.

ALLEGHENY FOAM FLOWER
Tiarella cordifolia

VIRGINIA SPIDERWORT
Tradescantia virginiana

THIMBLE FLOWER, BLUE See *Gilia*
THOROUGHWORT See *Eupatorium*

TIARELLA

T. cordifolia (Allegheny foam flower)

The Allegheny foam flower grows naturally in deciduous forests in much of eastern North America, from Nova Scotia and Ontario down into Michigan and Indiana, and in the Appalachians as far south as Georgia and Alabama. This plant is distinguished by a graceful stalk of fluffy white flowers 6 to 12 inches tall, rising above mounds of green foliage in late spring. Each flower measures about $^2/_5$ inch across and is made up of five tiny petals with 10 long stamens forming a feathery spray in the center. The flower heads and leaves grow singly atop separate stalks, all growing directly from the base of the plant. The foliage is slightly hairy and shaped like maple leaves, with three to seven lobes and scalloped edges; each leaf measures up to 4 inches across. The foliage remains green until late autumn or early spring, depending on the climate, finally turning red-orange, then withering as the new growth appears.

HOW TO GROW. The Allegheny foam flower requires a Deciduous Woodland environment. It grows best in light shade and moist, humus-rich soil, with an acid to neutral pH of 5.0 to 7.0. Adding leaf mold to the soil if none is present will help to create the proper growing conditions.

Propagate by transplanting the young plants that grow on runners sent out after the plant has flowered, much in the fashion of strawberries. Allegheny foam flower may also be propagated from seed sown in the fall.

TIDY TIPS, YELLOW DAISY See *Layia*

TRADESCANTIA

T. virginiana (Virginia spiderwort)

The individual blossoms of this perennial last only one day, but each plant produces an abundance of them through the spring and summer in the fields and woods as far north as Maine and Minnesota and as far south as Georgia and Missouri. The violet-blue flowers are 1½ to 3 inches wide. The stems grow 1 to 2 feet tall, bearing inch-wide leaves shaped like coarse blades of grass.

HOW TO GROW. This wildflower is suited to the Northeastern Coniferous and Deciduous Woodland environments. It does best in moist soil with a pH of 5.5 to 6.5 and in light shade. The spiderwort may be propagated by seeds sown in late summer, or by division of clumps in the early spring. Plant the clumps 12 to 15 inches apart, with the tips of the new growth at soil level.

TRAILING ARBUTUS See *Epigaea*

TRILLIUM

T. cernuum (nodding trillium); *T. erectum* (purple trillium); *T. grandiflorum* (snow trillium, great white trillium); *T. recurvatum* (prairie trillium); *T. undulatum* (painted trillium)

The trilliums, as the name implies, have their parts in threes: three petals, three sepals, three leaves. They are woodland perennials that bear flowers for up to a month in the spring. They produce a berry-like red fruit in the fall. The leaves are oval and usually pointed, with a clearly visible network of veins. Snow trillium tends to form clumps of up to eight stems from one rhizome and thus is desirable for massing and color effects in the garden. Most abundant in the northern Blue Ridge Mountain area, it is found from Maine to Georgia and in the Great Lakes region. The 3- to

6-inch-wide flower, borne on a stem 8 to 16 inches tall, is pure white or white tinged with pink, the white form fading to pink, then rose, as it withers. The leaves, 2½ to 6 inches long, are deep, clear green. There are forms of the snow trillium with double flowers. Purple trillium is actually maroon. Although its scent is unpleasant, the odor is detectable only at close range. Its 1- to 3-inch-wide flower stands erect on a 6- to 24-inch stem and in shape resembles that of snow trillium. It may produce several stems from one rhizome and form clumps. Purple trillium ranges from Newfoundland to North Carolina and Tennessee and is also found in lower Michigan; there is in addition a white form with narrower petals that grows in the southeastern states. Nodding trillium's name refers to the way its stem, 6 to 24 inches long, curves downward, placing the 1- to 2-inch-wide white or pink flower just below a canopy of 2- to 3-inch-long leaves. It is abundant in the Appalachians, but is found northward into New England and Quebec, and in the Great Lakes region and Manitoba. Prairie trillium, 6 to 18 inches high, is valued more for its silver-green mottled leaves, 2 to 4 inches long, than for its flower. The latter has erect brown-maroon petals, 1 inch long, that swell to a width of 2 inches, then meet at the tips; the sepals are purplish-green. It grows from Ohio and Minnesota to Alabama and Arkansas. Painted trillium, one of the most beautiful of the trilliums, has a white, wavy-edged flower, 1½ to 4 inches wide, with a fringe of rose-red around the throat. The flower emerges when the plant is only about 6 inches tall and if it is not pollinated will fade and wither before the plant reaches its full 12-inch height. Painted trillium is found in cold upland climates from Nova Scotia to Georgia and Missouri.

HOW TO GROW. Trilliums grow in a Deciduous Woodland environment. They do well in light to full shade, and all but painted trillium—whose special requirements are described below—need a moist, humus-rich, slightly acid to acid soil like that found around rhododendrons, azaleas and camellias. Snow trillium grows best in light shade and sandy loam with a pH of 6.0 to 7.0 and needs a 2-inch-deep layer of leaf mulch, aged manure, rotted wood or compost to protect it in winter; the mulch should be left on permanently. Purple trillium needs moderate to deep shade, a soil with a pH of 4.5 to 6.0, and a full layer of mulch as for snow trillium. Nodding trillium does best in full shade and a wet but well-drained soil with a pH of 5.0 to 6.0. It should be covered in the fall with a mulch of compost or leaves. Prairie trillium requires light to moderate shade—enough to protect it from the summer sun—and a soil with a pH of 6.0 to 7.0. The beautiful painted trillium has such rigid requirements—deep shade and a deep planting in cold, wet, peaty, sandy-bottom soil with a pH of 4.0 to 5.0—that it can be grown in the home garden only with difficulty. Trilliums can be propagated from seeds sown in the fall as soon as they ripen, but may require up to two years to germinate and another two to three years for the plants to bloom. Consequently, they are most often started from mature, blooming-age rhizomes purchased from nurseries, although the purple trillium can be propagated from rhizome offsets taken when the rhizome is four to six years old. The other trilliums are either too slow-growing for this method of propagation, or do not produce offsets. Plant rhizomes in the fall, 2 to 4 inches deep (except for painted trillium, whose rhizomes should be at least 5 inches deep). The eyes—buds for next season's growth—should face upward. Place rhizomes 5 to 8 inches apart.

TROUT-LILY See *Erythronium*
TULIP POPPY, MEXICAN See *Hunnemannia*

SNOW TRILLIUM
Trillium grandiflorum

For environments and climate zones, see maps, page 149.

WOOD MERRYBELLS
Uvularia perfoliata

MOUNTAIN CRANBERRY
Vaccinium vitis-idaea minus

TULIP, BUTTERFLY See *Calochortus*
TULIP, MARIPOSA See *Calochortus*
TULIP, PURPLE GLOBE See *Calochortus*
TURK'S-CAP LILY See *Lilium*
TURTLEHEAD See *Chelone*
TWINLEAF, AMERICAN See *Jeffersonia*
TWISTED STALK, ROSY See *Streptopus*

U

UVULARIA

U. perfoliata (wood merrybells, big merrybells, large-flow-ered bellwort); *U. sessilifolia* (little merrybells, sessile-leaved bellwort)

The merrybells are woodland plants found in the eastern half of North America. They are slender perennials with drooping, bell-shaped, yellow flowers, about 1 inch long, that bloom in early spring. The leaves of the plant characteristi-cally appear to be pierced by the upright stem. The wood merrybells, a native of the eastern mountains from Ontario south to Florida and Louisiana, grows 12 to 24 inches tall and has leaves 1½ to 4 inches long. The little merrybells, a more far-ranging species, grows from Quebec south to Geor-gia, and westward to Oklahoma and the Dakotas. A smaller plant than the wood merrybells, it reaches a height of only 6 to 8 inches and its leaves are seldom more than 2 inches long. Both species of merrybells are dainty plants that look best when they are grown in colonies.

HOW TO GROW. The merrybells need a Northeastern or Southeastern Coniferous Woodland environment, or a De-ciduous Woodland environment. They do best in a moist, humus-rich soil with a pH of 5.5 to 6.5, and in moderate to deep shade, preferably the shade provided by tall trees. Propagate by dividing the roots, in the spring or fall. Set wood merrybells 2 inches deep and 10 to 15 inches apart; set little merrybells 1 inch deep and 4 to 6 inches apart. Merry-bells can also be propagated from seed sown in the fall. They need a period of freezing to make them germinate the follow-ing spring. For additional plants, divide the rhizomes of es-tablished plants in the spring or fall, while they are dormant.

V

VACCINIUM

V. vitis-idaea minus (mountain cranberry)

A dwarf evergreen shrub, 4 to 8 inches high, the mountain cranberry grows across Canada and in the United States from northern New England to northern Minnesota. It blos-soms in early summer with clusters of tiny white or pink bell-shaped flowers ¼ inch long. But its greatest merits are its small, shiny, leathery leaves, about ⅔ inch long, and its red berries, about ½ inch across, which appear in the fall. The berries have the astringent taste of the common cranberry and can be used in cranberry recipes.

HOW TO GROW. The mountain cranberry needs a North-eastern Coniferous Woodland environment. It does well in either full sun or deep shade, but must have a moist, well-drained, acid soil, with a pH of 4.0 to 5.0, rich in peat. Set out plants in the spring so they can be well established be-fore winter. When using the mountain cranberry as a ground cover, space the plants about 1 foot apart; the creeping roots will send up new plants to fill the spaces in about two years. Plant shallowly, so that the roots are barely covered, but be sure to keep the soil moist. For more plants, divide the root clumps of the main plant, or propagate from seed collected and sown in late summer or early autumn when the fruits are ripe. Mountain cranberry grows slowly, eventually making a solid mat of glistening evergreen foliage.

VERBASCUM

V. blattaria (moth mullein); *V. thapsus* (flannel mullein)

Both these mulleins are biennials found in waste places all across the country. The moth mullein rises to a height of 3 to 4 feet from a large rosette of smooth green leaves, about 12 to 18 inches in diameter, and is topped by spikes of loosely spaced 1-inch white or yellow blossoms, which bloom from late spring to fall. Three long stamens project down from the central cup of the flower, suggesting the tongue and antennae of a moth, which gives this flower its name. The lower leaves are toothed and oblong, measuring about 8 to 10 inches long and 3 inches across. The flannel mullein is 2 to 6 feet tall, with many yellow flowers, ½ to 1 inch wide, on a compact spike. It blossoms from early summer to fall, but generally only a few flowers open at a time. Its basal leaves are up to 1½ feet long. The entire plant is covered with fine hairs, giving it a distinctive gray color and a woolly texture.

HOW TO GROW. The mulleins grow in any environment except that of the Desert and Wetlands. They do well in any soil except one that is cold and wet, and thrive in sun, although they also tolerate partial shade. The flannel mullein will survive in an extremely hot environment in dry rocky soil where other plants cannot grow. Propagate from seeds collected and sown in the fall. Thin moth mullein plants to stand 2 feet apart, flannel mullein 3 feet apart. Plants reseed themselves year after year.

VERBENA, SAND See *Abronia*

VIOLA

V. blanda (sweet white violet); *V. canadensis* (Canada violet); *V. papilionacea* (butterfly violet); *V. pedata* (bird's-foot violet); *V. pedunculata* (California violet); *V. pubescens* (downy yellow violet)

There are 500 or so members of the violet family, all of them spring-flowering perennials and all of them with a similar arrangement of petals—two upper petals, two side wings, and one flat lower petal that serves as a landing strip for the small insects that pollinate the blossoms. Three of this group of six species—the sweet white violet, butterfly violet, and bird's-foot—are what botanists call stemless because they have no central stem: their leaves and flowers spring directly from the top of the root. The sweet white violet is a tiny plant, only 2 to 4 inches tall, with faintly fragrant flowers, ½ inch long, with ½- to 1-inch-wide heart-shaped leaves. It grows in moist areas in Quebec, New England, the northern Midwest and the mountains of the Southeast. The Canada violet has a white flower, ¾ inch long, with a touch of yellow in the center of its petals and streaks of purple-brown. Its heart-shaped leaves are 2 to 4 inches long, and it grows 1 to 1½ feet tall, forming a bushy clump 2 feet wide. It is found over a wide geographical range: on the Pacific Coast from Oregon to Alaska; on the Atlantic Coast from Newfoundland to Alabama; and also in the Midwest and Southwest. The butterfly violet varies in color all the way from deep violet to white. It normally grows 3 to 6 inches high, but a vigorous butterfly violet may reach a height of 1 foot, with heart-shaped leaves up to 6 inches across. The flowers are about 1 inch long. It is scattered throughout the Northeast, the upper Midwest, and southward to Oklahoma and Georgia. The bird's-foot violet thrives in the sandy soil of pine barrens, prairies and railroad embankments. It grows 2 to 6 inches high, with leaves deeply segmented in the shape of a bird's foot. Its flowers are as much as 2 inches long and occur in two forms. In one, all the petals are the same light violet color; in the other, the two upper petals are deep

MOTH MULLEIN
Verbascum blattaria

BIRD'S-FOOT VIOLET
Viola pedata

For environments and climate zones, see maps, page 149.

violet and the three lower petals are a lighter shade. The bird's-foot violet is distributed throughout the East and Midwest, from Minnesota to Texas, and from southern Ontario south to Florida. The California violet has orange-yellow flowers, about 1 inch across, on 6- to 24-inch stems; the two upper petals are brown on the back. Its leaves are triangular, 1½ inches long. It is found on grassy slopes in the Coast Ranges below elevations of 2,500 feet from San Francisco to Baja California. The downy yellow violet has hairy stems, 8 to 12 inches high, with heart-shaped leaves up to 4 inches across; its flowers are marked with brown veins. It grows from Maine to Georgia in the East and is found in the Midwest in Oklahoma and Nebraska.

HOW TO GROW. Violets grow best in a Deciduous Woodland or Coniferous Woodland environment. Most require shade and well-drained, slightly acid, humus-rich soil with a pH of 6.0 to 7.0. Exceptions are the sweet white violet, which needs moist soil, and the bird's-foot and California violets, which do best in full sun and in dry, rocky, neutral soils.

Propagate violets from seed or by root division. Plant seeds in the fall, and transplant seedlings to stand about 6 to 12 inches apart. Take root divisions of sweet white violet by cutting off sections of runners; all other violets can be divided by cutting off sections of the root clump. Plant in early spring or fall, setting root clumps about 6 to 12 inches apart, so that the top of the root is at ground level. Mulch the Canada and downy yellow violets with 1 to 2 inches of leaf mold; mulch the sweet white violet very lightly to avoid smothering the small plant. The California and bird's-foot violets do not need to be mulched at all, and the butterfly violet needs no special care. In fact, it seeds itself and spreads so rapidly that the problem is often to control it.

VIOLET See *Viola*
VIOLET, DOGTOOTH See *Erythronium*

W

WARTBERRY FAIRY BELLS See *Disporum*
WATERLILY See *Nymphaea*
WINE-CUP See *Callirhoë*
WINTERGREEN See *Gaultheria*
WOOD LILY See *Lilium*
WOODS LARKSPUR, VIOLET See *Delphinium*
WOOD-SORREL See *Oxalis*
WOOD BETONY, EARLY See *Pedicularis*

X

XEROPHYLLUM
X. asphodeloidea (turkey-beard beargrass); *X. tenax* (common beargrass)

Both turkey-beard beargrass and common beargrass are summer-flowering perennials and both produce dense, lacy clusters of tiny white flowers on stems up to 5 feet tall. The clusters of turkey-beard beargrass are about 1 foot long; those of common beargrass are up to 2 feet long. Turkey-beard beargrass is found in sandy pine barrens from New Jersey to Georgia, and on dry, wooded mountainsides from Virginia to Tennessee and Georgia. The botanical name *xerophyllum* (dry leaf) describes the plant's stiff, narrow, rough-edged leaves that form a rosette around its base. In the turkey-beard beargrass these leaves are 6 inches long; the leaves of the common beargrass are up to 2 feet long and are used by the Indians in basket weaving. A specimen of either plant makes a striking accent in the wild garden.

HOW TO GROW. Turkey-beard beargrass is suited to the Deciduous and Southeastern Coniferous Woodland environ-

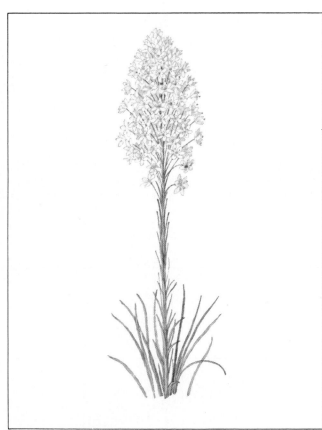

TURKEY-BEARD BEARGRASS
Xerophyllum asphodeloidea

ments, common beargrass to a Western Coniferous environment. Both species do well in sandy soil and filtered or full sunlight. Turkey-beard, however, requires an acid soil, pH 4.0 to 5.0; common beargrass, a neutral soil, pH 7.0. The plants grow from a rhizome, or tuberous root, and are propagated by division of those roots in early spring or fall. Plant the sections 2 feet apart, an inch below the soil surface or at the level of the parent plant. Common beargrass can also be propagated from seed started in fall in a cold frame. Both species of beargrass will withstand considerable drought because the hard, skinlike covering of their leaves slows evaporation and holds in moisture.

Y

YELLOW ADDER'S-TONGUE See *Erythronium*
YELLOW DAISY TIDY TIPS See *Layia*
YELLOW FALSE INDIGO See *Baptisia*

YUCCA
Y. filamentosa (Adam's-needle yucca)

The yucca, a perennial usually associated with the desert of the southwestern states, is also found in the East; Adam's-needle yucca grows on the coastal plain as far north as New Jersey. The stalk usually grows 3 to 4 feet tall, occasionally reaching 5 to 6 feet; in midsummer it bears a 2- to 4-foot-long flower head of creamy white bell-shaped blossoms. It has slender, tough, 1- to 2-foot-long, sharp pointed evergreen leaves with curly white threads growing out from the edges.

HOW TO GROW. Adam's-needle yucca is suited to most parts of the country. It does best in light, sandy, dry soil with a pH of 5.5 to 7.0, but will survive in almost any site. It flourishes in full or partial sun, but will grow in open shade. Additional plants can be propagated by division of the roots in spring or fall, and, rarely, from seeds. To propagate from seeds, sow them in spring or fall, barely covering the seeds with ¼ inch of soil. Adam's-needle yucca is well suited to beach-house gardens. It can also be used as a dramatic landscaping plant for a formal terrace or lawn.

Z

ZAUSCHNERIA
Z. californica (California fuchsia, hummingbird flower)

Although *Zauschneria* was named for an 18th Century Czech naturalist, J. P. J. Zauschner, this tender perennial is a native American wildflower. It grows on the dry slopes of the Pacific Coast Range from Oregon south to Mexico. It is a small, somewhat sprawling woolly-leaved plant, usually about 1 foot in height, rarely taller than 2½ feet. The tubular flowers, 1 to 1½ inches long, cluster loosely at the top of the stem and are usually pollinated by hummingbirds attracted by their red color. The plant blooms in late summer, and is an excellent candidate for planting in rock gardens and walls.

HOW TO GROW. California fuchsia needs a Semiarid Grassland or Western Coniferous Woodland environment. It does best in full sun and a spot sheltered from winter winds. A dry, sandy soil with a pH of 7.0 to 8.0 is essential. Water standing on the plant's roots is fatal, so it seldom survives damp eastern winters. Propagate from seed, from root divisions or from stem cuttings. Sow seeds in the spring, transplanting seedlings to stand 2 to 3 feet apart to allow for their spreading growth. Keep soil moist until seeds germinate. Divide roots in the spring, while the plant is still dormant. Take stem cuttings in the fall and keep them over the winter in a cold frame in Zones 5 and 6, to be transplanted into the garden the following spring.

ADAM'S-NEEDLE YUCCA
Yucca filamentosa

CALIFORNIA FUCHSIA
Zauschneria californica

For environments and climate zones, see maps, page 149.

The wildflower environments

Wildflowers succeed or fail on the basis of a complex mixture of factors—climate, rainfall, elevation, soil chemistry, companion vegetation—that together add up to a specific kind of environment. This environment can change in the space of a few yards or a few miles, but in general across the country there are nine basic types, ranging from the moist meadows and woodlands of the eastern third of the country to the dry grasslands and deserts of the West.

Every wildflower listed in the encyclopedia is keyed to one or more of these environments, and the simplest way to have a wildflower garden is to grow only those plants that are native to the environment in which you live. With experience, however, you may want to branch out and try wildflowers that grow in environments similar but not identical to your own. By using the information on the soil profiles of these nine environments, shown on pages 10-11, you can, for instance, modify your soil, making it more or less acid, or lighter or heavier, to suit the needs of a nonindigenous wildflower. Given the right combination of patience, time and energy, you can even create a microenvironment that is totally different from your own—growing waterlilies in the desert environment of Arizona, for example, or cacti in New Jersey.

The climate zones

How wildflowers grow depends, as it does for all plants, on climate. But given the right environment (above), wildflowers are generally more tolerant of temperature variations than their cultivated cousins. Painted trillium, for example, does as well in Nova Scotia as in Georgia, though the depth of winter cold in the two locales, as shown on the climate map, can vary by 30 degrees.

For wildflowers, in fact, the critical factor in climate is often as much altitude as latitude. Yellow jessamine, which flourishes in Myrtle Beach, South Carolina, in Zone 9, could probably be successfully introduced into a garden in Norfolk, Virginia, 200 miles to the north in Zone 8, because both lie on the coastal plain where the air is warmed by the Gulf Stream. But jessamine's chances of survival in Asheville, North Carolina, 200 miles to the west of Myrtle Beach, are relatively slim—because Asheville lies in the cool Appalachian highlands.

Finally, climate affects wildflowers according to species as well as genus: within any genus, some species are sturdier than others. *Aster spectabilis,* for example, thrives in Zones 5-7, while *Aster grandiflorus* grows only in Zones 7 and 8. In selecting wildflowers it is therefore important to check the climate preferences of the various species within a genus.

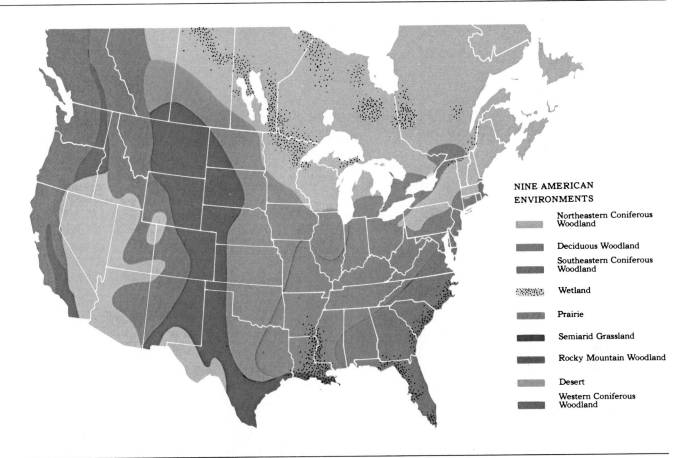

NINE AMERICAN
ENVIRONMENTS

Northeastern Coniferous
Woodland

Deciduous Woodland

Southeastern Coniferous
Woodland

Wetland

Prairie

Semiarid Grassland

Rocky Mountain Woodland

Desert

Western Coniferous
Woodland

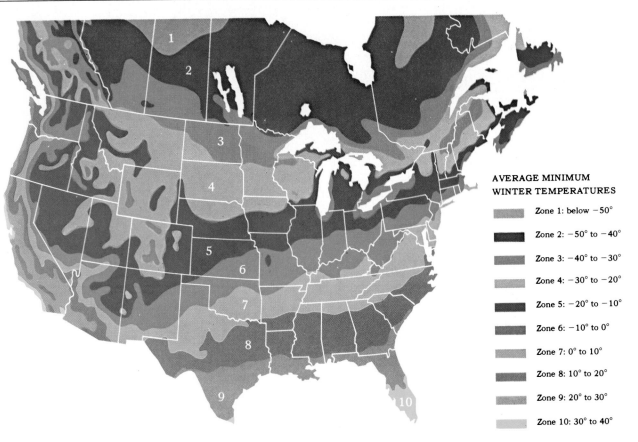

AVERAGE MINIMUM
WINTER TEMPERATURES

Zone 1: below −50°

Zone 2: −50° to −40°

Zone 3: −40° to −30°

Zone 4: −30° to −20°

Zone 5: −20° to −10°

Zone 6: −10° to 0°

Zone 7: 0° to 10°

Zone 8: 10° to 20°

Zone 9: 20° to 30°

Zone 10: 30° to 40°

Characteristics of 228 wildflowers

Species	White to green	Yellow to orange	Pink to red	Blue to purple	Multicolor	One per stem	Cluster	Under 2 inches	Over 2 inches	Spring	Summer	Fall	Under 1 foot	1 to 3 feet	Over 3 feet	Northeastern coniferous	Deciduous	Southeastern coniferous	Wetland	Prairie	Semiarid grassland	Rocky Mountain woodland	Desert	Western coniferous
ABRONIA UMBELLATA (sand verbena)	●		●			●	●	●		●	●	●	●										●	
ACTAEA ALBA (white baneberry)	●						●		●		●			●		●	●					●		●
ACTAEA RUBRA (red baneberry)	●						●		●		●			●		●	●					●		●
ALETRIS FARINOSA (star grass)	●					●	●	●			●			●		●	●		●					
ANEMONE CANADENSIS (Canada anemone)	●					●	●		●	●	●			●			●					●		
ANEMONE DELTOIDES (three-leaf anemone)	●				●	●		●		●	●		●				●					●		
ANEMONELLA THALICTROIDES (rue anemone)	●					●	●	●		●			●				●							
AQUILEGIA CAERULEA (Rocky Mountain columbine)				●	●	●			●		●			●			●					●		●
AQUILEGIA CANADENSIS (American columbine)		●	●			●			●	●				●		●	●	●				●		●
AQUILEGIA CHRYSANTHA (golden columbine)		●				●			●		●			●		●	●	●				●		●
AQUILEGIA FORMOSA (Sitka columbine)		●	●			●			●		●			●		●	●	●				●		●
ARGEMONE HISPIDA (hedgehog prickly poppy)	●		●			●			●		●			●							●	●	●	
ARGEMONE MUNITA (prickly poppy)	●					●			●		●				●						●	●	●	
ARISAEMA DRACONTIUM (green dragon)	●					●	●		●	●			●				●							
ARISAEMA TRIPHYLLUM (Jack-in-the-pulpit)	●					●	●		●	●			●				●							
ARUNCUS SYLVESTER (goatsbeard)	●						●	●			●				●		●							
ASARUM CANADENSE (Canada wild ginger)		●				●		●		●			●			●	●							
ASARUM SHUTTLEWORTHII (mottled wild ginger)		●				●		●			●		●			●	●							
ASARUM VIRGINICUM (heartleaf)		●				●		●			●		●			●	●							
ASCLEPIAS INCARNATA (swamp milkweed)	●		●				●	●	●		●	●		●	●		●		●	●	●			●
ASCLEPIAS SPECIOSA (showy milkweed)			●				●	●	●		●	●		●	●		●		●	●	●			●
ASCLEPIAS TUBEROSA (butterfly weed)		●					●		●		●			●			●		●	●	●			●
ASTER LINARIIFOLIUS (savory-leaved aster)			●			●		●			●	●		●			●					●		
ASTER NOVAE-ANGLIAE (New England aster)	●		●	●			●	●			●	●		●	●		●		●	●	●			
ASTER NOVI-BELGII (New York aster)	●		●	●			●	●			●	●		●	●		●		●	●	●			
ASTER PUNICEUS (swamp aster)			●	●			●	●			●	●		●	●		●		●	●	●			
ASTER SUBSPICATUS (aster subspicatus)				●			●	●			●	●		●	●		●		●	●	●			
BAERIA CHRYSOSTOMA HIRSUTULA (goldfields)		●					●	●		●			●											●
BAILEYA MULTIRADIATA (desert marigold)		●					●		●		●		●										●	
BAPTISIA TINCTORIA (yellow false indigo)		●				●	●	●			●			●		●	●	●						
BRODIAEA HYACINTHINA (white brodiea)	●					●	●	●			●			●						●	●		●	
BRODIAEA PULCHELLA (blue dicks)				●		●	●	●		●			●							●	●		●	
CALLIRHOE INVOLUCRATA (wine-cup)			●			●		●		●	●			●						●	●			
CALOCHORTUS AMOENUS (purple globe tulip)		●	●			●		●			●		●									●		
CALOCHORTUS VENUSTUS (Mariposa tulip)	●	●	●	●		●			●		●		●									●		
CALTHA PALUSTRIS (marsh marigold)		●					●	●		●			●			●	●		●					●
CAMASSIA LEICHTLINII (Leichtlin camass)	●		●			●	●	●		●				●										●
CAMASSIA QUAMASH (common camass)	●		●			●	●	●		●			●											●
CAMPANULA DIVARICATA (Allegheny bellflower)			●			●	●		●		●			●		●	●	●		●		●		
CAMPANULA ROTUNDIFOLIA (bluebells of Scotland)			●			●	●		●		●	●		●		●	●	●		●		●		
CASTILLEJA COCCINEA (Indian paint brush)		●	●			●	●	●		●	●		●				●							
CASTILLEJA FLAVA (yellow Indian paint brush)		●	●			●	●	●			●		●									●	●	
CASTILLEJA INTEGRA (orange paint brush)			●			●	●	●			●		●									●	●	
CAULOPHYLLUM THALICTROIDES (blue cohosh)	●	●				●	●	●		●				●			●							
CHELONE GLABRA (white turtlehead)			●			●		●	●		●	●		●			●							
CHELONE LYONI (pink turtlehead)			●			●		●	●		●	●		●			●							
CHIMAPHILA MACULATA (striped pipsissewa)	●		●			●	●	●			●		●			●		●						●
CHIMAPHILA UMBELLATA (common pipsissewa)	●		●			●	●	●			●		●			●		●						●
CIMICIFUGA AMERICANA (American bugbane)	●					●	●	●			●	●		●			●							
CIMICIFUGA RACEMOSA (cohosh bugbane)	●					●	●		●		●			●	●		●							

	FLOWER COLOR					FLOWER TYPE		FLOWER SIZE		BLOOMING SEASON			PLANT HEIGHT			ENVIRONMENT								
	White to green	Yellow to orange	Pink to red	Blue to purple	Multicolor	One per stem	Cluster	Under 2 inches	Over 2 inches	Spring	Summer	Fall	Under 1 foot	1 to 3 feet	Over 3 feet	Northeastern coniferous	Deciduous	Southeastern coniferous	Wetland	Prairie	Semiarid grassland	Rocky Mountain woodland	Desert	Western coniferous
CLARKIA AMOENA (farewell-to-spring)	●		●	●			●		●		●			●										●
CLARKIA ELEGANS (rose clarkia)			●	●		●	●				●			●										
CLAYTONIA VIRGINICA (Virginia spring beauty)	●		●			●	●	●		●				●			●							
CLINTONIA BOREALIS (yellow clintonia)		●				●	●	●		●			●			●	●							
CLINTONIA UMBELLULATA (speckled beadlily)	●					●	●		●				●			●	●							
COLLINSIA HETEROPHYLLA (collinsia)	●		●	●		●	●				●			●		●	●	●		●	●	●		●
COPTIS GROENLANDICA (common goldthread)	●					●		●		●			●			●	●							●
COPTIS TRIFOLIA (Alaska goldthread)	●					●		●		●			●			●	●							●
COREOPSIS LANCEOLATA (lance coreopsis)		●				●			●		●			●							●			
COREOPSIS MARITIMA (Pacific coreopsis)		●				●			●		●			●								●		
CORNUS CANADENSIS (bunchberry)	●						●	●			●		●			●	●							●
CYPRIPEDIUM ACAULE (pink lady's slipper)	●		●			●			●		●			●		●	●							●
CYPRIPEDIUM ARIETINUM (ramshead lady's slipper)	●					●		●	●	●				●		●	●							●
CYPRIPEDIUM CALCEOLUS (yellow lady's slipper)		●			●		●	●	●	●				●		●	●							●
CYPRIPEDIUM CALIFORNICUM (California lady's slipper)	●	●				●	●		●		●			●		●	●							●
CYPRIPEDIUM CANDIDUM (white lady's slipper)	●					●		●	●	●		●		●		●	●							●
CYPRIPEDIUM REGINAE (showy lady's slipper)	●		●				●	●	●		●			●		●	●							●
DARLINGTONIA CALIFORNICA (California pitcher plant)			●			●			●		●			●										●
DELPHINIUM CARDINALE (cardinal larkspur)			●			●	●		●		●			●										●
DELPHINIUM DECORUM (yellow tinge larkspur)				●		●	●	●		●	●		●											●
DELPHINIUM MENZIESI (Menzies larkspur)			●			●	●	●		●	●		●											●
DELPHINIUM PARRYI (Parry larkspur)				●		●	●	●			●			●										●
DICENTRA CANADENSIS (squirrel corn)	●					●	●	●			●		●				●							
DICENTRA CUCULLARIA (Dutchman's breeches)	●					●	●	●		●				●			●							
DICENTRA EXIMIA (fringed bleeding heart)			●			●	●	●		●	●	●	●				●							
DISPORUM LANUGINOSUM (hairy fairy bells)		●				●	●	●		●				●		●	●	●				●		●
DISPORUM TRACHYCARPUM (wartberry fairy bells)	●					●	●	●		●				●		●	●					●		●
DODECATHEON AMETHYSTINUM (jewel shooting star)			●			●	●	●		●			●							●				
DODECATHEON CLEVELANDII (Cleveland shooting star)			●			●	●	●		●				●						●				
DODECATHEON MEADIA (common shooting star)	●		●	●			●	●		●				●						●				
DROSERA ROTUNDIFOLIA (roundleaf sundew)	●		●			●		●			●		●			●	●	●	●			●	●	●
ECHINACEA ANGUSTIFOLIA (narrow-leaved coneflower)			●	●		●		●			●	●	●							●				
ECHINACEA PURPUREA (purple coneflower)			●			●			●		●	●	●							●				
EPIGAEA REPENS (trailing arbutus)	●		●			●	●	●		●			●				●							
EPILOBIUM ANGUSTIFOLIUM (fireweed)			●	●		●	●	●			●				●	●	●	●						●
ERIOGONUM CROCATUM (wild buckwheat)		●				●	●	●			●		●									●		
ERYTHRONIUM ALBIDUM (white fawn lily)	●					●		●		●			●				●							
ERYTHRONIUM AMERICANUM (common fawn lily)		●				●		●		●			●				●							
ERYTHRONIUM GRANDIFLORUM (lamb's-tongue fawn lily)		●				●		●	●	●				●			●							
ERYTHRONIUM MONTANUM (avalanche lily)	●					●	●	●		●				●			●							
ERYTHRONIUM REVOLUTUM (mahogany fawn lily)	●		●	●		●	●	●		●				●			●							
ESCHSCHOLZIA CALIFORNICA (California poppy)		●				●			●	●	●	●	●										●	
EUPATORIUM COELESTINUM (mistflower)	●		●				●	●			●	●		●			●			●				
EUPATORIUM PERFOLIATUM (boneset)	●		●				●	●			●	●		●		●	●							
EUPATORIUM PURPUREUM (bluestem)	●		●				●	●			●	●			●		●			●				
FRAGARIA VIRGINIANA (Virginia strawberry)	●					●	●	●		●			●				●			●				
FRITILLARIA BIFLORA (chocolate lily)			●			●	●	●		●			●									●		●
FRITILLARIA LANCEOLATA (checker lily)			●			●	●	●		●			●									●		●
FRITILLARIA PUDICA (yellow fritillary)		●	●			●	●	●		●			●									●		●
GAILLARDIA ARISTATA (blanketflower)		●				●			●		●		●							●		●		

	FLOWER COLOR					FLOWER TYPE		FLOWER SIZE		BLOOMING SEASON			PLANT HEIGHT			ENVIRONMENT								
	White to green	Yellow to orange	Pink to red	Blue to purple	Multicolor	One per stem	Cluster	Under 2 inches	Over 2 inches	Spring	Summer	Fall	Under 1 foot	1 to 3 feet	Over 3 feet	Northeastern coniferous	Deciduous	Southeastern coniferous	Wetland	Prairie	Semiarid grassland	Rocky Mountain woodland	Desert	Western coniferous
GALAX APHYLLA (galax)	●					●	●		●				●				●							
GAULTHERIA PROCUMBENS (checkerberry wintergreen)	●					●	●			●		●				●	●	●						
GENTIANA ANDREWSII (Andrews gentian)	●		●			●		●			●	●	●			●	●	●						
GENTIANA CRINITA (fringed gentian)			●		●			●			●	●	●			●	●	●						
GERANIUM MACULATUM (spotted geranium)			●			●	●		●	●			●			●	●	●						
GERANIUM ROBERTIANUM (herb Robert)			●			●	●		●	●	●		●			●	●	●						
GEUM MACROPHYLLUM (large-leaf geum)		●				●	●	●		●	●			●		●				●		●		
GEUM TRIFLORUM (prairie smoke)	●	●	●			●	●	●		●			●	●		●	●			●		●		
GILIA CAPITATA (blue thimble flower)	●			●		●		●		●	●		●									●		
GILIA RUBRA (red gilia)				●		●	●		●	●	●				●							●		
GILLENIA TRIFOLIATA (bowman's root)			●			●	●		●		●			●		●	●	●						
GOODYERA PUBESCENS (downy rattlesnake plantain)	●					●	●		●		●			●		●	●	●						
GOODYERA TESSELATA (checkered rattlesnake plantain)	●					●	●		●		●			●		●	●							
GRINDELIA ROBUSTA (shore grindelia)		●				●	●		●		●	●		●										●
HELENIUM AUTUMNALE (common sneezeweed)		●	●			●	●		●		●	●			●	●	●	●						●
HELENIUM BIGELOVII (Bigelow sneezeweed)		●	●				●		●		●			●		●	●	●						●
HELIANTHUS DECAPETALUS (golden thin-leaved sunflower)		●			●		●		●		●	●		●	●	●	●							
HEPATICA ACUTILOBA (sharp-lobed hepatica)	●		●	●		●		●		●			●			●	●	●						
HEPATICA AMERICANA (round-lobed hepatica)	●		●	●		●		●		●			●			●	●	●						
HERACLEUM MAXIMUM (cow parsnip)	●					●	●		●		●			●					●					
HEUCHERA MICRANTHA (small-flowered alumroot)	●		●			●	●	●	●				●											●
HEUCHERA SANGUINEA (coral bells)			●			●	●		●		●		●									●		
HIBISCUS CALIFORNICUS (California rose mallow)	●		●			●		●		●	●		●					●						
HIBISCUS MOSCHEUTOS (rose mallow)	●		●			●		●		●	●			●					●					
HOUSTONIA CAERULEA (bluet)	●			●		●	●	●		●			●			●	●	●						
HUNNEMANNIA FUMARIAEFOLIA (Mexican tulip poppy)		●				●		●		●	●		●										●	
HYDRASTIS CANADENSIS (golden seal)	●					●		●		●			●			●	●	●						
HYPOXIS HIRSUTA (common golden star grass)		●				●		●		●	●		●	●		●	●		●					
IRIS CRISTATA (crested iris)	●			●		●		●	●	●	●		●				●							
IRIS DOUGLASIANA (Douglas iris)			●	●		●		●	●	●			●			●								
IRIS VERNA (vernal iris)			●	●		●		●		●	●		●				●	●						
IRIS VERSICOLOR (blue flag iris)				●		●		●	●	●	●			●		●								
JEFFERSONIA DIPHYLLA (American twinleaf)			●			●		●		●			●	●		●	●							
LAYIA PLATYGLOSSA (yellow daisy tidy tips)	●	●				●		●		●			●							●				●
LEWISIA COTYLEDON (Siskiyou lewisia)	●		●			●	●			●			●									●		
LEWISIA REDIVIVA (bitter-root)			●			●	●		●				●									●		
LIATRIS PYCNOSTACHYA (Kansas gay-feather)	●		●	●		●	●			●	●			●		●				●				
LIATRIS SCARIOSA (tall gay-feather)	●		●	●		●	●			●	●			●		●				●				
LIATRIS SPICATA (spike gay-feather)	●		●	●		●	●			●	●			●		●			●					
LILIUM CANADENSE (Canada lily)		●	●			●			●		●			●	●	●	●	●		●				●
LILIUM PARDALINUM (leopard lily)				●		●		●	●		●			●	●	●	●	●		●				●
LILIUM PHILADELPHICUM (wood lily)		●	●			●			●		●			●	●	●	●	●		●				●
LILIUM SUPERBUM (Turk's-cap lily)			●			●		●			●	●		●	●	●	●	●		●				●
LIMNANTHES DOUGLASI (Douglas meadow foam)	●		●		●		●	●		●			●											●
LOBELIA CARDINALIS (cardinal flower)			●			●	●		●		●	●		●					●					
LOBELIA SYPHILITICA (great blue lobelia)	●			●		●	●		●		●			●					●					
LUPINUS HARTWEGI (Hartweg lupine)				●		●	●		●	●			●									●		
LUPINUS NANUS (sky lupine)				●		●	●		●				●									●		
LUPINUS TEXENSIS (Texas bluebonnet)			●			●	●	●		●	●		●									●		
MEDEOLA VIRGINICA (cucumber root)		●				●	●		●		●		●	●		●	●							

	FLOWER COLOR					FLOWER TYPE		FLOWER SIZE		BLOOMING SEASON			PLANT HEIGHT			ENVIRONMENT								
	White to green	Yellow to orange	Pink to red	Blue to purple	Multicolor	One per stem	Cluster	Under 2 inches	Over 2 inches	Spring	Summer	Fall	Under 1 foot	1 to 3 feet	Over 3 feet	Northeastern coniferous	Deciduous	Southeastern coniferous	Wetland	Prairie	Semiarid grassland	Rocky Mountain woodland	Desert	Western coniferous
MENTZELIA LAEVICAULIS (blazing star)		●			●	●			●		●	●	●								●		●	
MENTZELIA LINDLEYI (Lindley blazing star)		●				●		●	●	●				●							●		●	
MERTENSIA VIRGINICA (Virginia bluebell)				●		●	●			●				●			●							
MIMULUS AURANTIACUS (bush monkey flower)		●	●			●		●	●	●				●										●
MITCHELLA REPENS (partridgeberry)	●		●			●	●				●					●	●	●						●
MONARDA DIDYMA (bee balm)			●		●		●		●		●	●		●			●							●
MONARDA FISTULOSA (wild bergamot)	●		●		●		●				●	●		●						●				
NEMOPHILA MACULATA (spotted nemophila)				●	●		●	●			●		●											●
NEMOPHILA MENZIESI (baby-blue-eyes)				●		●		●		●	●		●											●
NYMPHAEA ODORATA (American waterlily)	●		●			●			●		●		●						●					
OENOTHERA FRUTICOSA (common sundrop)		●				●	●			●				●		●	●	●						
OENOTHERA HOOKERI (Hooker evening primrose)		●	●			●	●			●				●		●	●	●						
OPUNTIA COMPRESSA (compressed prickly-pear cactus)		●				●		●		●		●									●		●	
OPUNTIA FRAGILIS (fragile prickly-pear cactus)	●	●				●		●		●		●									●		●	
OPUNTIA POLYCANTHA (many-spined prickly-pear cactus)		●				●		●		●		●									●		●	
ORTHOCARPUS COPELANDII (Copeland's owl's clover)	●			●		●	●			●		●												●
ORTHOCARPUS PURPURASCENS (owl's clover)				●		●	●		●			●												●
OXALIS ACETOSELLA (common wood-sorrel)	●			●		●		●		●	●		●			●	●	●		●				
OXALIS VIOLACEA (violet wood-sorrel)			●			●	●		●	●	●		●			●	●	●		●				
PANAX QUINQUEFOLIUS (American ginseng)	●					●	●				●		●				●							
PEDICULARIS CANADENSIS (early wood betony)				●		●	●	●		●	●		●			●	●	●						
PENSTEMON BARBATUS (beardlip penstemon)			●			●			●		●			●							●		●	
PENSTEMON CORDIFOLIUS (vine penstemon)		●	●			●			●		●			●							●		●	
PENSTEMON PALMERI (Palmer's penstemon)	●					●		●			●			●							●		●	
PENSTEMON SPECTABILIS (showy penstemon)			●	●		●		●			●			●							●		●	
PHACELIA CAMPANULARIA (California bluebell)				●		●			●	●			●								●			
PHACELIA GRANDIFLORA (bee phacelia)			●	●		●		●		●				●							●			
PHACELIA TANACETIFOLIA (wild heliotrope)				●		●		●		●				●							●			
PHLOX DIVARICATA (wild sweet William)				●		●		●		●			●	●			●							
PHLOX STOLONIFERA (creeping phlox)			●	●		●		●		●			●	●			●							
PODOPHYLLUM PELTATUM (common May apple)	●						●		●	●				●		●	●	●						
POLEMONIUM REPTANS (creeping Jacob's-ladder)				●		●		●		●	●			●		●	●	●						
POLYGONATUM BIFLORUM (small Solomon's seal)	●					●		●		●				●		●	●	●		●				
POLYGONATUM COMMUTATUM (great Solomon's seal)	●					●		●		●				●		●	●	●		●				
RHEXIA VIRGINICA (common meadow beauty)			●			●		●			●			●					●					
ROMNEYA COULTERI (Matilija poppy)	●					●			●		●				●						●			
RUDBECKIA HIRTA (black-eyed Susan)				●	●		●		●		●			●						●				
SALVIA AZUREA (blue sage)				●		●		●			●	●		●						●	●			
SALVIA CLEVELANDII (Cleveland's sage)				●		●		●			●			●						●	●			
SANGUINARIA CANADENSIS (bloodroot)	●					●		●		●			●				●							
SARRACENIA FLAVA (trumpet pitcher plant)		●					●		●	●	●			●					●					
SARRACENIA PURPUREA (common pitcher plant)			●			●		●		●			●						●					
SAXIFRAGA VIRGINIENSIS (Virginia saxifrage)	●					●	●			●			●				●							
SEDUM ACRE (goldmoss sedum)		●				●		●			●		●				●							
SEDUM TERNATUM (mountain sedum)	●					●		●		●			●				●							
SHORTIA GALACIFOLIA (Oconee bells)	●		●			●		●		●			●					●						
SISYRINCHIUM ANGUSTIFOLIUM (common blue-eyed grass)			●			●		●		●	●			●		●	●	●		●	●	●		●
SISYRINCHIUM BELLUM (western blue-eyed grass)			●			●		●		●				●		●	●	●		●	●			●
SISYRINCHIUM CALIFORNICUM (golden-eyed grass)		●				●		●			●			●		●	●	●		●	●			●
SMILACINA RACEMOSA (feather Solomon plume)	●					●		●		●				●			●					●		

Species	White to green	Yellow to orange	Pink to red	Blue to purple	Multicolor	One per stem	Cluster	Under 2 inches	Over 2 inches	Spring	Summer	Fall	Under 1 foot	1 to 3 feet	Over 3 feet	Northeastern coniferous	Deciduous	Southeastern coniferous	Wetland	Prairie	Semiarid grassland	Rocky Mountain woodland	Desert	Western coniferous
SOLIDAGO CALIFORNICA (California goldenrod)		•					•	•				•		•										•
SOLIDAGO CANADENSIS (Canada goldenrod)		•					•	•			•	•		•										•
STREPTOPUS ROSEUS (rosy twisted stalk)			•	•		•		•		•	•			•		•	•							
THALICTRUM DIOICUM (early meadow rue)			•			•	•	•		•				•		•	•	•						
THALICTRUM POLYCARPUM (Sierra meadow rue)	•					•	•	•		•				•	•	•	•	•						•
THERMOPSIS CAROLINIANA (Carolina thermopsis)		•					•	•		•					•		•							
TIARELLA CORDIFOLIA (Allegheny foam flower)	•						•	•		•			•				•							
TRADESCANTIA VIRGINIANA (Virginia spiderwort)				•			•		•	•	•			•			•	•		•				
TRILLIUM CERNUUM (nodding trillium)	•	•				•			•	•				•			•							
TRILLIUM ERECTUM (purple trillium)		•		•		•			•	•				•			•							
TRILLIUM GRANDIFLORUM (snow trillium)	•	•				•			•	•				•			•							
TRILLIUM RECURVATUM (prairie trillium)				•	•	•			•	•			•				•							
TRILLIUM UNDULATUM (painted trillium)				•	•	•			•		•		•				•							
UVULARIA PERFOLIATA (wood merrybells)		•				•		•		•				•		•	•	•						
UVULARIA SESSILIFOLIA (little merrybells)		•					•	•		•				•		•	•	•						
VACCINIUM VITIS-IDAEA MINUS (mountain cranberry)	•		•				•	•			•		•			•								
VERBASCUM BLATTARIA (moth mullein)	•	•					•	•		•	•	•		•						•		•		
VERBASCUM THAPSUS (flannel mullein)		•					•	•			•	•		•						•		•		
VIOLA BLANDA (sweet white violet)	•					•		•		•			•	•	•									•
VIOLA CANADENSIS (Canada violet)			•	•		•		•			•		•				•							•
VIOLA PAPILIONACEA (butterfly violet)	•		•	•		•		•		•			•	•										•
VIOLA PEDATA (bird's-foot violet)			•	•		•		•		•			•											•
VIOLA PEDUNCULATA (California violet)			•	•		•		•		•		•	•											•
VIOLA PUBESCENS (downy yellow violet)		•				•		•		•			•	•		•	•							•
XEROPHYLLUM ASPHODELOIDEA (turkey-beard beargrass)	•					•	•		•		•		•				•							
XEROPHYLLUM TENAX (common beargrass)	•					•	•		•		•		•											•
YUCCA FILAMENTOSA (Adam's-needle yucca)	•					•	•		•		•		•	•	•	•					•	•	•	•
ZAUSCHNERIA CALIFORNICA (California fuchsia)			•			•	•		•		•		•									•		•

Bibliography

Aiken, George D., *Pioneering with Wildflowers*. Prentice Hall, 1968.

Allen, Durward L., *The Life of Prairie and Plains*. McGraw-Hill, 1967.

Arnberger, L. P., *Flowers of the Southwest Mountains*. Southwestern Monuments Association, 1964.

Birdseye, Clarence and Eleanor G., *Growing Woodland Plants*. Oxford University Press, 1951.

Brooklyn Botanic Garden, *Gardening with Wild Flowers; A Handbook*. 1974.

Brown, Vinson, *Reading the Woods*. The Stackpole Co., 1969.

Bruce, Hal, *How to Grow Wildflowers and Wild Shrubs and Trees in Your Own Garden*. Alfred A. Knopf, 1976.

Clements, Edith S., *Flowers of Mountain and Plain*. H. D. Wilson Co., 1926.

Conrad, Henry S., *The Waterlilies: A Monograph of the Genus Nymphaea*. Carnegie Institute of Washington, 1905.

Correvon, Henry, *Rock Gardens and Alpine Plants*. Macmillan, 1930.

Craighead, J. G., Craighead, F. C. Jr., and Davis, R. J., *A Field Guide to Rocky Mountain Wildflowers*. Houghton Mifflin, 1963.

Dana, Mrs. William Starr, *How to Know the Wild Flowers*. Dover, 1963.

Dodge, Natt N., *Flowers of the Southwest Deserts*. Southwestern Monuments Association, 1969.

Dodge, Natt N., *Roadside Wildflowers of the Southwestern Uplands*. Southwest Parks and Monuments Association, 1970.

Dorman, Caroline, *Wildflowers of Louisiana*. Louisiana Department of Conservation, 1942.

Durand, Herbert, *Taming the Wildings; A Book of Cultural Information for Lovers of Our Wild Flowers, Wild Bushes and Ferns. . . .* Putnam, 1923.

Durand, Herbert, *Wild Flowers and Ferns: In Their Homes and in Our Gardens*. Putnam, 1925.

Foley, D. J., *Gardening by the Sea*. Chilton Books, 1965.

Graetz, K. E., *Seacoast Plants of the Carolinas*. University of North Carolina, 1974.

Haskins, Leslie L., *Wildflowers of the Pacific Coast*. Binfords & Mort, Publishers, 1934.

Hausman, E. H., *Beginners Guide to Wild Flowers*. G. P.

Putnam's Sons, 1948.

Hersey, Jean, *The Woman's Day Book of Wildflowers*. Simon and Schuster, 1976.

Hull, Helen S., *Wild Flowers for Your Garden*. M. Barrows, 1955.

Ketchum, Richard M., *The Secret Life of the Forest*. American Heritage Press, 1970.

Kramer, Jack, *Natural Gardens; Gardening with Native Plants*. Scribner, 1973.

Küchler, A. W., *Potential Natural Vegetation of the Conterminous United States*. American Geographical Society, 1964.

Lenz, Lee W., *Native Plants for California Gardens*. Rancho Santa Ana Botanic Garden, 1956.

McKenny, Margaret, *The Wild Garden*. Doubleday, Doran, and Company, 1936.

MacKenzie, Katherine, *Wild Flowers of the Northeast*. Tundra Books, 1976.

MacKenzie, Katherine, *Wild Flowers of the Midwest*. Tundra Books, 1976.

Menninger, E. A., *Seaside Plants of the World*. Hearthside Press, 1964.

Munz, Philip A., *California Mountain Wildflowers*. University of California Press, 1963.

Munz, Philip A., *California Spring Wildflowers*. University of California Press, 1972.

New England Wild Flower Notes. New England Wild Flower Society, 1974.

Orr, Robert T. and Margaret, *Wildflowers of Western America*. Knopf, 1974.

Parsons, M. E., *Wildflowers of California*. Dover, 1966.

Peterson, R. T., and McKenny, M., *Field Guide to Wildflowers of Northeastern and North-Central North America*. Houghton Mifflin, 1968.

Rickett, Harold William, *The Odyssey Book of American Wildflowers*. Odyssey Press, 1964.

Rickett, Harold William, *Wild Flowers of the United States:*

Volume One: The Northeastern States. McGraw-Hill, 1965.
Volume Two: The Southeastern States. McGraw-Hill, 1967.
Volume Three: Texas. McGraw-Hill, 1969.
Volume Four: The Southwestern States. McGraw-Hill, 1970.
Volume Five: The Northwestern States. McGraw-Hill, 1971.
Volume Six: The Central Mountains and Plains. McGraw-Hill, 1973.

Roberts, Harold and Rhoda, *Colorado Wild Flowers*. Denver Museum of Natural History, 1967.

Robinson, W., *Alpine Flowers for the Garden*. John Murray, 1910.

Sharpe, G. W., *100 Wildflowers of Glacier National Park*. Glacier Natural History Association, 1952.

Sperka, Marie, *Growing Wildflowers; A Gardener's Guide*. Harper & Row, 1973.

Steffek, Edwin F., *Wild Flowers and How to Grow Them*. Crown Publishers, 1963.

Steyermark, J. A., *Spring Flora of Missouri*. Lucas Bros. Publishers, 1940.

Stupka, Arthur and Eastern National Park and Monument Association, *Wildflowers in Color*. Harper & Row, 1965.

Taylor, Kathryn S. and Hamblin, Stephen F., *Handbook of Wild Flower Cultivation*. Macmillan, 1963.

Taylor, Norman, *Wild Flower Gardening*. Van Nostrand, 1955.

Tenenbaum, Frances, *Gardening with Wild Flowers*. Scribner, 1973.

Thompson, Dorothea S., *Creative Decorations with Dried Flowers*. Hearthside Press, Inc., 1965.

Ward, Grace B. and Onas M., *190 Wild Flowers of the Southwest Deserts in Natural Color*. Best-West Publications.

Warnock, B. H., *Wildflowers of the Big Bend Country, Texas*. Syl Ross University, 1970.

Wherry, Edgar T., *Wild Flower Guide, Northeastern and Midland United States*. Doubleday & Co., 1948.

Picture credits

The sources for the illustrations in the book are shown below. Credits from left to right are separated by semicolons, from top to bottom by dashes. Cover—Sonja Bullaty. 4—Courtesy of WGBH Educational Foundation; Frederick Allen; Richard Crist. 6—Sonja Bullaty. 10, 11—Drawings by Paul Breeden. 14—Drawings by Matt Greene. 19—Bob Waterman. 20, 21—Terence Moore. 22, 23—Wolf von dem Bussche except bottom right Eugene and Margarita Cline. 24, 25—Michael Mauney. 26, 27—Sonja Bullaty. 28, 29—Bernard Askienazy. 30—Brent D. McCullough. 35—Sonja Bullaty; Fred Case—Leo Touchet (2). 36—Dan Budnik; Fred Case (2)—Dan Budnik except center Fred Case. 37—Dan Budnik; Fred Case (2)—Fred Case (2); Dan Budnik. 40, 42—Drawings by Matt Greene. 44—Bernard Askienazy. 46 through 53—Drawings by Matt Greene. 55 through 57—Entheos. 60—Farrell Grehan from the National Audubon Society Collection/Photo Researchers, Inc. 62 through 73—Drawings by Matt Greene. 75—Brent D. McCullough. 76—Brent D. McCullough; Yeager and Kay from the National Audubon Society Collection/PR. 77—Miriam Reinhart from the National Audubon Society Collection/PR; Ken Brate from the National Audubon Society Collection/PR—Leonard Lee Rue III from the National Audubon Society Collection/PR. 78—Ken Brate from the National Audubon Society Collection/PR; Mary Thacher from the National Audubon Society Collection/PR—Ken Brate from the National Audubon Society Collection/PR. 79—Noble Proctor from the National Audubon Society Collection/PR; Brent D. McCullough. 80—Brent D. McCullough; Ken Brate from the National Audubon Society Collection/PR. 81—Ken Brate from the National Audubon Society Collection/PR. 82 through 147—Encyclopedia illustrations by Richard Crist except where indicated. 149—Maps by Adolph E. Brotman.

Acknowledgments

The index for this book was prepared by Anita R. Beckerman. For their help in the preparation of this book, the editors wish to thank the following: Els Benjamin, Horticulturist, Brookside Gardens, Wheaton, Md.; James Buckler, Smithsonian Institution, Washington, D.C.; Selma Bunks, Westport, Conn.; Laura Byers, Librarian, Dumbarton Oaks, Washington, D.C.; O. R. Carter, U.S. Soil Conservation Service, Hyattsville, Md.; M. L. Carver, Alpines West Nursery, Spokane, Wash.; Morris Clint, Palm Gardens Nursery, Brownsville, Texas; Dr. Robert De Filipps, Smithsonian Institution, Washington, D.C.; Robert Haehle, Director, Brookside Botanical Gardens, Wheaton, Md.; Elizabeth C. Hall, Senior Librarian, Horticultural Society of New York, New York City; Craig T. Keys, National Arboretum, Washington, D.C.; W. P. Lee, Lee Nursery, Panama City, Fla.; Bruce Lund, Director, Broadmoor Sanctuary (Massachusetts Audubon Society), South Natick, Mass.; Sheldon Miller, Miller's Hardware, Alexandria, Va.; Eugene Mincemoyer, Mincemoyer's Nursery, Jackson, N.J.; Mary O'Gorman, New York City; Richard H. Pough, Pelham, N.Y.; Clyde Robin, Castro Valley, Calif.; Michele Sengsourinh, Smithsonian Institution, Washington, D.C.; George Sharpley, Garden Spot, Manteo, N.C.; Gordon Smith, Edward Gottlieb & Associates, Ltd., Washington, D.C.; Robert I. Spake, County Extension Chairman, Agricultural Extension Service, Manteo, N.C.; Jane Steffey, American Horticultural Society, Mt. Vernon, Va.; Carl Stephens, The Shop in the Sierra, Midpines, Calif.

Index

*Numerals in italics indicate an
illustration of the subject mentioned.*